working memory capacity

ESSAYS IN COGNITIVE PSYCHOLOGY

North American Editors:
Henry L. Roediger, III, *Washington University in St. Louis*
James R. Pomerantz, *Rice University*

European Editors:
Alan D. Baddeley, *University of York*
Vicki Bruce, *University of Edinburgh*
Jonathan Grainger, *Université de Provence*

Essays in Cognitive Psychology is designed to meet the need for rapid publication of brief volumes in cognitive psychology. Primary topics will include perception, movement and action, attention, memory, mental representation, language, and problem solving. Furthermore, the series seeks to define cognitive psychology in its broadest sense, encompassing all topics either informed by, or informing, the study of mental processes. As such, it covers a wide range of subjects including computational approaches to cognition, cognitive neuroscience, social cognition, and cognitive development, as well as areas more traditionally defined as cognitive psychology. Each volume in the series will make a conceptual contribution to the topic by reviewing and synthesizing the existing research literature, by advancing theory in the area, or by some combination of these missions. The principal aim is that authors will provide an overview of their own highly successful research program in an area. It is also expected that volumes will, to some extent, include an assessment of current knowledge and identification of possible future trends in research. Each book will be a self-contained unit supplying the advanced reader with a well-structured review of the work described and evaluated.

Titles in preparation

Gallo: *Associative Illusions of Memory*
Gernsbacher: *Suppression and Enhancement in Language Comprehension*
Park: *Cognition and Aging*
Mulligan: *Implicit Memory*
Surprenant & Neath: *Principles of Memory*
Brown: *Tip-of-the-tongue Phenomenon*

Recently published

McNamara: *Semantic Priming*
Brown: *The Déjà Vu Experience*
Coventry & Garrod: *Seeing, Saying, and Acting*
Robertson: *Space, Objects, Minds, & Brains*
Cornoldi & Vecchi: *Visuo-spatial Working Memory and Individual Differences*
Sternberg et al.: *The Creativity Conundrum*
Poletiek: *Hypothesis-testing Behaviour*
Garnham: *Mental Models and the Interpretations of Anaphora*
Engelkamp: *Memory for Actions*

For continually updated information about published and forthcoming titles in the Essays in Cognitive Psychology series, please visit: **www.psypress.com/essays**

working memory capacity

NELSON COWAN

PSYCHOLOGY PRESS
NEW YORK AND HOVE

Published in 2005 by
Psychology Press
Taylor & Francis Group
270 Madison Avenue
New York, NY 10016

Published in Great Britain by
Psychology Press
Taylor & Francis Group
27 Church Road
Hove, East Sussex BN3 2FA

Printed in the United States of America on acid-free paper
10 9 8 7 6 5 4 3 2 1

International Standard Book Number-10: 1-84169-097-X (Hardcover)
International Standard Book Number-13: 978-1-84169-097-1 (Hardcover)
Library of Congress Card Number 2005007015

Library of Congress Cataloging-in-Publication Data

Cowan, Nelson.
    Working memory capacity / Nelson Cowan.
        p. cm. -- (Essays in cognitive psychology)
    Includes bibliographical references and index.
    ISBN 1-84169-097-X (hardcover : alk. paper)
    1. Short-term memory. I. Title. II. Series.

BF378.S54C69 2005
153.1'3--dc22   2005007015

Taylor & Francis Group
is the Academic Division of T&F Informa plc.

Visit the Taylor & Francis Web site at
http://www.taylorandfrancis.com

and the Psychology Press Web site at
http://www.psypress.com

CONTENTS

Preface

The material in this book is an elaboration and explanation of material I published in the *Behavioral and Brain Sciences* in 2001 (erroneously dated 2000 on the first page, often causing confusion), entitled "The magical number 4 in short-term memory: A reconsideration of mental storage capacity." In my reading of the research literature on the small amount of information that can be kept in mind at one time, or *working memory*, I truly felt as if I kept meeting up with the numbers 3 and 4. People can retain for immediate use three or four unlinked, separate items, or chunks, of information at once. In a similar manner, George Miller (1956) was famously persecuted by the number 7. One important difference is that Miller did not really mean it. As he mentioned in an autobiographical article (Miller, 1989), he introduced the magical number 7 in a tongue-in-cheek fashion to allow him to link together two lines of his own research that he perceived as having little in common. Many readers have failed to perceive the situation in that manner and have accepted the number 7 at face value. Many others, particularly those specializing in cognitive psychology, have instead dismissed the possibility of a constant working memory capacity altogether.

If we are to detect simplifying principles in psychological science, as in other sciences, we should avoid being so "sophisticated" in our understanding, so sure that many factors must interact, that we shy away from the possibility that there actually are constants to be discovered. We have to stick our necks out a bit to propose these constants as hypotheses when they seem warranted, and risk being viewed by some investigators as naive. It seems to me, from my reading of the literature, that, when the grouping or chunking of stimulus materials is known, the average adult can retain three to four chunks in working memory, and that this near-constant capacity of working memory holds true across a wide range of test situations.

The magical number 7 typically may reflect a common situation in which chunks of information are rapidly formed by combining sets of two or three adjacent words, making about three or four mental chunks out of five to nine presented words (for example, in telephone numbers, which appear with spaces between potential groups of digits).

This book explains the evidence for these theoretical proposals about capacity limits, puts them in a theoretical perspective (based largely on my 1988 article in *Psychological Bulletin* and my 1995 book, *Attention and memory: An integrated framework*), compares them with other, competing perspectives, and takes a shot at proposing why capacity limits occur. Finally, it illustrates the practical importance of capacity limits. I may be in error in some of my suppositions and reasoning, but I am sure that research on this topic is centrally important to the cognitive, developmental, and neurological sciences.

In this book, also, an important link is drawn between working memory capacity defined as how many separate concepts can be kept accessible at once, and working memory capability defined as how well attention can be used to keep a task goal active in the presence of interference. Both types of ability may draw on a common attentional capability. The focus of attention may *zoom out* to apprehend a field of items, up to a limit of about four, or *zoom in* to hold on to a goal in the face of interference, along with the minimum necessary data.

It feels to me as if the book is less in need of a preface than the 2001 *Behavioral and Brain Sciences* article on which it is loosely based. The review process for that article was unusually rigorous compared with most journal articles. There were eight excellent peer reviews and then a second round of eight more excellent peer reviews, some from different reviewers than were used the first time, and a third round of five reviews. The editor of the journal, Stevan Harnad, subsequently contributed many of his own excellent editorial points. The accepted article then served as the basis for 39 very thoughtful peer commentaries that appeared with my target article and were followed by my integrated response. I am extremely grateful to all of those reviewers and commentators, because the end result of all of the hard work was a source that is a compendium of viewpoints on working memory capacity limits.

The only trouble with such a compendium is that it can be tedious to pick out and organize all of the issues that were raised and to understand them in light of one another, and in light of more recent evidence. That is where this book comes into play. Some of the evidence is abridged here to highlight the themes and issues, which I have attempted to bring up to date. For the serious scholar of working memory, this book can be used as a portal that can also be supplemented with further remarks that Cowan (2001) and commentators made, and with more recent publications.

When I agreed to write this book in 2002, I felt as if I had a somewhat parochial view to advance. I am shocked at what has happened in the field since then. A tidal wave of excellent new research on capacity limits is coming out so that truly, important information has been coming faster than I could incorporate it into the book. Also, I feel as if this is one of the first areas in which neuroimaging research is fulfilling its promise by providing strong clues about the nature of the cognitive processing system. My reaction is to hope only that I can convey some of the exhilaration in the field at this time.

The work was supported by NIH Grant R01 HD-21338, which began as a New Investigator Research Award in 1984 and has continued almost uninterrupted. Two readers of the book, Alan Baddeley and Klaus Oberauer, were immeasurably helpful, as were readings of the next draft by two graduate students, Zhijian Chen and Candice Morey, and by my colleague, Moshe Naveh-Benjamin. Members of my department at the University of Missouri provided encouragement and moral support. I had relevant discussions with Steven Hackley, Jon King, Richard Morey, Jeffrey Rouder, and Ken Sher. The book would not have been possible without an excellent research team (with undergraduates, graduate students, postdoctoral fellows, and a research associate), including Michael Bunting, Michael Carr, Zhijian Chen, Anna Hismjatullina, Sam Mattox, Matthew Moreno, Candice Morey, J. Scott Saults, and, formerly, Linda Day, Emily Elliott, Timothy Keller, Lara Nugent, Troy Johnson, and Noelle Wood, among others in various capacities and for various amounts of time. Recent collaboration with John Towse and Graham Hitch has been helpful. I also deeply appreciate the support of my wife, Jean Ispa, and our children, Alex, Zac, and Simone.

At various times in my life, I have reflected on what is possible to achieve and what is unrealistic. It seems to me that a contributor to a scientific field usually can advance an understanding of a handful of phenomena (four?) at best. I hope that the line of research summarized in this book is seen as one of my most important scientific endeavors.

Nelson Cowan
Columbia, Missouri
September, 2005

CHAPTER 1

The Problem of Capacity Limits

□ WORKING MEMORY CAPACITY AND THE FULL BRAIN

In a cartoon in *The Far Side* by Gary Larson, a bewildered student raises his hand to ask, "Mr. Osborne, may I be excused? My brain is full." Now, analyzing a joke runs the risk of ruining it. Yet, in this case, it seems instructive that there is something funny about the idea of a human brain being full. It seems to be common knowledge that every experience leaves an indelible mark on our memories. Unlike a computer, the normal human brain never reaches a point at which new experiences can no longer be committed to memory; the brain cannot be full. At the same time, one can be overwhelmed by new information—to the point that it seems to be too much to comprehend, too confusing or complex to file away in memory. It is that feeling, one might presume, that made Larson's character want to leave the classroom.

The feeling of being overwhelmed by a lot of new information can occur because of the special type of memory that is typically termed *working memory*. It refers to the relatively small amount of information that one can hold in mind, attend to, or, technically speaking, maintain in a rapidly accessible state, at one time. The term *working* is meant to indicate that mental work requires the use of such information. For example, if I asked you to retrieve a book from a locked room in the psychology building and I told you that the room is on the third floor, that it is the second office to the right of the elevator but that I don't recall the room number, that the key is in my mailbox in the mail room at the opposite end of the hall on that floor, and that the book is by an author named Smith and was published in 1985, you would have to consider all of that information to retrieve the book. Your best option might be to form an imaginary map of the situation with some verbal details filled in (or even a written map, if the writing materials were available) and to refer to that map. However, you might be unable to do so and might have difficulty keeping all of the relevant information in mind, leading to that uncomfortable feeling of, as it were, a full brain. If some of the information is forgotten (that is, if working memory proves inadequate), it still may be possible to muddle through the situation, but often with mishaps or mistakes along the way. The purpose of this book is to address the question of how to measure the amount of information that can be held in mind successfully at one time, or working memory capacity.

This concept of working memory and its limits is a key part of the human condition. The vast wealth of wisdom and experience that one has at one's disposal is like a well-equipped tool shop, but, when it is time to solve a problem, we struggle to find all of the best tools for the job and to carry them to where they are needed. We need working memory in language comprehension, to retain earlier parts of a spoken message until they can be integrated with the later parts; in arithmetic, to retain partial results until the rest of the answer can be calculated; in reasoning, to retain the premises while working with them; and in most other types of cognitive tasks. Moreover, we need working memory not only to hold new information that has been given to us, but also to integrate it with old information. For example, take the aforementioned case of retrieving a book from an office. If you already are familiar with the layout of the building and can retrieve that information from memory, the new information can be associated with your mental image of the third floor to make it easier to remember, in an integrated, maplike form. It may take effort to achieve that integration, but the information then becomes easier to use and later to retrieve from memory.

Because working memory is limited, there sometimes is important mental work that fails to get done; multiple ideas or facts fail to become integrated as they should. Consequently, people occasionally retain inconsistent memories. For example, you may have planned for a week or so to pick up a certain rare type of vegetable for a dish you are planning to cook for some guests. You may then learn that the guests cannot come and that the dinner is going to be postponed for a month. Still, learning that is not necessarily sufficient to make you revise your shopping plans. It may be only when the shopping plans and the postponement of the dinner are present in working memory at the same time that you suddenly realize that there is no longer a good purpose to buy the rare vegetable.

Psychologists have been studying and thinking about concepts similar to working memory for a long time—at least as long as the modern field of experimental psychology has existed, for slightly more than 100 years. Yet, there still is little agreement about just how much information can be held in working memory at one time. In experiential terms, what is the limit on how much can be experienced at once or on how much we can be conscious of at once? These are the types of fundamental questions that will be considered in this book. They help to define what it means to be a human being and they get at processes that profoundly affect the capabilities and limitations of our thought processes.

☐ BROAD AND NARROW DEFINITIONS OF CAPACITY

We have asked, fundamentally, what is the human limit in working memory capacity. Now it is important to refine the question. According to a very broad definition, working memory capacity is simply the ability to remember things in an immediate-memory task (a task with no delay between the end of the presentation of items to be recalled and the period of recall itself). For example, if given a list of words to recall, if one recalls six of the words, one's capacity would be six words; if one recalls three words, one's capacity would be three words; and so on. It has to be said that that is not a very satisfactory definition of capacity because there is no reason to believe that it could lead to any information beyond what we already know from the data. When we ask about capacity in a narrower sense, we are asking not about the ability of the entire processing system in the task, but rather about the ability of a specific component of the system. The narrower component with which this book is most concerned is the amount that an individual can hold in mind at one time, which I think to be synonymous with the individual's focus of attention. Given that this component has a lot to do with the experience of being human, its potential value is easy to understand. The trouble is, when it comes to the human mind, the components are not visible and easily separable from one another, making this a very difficult type of issue to address. If it were easy, this book would not be necessary.

Occasionally (starting now), I will use analogies to communicate ideas that may offer some insights. Suppose someone asks about the capacity of a ferry boat. Imagine that the boat will take people only in vehicles and that the boat is limited only in how many vehicles it can take on board.

The practical capacity of the boat might be defined as how many people it will hold. However, the answer depends on how many people are packed into each vehicle. If the boat remains at the dock until it is full (after which no more vehicles are admitted) and then departs on its journey, the number of people transported each time will vary within a certain range. However, a person will understand that variation better if he or she knows about the boat's fundamental limit in terms of vehicles. So, the limit in terms of vehicles is a narrow sense of capacity and understanding that limit lends insight to our understanding, even if we are ultimately more interested in the practical question of how many people can be transported. Of course, for practical purposes, someone also might want to know what other means of transportation are available for crossing the body of water or, in terms of working memory, what mental processes are available for holding information for a task at hand.

To appreciate the benefit of analyzing performance into fundamental components, consider a seminal study related to working memory that was conducted by Sperling (1960). In that study, arrays of letters and other characters were briefly flashed on a computer screen. The task was to record the character array or some designated portion of it. When held responsible for the entire array, subjects were able to recall only about four items, no matter how many items the array held. That result is illustrated in Figure 1.1.

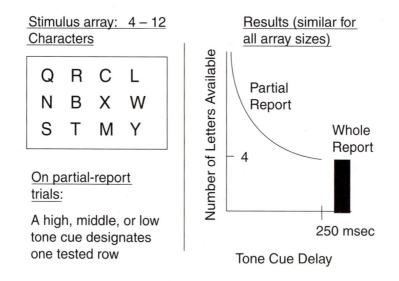

FIGURE 1.1 An illustration of the method and results of Sperling (1960).

When subjects were held responsible for the entire array, they could recall only about 4 of the characters on average, no matter how many the array contained (between 4 and 12). However, in some conditions, a tone was presented very soon after the array ended, indicating which of three rows was to be recalled. This procedure served the purpose of sampling from the information available to the subject, rather than requiring a full reporting of it. With such a tone cue, subjects were able to recall up to three or four items *from the designated row*. At this point, it was necessary to postulate two different capacities. The information from the entire array, or most of it at least, was said to be held in a vivid, but transient, sensory memory. This accounted for the fact that subjects' memory for a row of characters designated by a partial-report tone cue was excellent. Apparently, the sensory memory of the entire stimulus array managed to persist from the time of the array to the time of a closely following tone cue (although the more delayed the tone cue was, up to a quarter second or so, the more diminished the sensory memory became). However, there was some additional limit on working memory that made it impossible for subjects to report more than about four items on average from whatever set was relevant. Later, we will see that this capacity limit appears to be typical of a very fundamental component of the processing system: it turns out to be a capacity limit narrowly defined, which may result from a limit in the capacity of the focus of attention (Cowan, 2001).

☐ IN SEARCH OF CAPACITY MEASURES

A historical moment in the history of experimental psychology occurred when Jevons (1871) rolled some black beans onto a table and tried to estimate the number without actually counting the beans. His motivation included this quotation from Sir William Hamilton: "Supposing that the mind is not limited to the simultaneous consideration of a single object, a question arises, How many objects can it embrace at once? .... I find this problem stated and differently answered by different philosophers, and apparently without a knowledge of each other" (p. 281). Jevons went on to state that:

> This subject seemed to me worthy of more systematic investigation, and it is one of the very few points in psychology which can, as far as we yet see, be submitted to experiment. I have not found it possible to decide conclusively in the manner Hamilton suggests, whether 4 or 5 or 6 is the limit, nor do imaginative acts of experiment seem likely to advance exact knowledge. Probably the limit

is not really a definite one, and it is almost sure to vary somewhat in different individuals. (p. 281)

Jevons noted that "The whole value of the experiment turns upon the rapidity of the estimation, for if we can really count five or six by a single mental act, we ought to be able to do it unerringly at the first momentary glance" (p. 281). In more than 1,000 trials, three and four items were unerringly enumerated, whereas increasingly larger proportions of error occurred for higher numbers. (The proportion of trials correct was .95 for five beans, .82 for six beans, .72 for seven beans, .56 for eight beans, and continued to decline for higher numbers of beans.) In later chapters, we will revisit this basic technique with more recent research on what has come to be known as the process of *subitizing*, or enumerating objects without actually counting. For now, this first study serves as an interesting historical backdrop for a broader debate about psychological theories.

In particular, there has long been a heated debate about whether it is reasonable to expect to find constants in psychology, such as a constant working memory capacity limit in the enumeration task. This debate was characterized very well by Carr (1933), with respect to enumeration and then to constants of learning, in the abstract to his article:

> There are two opposed attitudes toward experimental problems in psychology, one the "constancy" attitude, the other the "relativity" attitude. The former assumes the presence of constants which are the true values even though disturbed or hidden from view because of the variable distractive conditions which cannot be controlled. The latter attitude directs attention to the variations, and attempts to determine how and why the obtained value varies with the conditions of which it is a function.

The present work takes one sort of constancy attitude toward capacity. Now, what would be a motivation for doing so? Clearly, if a constant can be found, it greatly simplifies the theory of human performance. Finding the simplest theory that is adequate to explain the data is a basic goal of science. Moreover, it appears to be the case that, even if a constant exists, it typically will be obscured by the "variable distractive conditions" that Carr mentioned.

Cowan (2001) used the example of the gravitational constant. Although it seems obvious now that we know about it, discovery of the gravitational constant actually was a magnificent achievement. Scientists could have argued that no such regularity existed. Feathers fall to the ground much slower than pebbles, and both birds and arrows can stay in the air for a very long time. The gravitational constant was not discovered until Tycho Brahe collected extensive data on planetary movement, which counts as a type of motion in the absence of wind resistance. Johannes Kepler used such evidence to establish regularities or laws of planetary motion, without understanding the principles behind the regularities. Only then could Isaac Newton discover the gravitational constant. To be sure, such a constant still had to be tied in to other forces in the universe, and the work of Albert Einstein went a long way toward achieving that integration. Nevertheless, progress could not be made until the variable distractive conditions (wind resistance, in this case) could be identified and controlled.

What might be the variable distractive conditions for working memory capacity, and what might be the nature of the constant? As the ferry boat analogy suggested, there may be multiple ways in which a working memory mechanism can be used (in the analogy, few versus many people in each vehicle on the ferry) or multiple mechanisms capable of holding information (in the analogy, a bridge that can be taken across the water). To study any one mechanism, it has to be isolated from the other holding mechanisms.

The one mechanism on which I will concentrate, and the one that may be of greatest interest theoretically, is the capacity of the focus of attention. I will assume that this focus of attention matches the subjective or phenomenological idea of the information of which one is aware at a given moment. According to philosophical and empirical details, some would question this equivalence but that amount of quibbling is neither possible nor necessary for the present concerns, in my judgment; scientific work often must depend on a partly intuitive understanding of some basic concepts.

Why is the focus of attention of interest? For several reasons. First, because it may help to measure the extent of what we, as human beings, intuitively take to be the contents of the mind; it is the material about which we think, or what James (1890) termed the *trailing edge of consciousness*. Second, the focus of attention and its contents are of interest if Baars (1988) is correct in assuming that links are formed between all of the information held in that focus at the same time (also Baars & Franklin, 2003). The way in which new ideas are entered into the memory system would appear to be that already known ideas are hooked together in a new way; that is, a central premise of a seminal article in cognitive psychology (Miller, 1956). However, the ability to hook ideas together may depend on their residing in the focus of attention at the same time.

A simple example, based on Köhler's (1917, 1924, 1927) famous experiments with apes, may help. Imagine that you are placed in a room with a treat tied to a string hanging from the ceiling, slightly too high to reach, in the northeast corner of the room, and nothing else in the room except a strong wooden box in the southwest corner. If you are able to keep in mind the treat and the box at the same time, it probably will occur to you to move the box under the treat to climb on it and get the treat. This type of insight sometimes occurred to apes, albeit much less readily than it would occur to adult humans. For either animal, though, when the insight does occur without one actually seeing the box and the treat in the same visual field, presumably it occurs on the basis of a focus of attention that includes the treat and the box together, combined into a unified mental image or scheme.

Many concepts should require more than two parts be coordinated. For example, full understanding and use of the English verb "to give" requires that one hold in mind and coordinate not only the action, but also three nouns playing different roles: the giver, the object to be transferred, and the recipient.

The coordination of multiple parts also is presumably important for entering new units into long-term memory. How does one commit a telephone number to memory, for example? Sequences of two to four digits at a time can be memorized. In our town, the digits "573" form the local area code, so learning a new telephone number that begins with that area code is not a problem for me anymore. We may commit to memory additional chunks of information such as "634" and "5789." Then we are in a good position to commit new, larger chunks to memory, such as "573-634-5789." Telephone numbers are parsed that way, making the memorization task easier.

What, then, would be the variable distractive conditions that would prevent us (as psychological researchers) from measuring the contents of the focus of attention? There are several, at least. First, the units may be unclear. We don't usually have good information about how the information is grouped into units or chunks. Did a particular person actually memorize "5789," or was it "57-89" or "578-9"? Typically, we don't know. Therefore, if these chunks form the units that are held in mind, we cannot easily count them.

Second, there are other holding mechanisms discussed in the literature that have to be taken into account. Broadbent (1958) and Sperling (1960) discussed a memory for large amounts of unanalyzed sensory information, such as information about how a stimulus field looked, sounded, or felt. That information presumably exists even for spoken channels that are unattended at the time of their presentation, or printed multiple-character arrays that are presented too briefly for all of the characters to be read and memorized. Would it be possible for an individual to recall everything that was present in the focus of attention and then turn attention to the sensory memory of other stimuli, "refilling" attention and then recalling its new contents? If so, that process would tend to inflate our estimates of the capacity of the focus of attention.

Third, it may be possible to use strategies that can "recirculate" information so that it does not have to remain steadily in the focus of attention to remain accessible. Baddeley (1986) discussed the literature on the ability to rehearse covertly verbal materials by saying them to oneself repeatedly. At least in older children and adults, this process can be carried out semiautomatically, without a very concentrated use of attention (Guttentag, 1984).

Fourth, and finally, there is no agreed-on objective index of the focus of attention. One can discuss properties such as the faster access to information inside of the focus of attention compared with information outside of the focus (McElree, 2001; Oberauer, 2002) or the resistance of information in the focus of attention to proactive interference from similar materials (Cowan, Johnson, & Saults, in press; Craik & Birtwhistle, 1971; Halford, Maybery, & Bain, 1988). However, these different criteria do not always yield the same results, leading to a clear distinction between information in versus out of the focus of attention. It is my conjecture that these different criteria will yield comparable outcomes after certain methodological problems are solved, but that conjecture has not yet been proven.

It seems, then, that the road toward measuring a specific capacity is likely to be a long, bumpy, and winding one. On the positive side, we have been able to identify several of the major factors that may complicate or contaminate the measurement and have come up with some fairly convergent results. On the negative side, it seems as if it might be a difficult task to be able to control the influence of all of these distractive conditions to measure capacity, and there could be other such factors that have not been identified.

There even is controversy regarding which tasks should be counted as working memory tasks. For example, some evidence suggests that subitizing could be carried out without holding the objects in the field separately in mind. Instead, one could match the spatial pattern of objects to a known configuration, such as the arrangement of dots on a die. There is evidence that makes this approach plausible (Logan & Zbrodoff, 2003; Tuholski, Engle, & Baylis, 2001). Yet, other evidence suggests that elderly adults cannot subitize as many objects as can young adults (Basak & Verhaeghen, 2003). It is known that elderly adults lose working memory abilities relative to young adults, but there is no reason to suspect that elderly adults lose knowledge about patterns they once had memorized. Also, Trick, Audet, and Dales (2003) found similar subitizing limit even in the case in which the objects moved around on the screen, demonstrating a link between subitizing and another capacity-limited skill: tracking moving objects.

Perhaps a compromise solution is possible; for example, working memory capacity may be needed to learn the patterns in the test situation.

Often, working memory can be observed only in its interaction with other complex systems, as Broadbent (1971) pointed out long ago. So, the goal of analyzing working memory within the processing system will be a challenging one.

□ THREE ATTITUDES: NAIVE CONSTANCY, RELATIVITY, AND REFINED CONSTANCY

With the possibilities and difficulties kept in mind, now let us return to Carr's (1933) classic discussion. He returns to the old topic of the span of apprehension: "How many spatially discrete objects can one visually apprehend at once? The question implies that there is a numerical constant involved which it is our duty to discover. Titchener … and Pillsbury … report this number to be 4 or 5" (p. 514). Call this simple quest for a constant *naïve constancy*.

Through subtle ridicule, Carr then captures well a denigration of the quest for constants that, in my experience, clearly persists in the field:

> What shall we do with these numbers when we get them? Is their attainment the goal of our science? Will they give us scientific elation and peace of mind? Will our students be thrilled by such knowledge? Do we obtain these numerical facts in order to explain them? If the number apprehended is a constant, must not that fact be contingent upon some fixed characteristic of the optical apparatus? What are those limiting characteristics? (p. 514)

The antidote to this approach is relativity:

> The opposing attitude is that of *relativity*. It assumes that the number apprehended is a function of the particular conditions employed, and that the obtained value will vary with these conditions. The experimental procedure is as follows. The value for an arbitrarily selected set of conditions is first obtained. These conditions are then systematically varied in the attempt to discover which are effective and which are non-effective. The attempt is made—not to hold the number constant—but to control it as much as possible—to vary it within its maximal and minimal limits. The interest of the experimenter is not in the numbers, but in the list of effective factors and their kind and degree of influence. (p. 515)

To Carr (1933), this approach seems to prevail:

> Is the number of objects apprehended a constant or a highly variable quantity? To my mind the facts at hand indicate a high degree of relativity. If the objects are clear-cut, distinct, homogeneous, and arranged in a square, 36 may be readily apprehended. ... The number apprehended is highly relative to the conditions of the experiment. (p. 515)

Fair enough; but it is still important to ask what the end point of this type of investigation may be. Are we then supposed to be satisfied with the conclusion that the span of apprehension simply varies widely? To do so seems an admission of defeat. The real glory may come in finding constancy within the relativity. For example, although Albert Einstein gave us relativity in the field of physics, one result of his inquiry was the postulation of an apparently inviolable constant, the speed of light in a vacuum. Another well-known outcome that could be considered to be constant was the rate of conversion between matter and energy ($E = mc^2$).

So we come to the possibility of *refined constancy*, or constants formulated with respect to relevant varying conditions. Yes, it may be possible to apprehend 36 objects arranged in an orderly fashion, at least after some practice with the pattern. If so, however, perhaps there is a conversion rate. Considerable order among the set is needed if 36 objects are to be apprehended. For example, it may be that there is a design with four rows of dots, each containing three sets of three dots. Then, if the array is presented long enough for those facts to be understood, it is possible to conclude that there are 36 items. However, that process may occur through a series of steps, during each of which only about three or four items are apprehended. At one step, the lower-level set size of three dots is noticed. At the next step, the row size of three of these sets is noticed, and at another moment, the four rows are noticed. So it remains possible that a constant can be extracted from the morass. There may be only 3 or 4 objects apprehended at each single moment within the process of enumerating the 36 dots.

To explore the possibility that a basic constant such as the span of apprehension, or in other words the capacity of the focus of attention, exists, it is necessary to understand the "various distractive conditions" that may apply. By investigating the research on the human information-processing system as it has been applied to the concept of working memory, we may gain a context to search for constancy of capacity.

In the analogy regarding the capacity of a ferry boat, suppose that one could not observe the cars going into the ferry (perhaps because it was proprietary information?), but only had an estimate of the people arriving at the city on the opposite shore, whether by ferry boat or by another means such as a bridge. That estimate would serve some practical purposes, such as planning the amount of food needed in the city. However, if one wanted to understand the fundamental capability of the system, a more controlled approach would have to be taken. For example, the city could temporarily close the bridge and also limit the ferry voyages to one person per vehicle. Then the number of people arriving in the city would serve as an estimate of how many vehicles fit on the boat. This stretched analogy helps to dramatize the situation in human cognition in which a basic mechanism of working memory capacity, narrowly defined, is not apparent to the eye but can be investigated if we know enough about the processing system in which the mechanism is ensconced. One such basic mechanism is that associated with conscious awareness of the stimuli and a capacity-limited, primary memory.

The next section investigates working memory limits broadly defined, with reference to terminology commonly used within the field of working memory. Then, investigations of capacity limits will be described in preparation for the present theoretical approach to capacity in chapter 2.

☐ HISTORY OF WORKING MEMORY RESEARCH: ALTERNATIVE TERMS AND CONCEPTS

Almost no aspect of working memory has been without lively controversy, and the controversy proves to be quite relevant to the issue of the capacity of working memory. The work and debate has been known by different terms, each of which underlies a different way of thinking about aspects of working memory. A history of terms and definitions is intertwined with a history of research.

Primary and Secondary Memory

Working memory is a concept that has been evident in some form to various philosophers. As Logie (1996) pointed out, John Locke (1690) distinguished between a faculty of mind that he termed *contemplation* or bringing an idea to mind, and *memory*, or the power to revive an idea after it has disappeared from the mind. Relevant concepts appeared in the late 19th century in the works of one of the first experimental psychologists, Wilhelm Wundt, much of which was never translated from German into

English. In the United States, William James (1890), who was aware of Wundt's work, distinguished between *primary memory* and *secondary memory*. The latter refers to the vast amount of information stored from a lifetime of experience, whereas primary memory refers to "the trailing edge of the conscious present," clearly a much more narrowly limited amount of information.

The term *primary memory* was made more popular within experimental psychology by an influential article by Waugh and Norman (1965) in which a mathematical formula was used to distinguish the special contribution of primary memory. That study, like many others in the field, made use of a tradition going back at least to Ebbinghaus (1895/1964), in which the stimuli to be remembered were unconnected lists of verbal items (such as words or nonsense syllables) in a random order. This sort of experiment is deemed useful even though, in the real world, memory for words in a sentence or memory for other realistic stimuli depends on making logical connections between the elements, drawing heavily on experience to do so. The experimental rationale is that one can gain a better understanding of some of the underlying memory processes by minimizing associations between items to be recalled; effects of coherent connections can then be added on to that. Waugh and Norman used series of random digits, and their mathematical formula capitalized on the finding that memory for the most recent few items in a list is superior to memory for prior items, from the middle of the list (the *recency effect*). It was assumed that the advantage for the most recent items occurred because those items were present in primary memory, which could be used along with secondary memory. Presumably, though, prior items had been displaced from primary memory. It was estimated on this basis that only a few items could be held in primary memory at a time.

An apparent problem for the approach of Waugh and Norman (1965) is that items at the beginning of a list also typically are recalled better than the middle items (the *primacy effect*), even though those initial items should have been displaced from primary memory. A possible solution to that problem comes from the finding that covert rehearsal greatly favors items near the beginning of the list; when individuals are asked to rehearse aloud, they produce those items repeatedly, much more often than they produce items in the list (Rundus, 1971; Tan & Ward, 2000). Therefore, the items that are recalled the most may be those that either were presented last or were re-presented last by the experimental subject's own covert mental processes. This sort of analysis suggests that the estimate of the contents of primary memory should take into account primacy effects, not just recency effects.

One consequence of this covert rehearsal is that, if one asks participants at the end of a study of list memory to re-recall all of the words from all of the lists in a surprise test, they recall the words from the beginning of the lists best of all, the middle items next best, and the most recent items from the various lists more poorly, a phenomenon known as the *negative recency effect* (Craik, Gardiner, & Watkins, 1970). This effect stands in stark contrast to the excellent performance on the most recent items in immediate free recall, the ordinary recency effect. Presumably, the act of rehearsing items helps form a stable mental representation in memory for later recall. The most recent few items in each list are not as often rehearsed in that manner because they can be recalled directly from primary memory without such rehearsal. In the final free recall test, though, the primary memory representation of these items no longer exists and a long-term memory has not been formed through rehearsal, either.

Although few would totally deny the distinction between primary and secondary memory mechanisms as William James (1890) described them, researchers often have questioned whether the distinction is truly important to consider when predicting performance on memory tasks. Some have argued for a memory system that is seamless and unified and have looked toward the hope of accounting for performance on all memory tasks with a single set of principles and laws, regardless of the circumstances or test delays (e.g., Brown, Preece, & Hulme, 2000; Crowder, 1993; McGeoch, 1932; Melton, 1963; Nairne, 2002; Neath & Surprenant, 2003; Wickelgren, 1975). The viability of this approach hinges on several questions: (1) whether there is an advantage for items to be recalled before a certain fixed amount of time has passed (at least, after the items are no longer attended) and a drop-off or decay of memory at approximately a fixed rate; and (2) whether there is a mechanism that holds information with a limited capacity, so that new information can be entered only by replacing other information. The unified-memory alternative to these two principles is, respectively, that memory drops off at a rate that is totally dependent on the schedule of presentation of items that has been used (e.g., Logan, 2004; Waugh & Norman, 1965) and that interference between items occurs but not because of a limited capacity (e.g., Nairne & Neath, 2001).

There are now several critiques suggesting that the unitary approach is not sufficient (Cowan, 1995, 1999; Davelaar, Goshen-Gottstein, Ashkenazi, Haarman, & Usher, 2005; Healy & McNamara, 1996). There are many phenomena that, although supporting a unitary system at first glance, appear to show subtle dissociations between short- and long-term memory when examined more closely. For example, Bjork and Whitten (1974) and Tzeng (1973) showed that recency effects could be obtained even with a long distracting task, lasting many seconds, after each item. The distracting tasks should make it impossible for a temporary memory representation to be responsible; therefore, other principles must be responsible for the recency effect that occurs in such circumstances. However, there may be multiple mechanisms responsible for recency effects, only some of which pertain to a temporary or short-term representation. Other aspects of the pattern of responses are not the same when words are presented with interleaved distracting tasks. For example, whereas there is an advantage in memory for lists of short words when the words are presented together, presumably because of a rehearsal mechanism operating in short-term memory (Baddeley, 1986), there is an advantage in memory for lists of long words when the words are presented with intervening distracting tasks (Cowan, Wood, & Borne, 1994; Cowan, Wood, Nugent, & Treisman, 1997). Also, when words are presented together, the last few are not deeply processed so that a "negative recency" effect occurs in final free recall (Craik et al., 1970); but this does not happen when the words were initially presented with intervening distracting tasks (for a review see Davelaar et al., 2005). Cowan (1995) and Davelaar et al. (2005) reviewed other such examples in the literature. Davelaar et al. also predicted and obtained a new dissociation, confirming that the recency effect was devoid of proactive interference in immediate free recall (Craik & Birtwhistle, 1971), but not in the presence of distractor tasks between items presented for free recall.

Nevertheless, many studies indicate that it is difficult to find direct evidence of a process in which information decays as a function of the amount of elapsed time (Cowan, Beschin, & Della Sala, 2004; Cowan, Saults, & Nugent, 2001; Nairne, 2002; Winkler, Schröger, & Cowan, 2001). If there is no such thing as decay, the unitary and dual approaches can still quibble about whether interference that takes place over time supports a temporary-memory process or not. For the most part, in this book, the arguments for and against decay will be circumvented.

Instead, the emphasis is on a system that has a limited capacity. It, too, could be under attack from unitary memory theory, inasmuch as one might predict a limited number of items recalled on the basis of unitary principles in particular test situations. What I will attempt to demonstrate, however, is that a simpler account for all of the existing evidence is one in which at least one particular mental mechanism, perhaps the focus of attention, has a limited capacity that can be measured as a fixed number of objects or chunks. This type of mechanism provides support for James' (1890) distinction between primary and secondary forms of memory.

Immediate and Mediate Memory

Another term in early use was *immediate memory*. This refers to memory in situations in which recall is requested as soon as the stimulus sequence ends. It can be compared with *mediate memory*, or memory when there is material interposed between the target stimulus sequence and the response. It is hard to trace the origins of such terms. However, in a literature search using a database that covers journal articles and some books back to 1872, I found that the earliest entry for "immediate memory" was Winch (1904) in his study of school children. One limitation of this term is that it implies that the memory faculty includes only items just presented. If information is recalled from secondary memory back into primary memory, that does not fall within the definition of immediate memory. Therefore, though it is well-suited to a description of an important type of test situation, it does not seem broad enough for a principled discussion of the mental faculties that underlie performance in such tests.

Short- and Long-Term Memory

The term *short-term memory* and its complement, *long-term memory*, have been very popular. Again, it is not clear when these terms first were used. Thorndike (1910) discussed "memory over short and long intervals," and the terms short- and long-term memory were widely used to reflect these two situations. The implication from research early on in cognitive psychology (e.g., Broadbent, 1958; Brown, 1958, 1959; Miller, 1956; Peterson & Peterson, 1959) was that a special process of some sort was needed to account for the recall of information in the short term. One problem with that term is that its intended meaning differs somewhat from the way in which it has come to be understood by the public. Various studies (e.g., Peterson & Peterson, 1959) suggested that there is a special access to information for up to about a 30-s period; consequently, that was the period typically labeled short-term memory by cognitive psychologists. In contrast, when I hear nonpsychologists talk about short-term memory, they typically are referring to information acquired within about a day, as opposed to information learned previously. That is a potentially important distinction and there should be terms for it, but it is not what was intended in the field of cognitive psychology by short- and long-term memory. This is one reason not to continue using these terms. They cause confusion.

The term short-term memory also became associated, in time, with a simplified notion of performance in which items that were to be remembered in the short term were all placed in a simple location in the mind to be retrieved, intact, later. That was not really the fault of the early researchers whose seminal works incorporated such a simplified metaphor in one way or another (e.g., Atkinson & Shiffrin, 1968; Broadbent, 1958; Miller,

1956); there was no reason to use a metaphorical model that was more complex than the phenomena the researchers were trying to explain. Nevertheless, the term short-term memory does not appear to express the multifaceted nature of temporary retention processes as we now commonly conceive of them.

Figure 1.2 depicts fundamental properties of the working memory system as conceived in three ways, the first of which relates to the present section. It is the processing diagram sketched in a footnote by Broadbent (1958) and later elaborated on by Atkinson and Shiffrin (1968), which Baddeley (1986) termed the *modal model* because a number of early models were similar.

The modal model shown at the top of Fig. 1.2 is based on findings that people could only pay attention to a limited amount at once, usually a single channel of information, but still could retrieve information from a stimulus on any unattended channel or source if attention was switched to it quickly enough afterward (Broadbent, 1958). The model therefore posits a passive memory of limited duration but unlimited capacity (i.e., holding an unlimited amount of information at one time) feeding information into a capacity-limited store. This, in turn, feeds information into a long-term or secondary store.

The arrows in Fig. 1.2 represent the transfer of information from one structure to another. The passive memory of unlimited capacity was presumably sensory in nature, and therefore has been labeled sensory storage. The model apparently allowed that sensory information might be generated in the long term and capacity-limited stores together and passed back down into the sensory store; thus, the two-way arrows between the capacity-limited store and sensory storage. This differs from the usual assumption that sensory memory can come only from the senses and cannot be completely replicated through mental processes such as imagery (see Cowan, 1995, for a review of this issue). So, perhaps the first store in the model should be viewed as a composite of sensory information from all sources, external and internal. The feedback of information from long-term storage to the limited-capacity store is essential if people are going to relate the incoming stimuli to known categories (i.e., to recognize things that they experience).

Some kind of filtering device was assumed to allow only a certain amount to pass from the unlimited store to the limited store, and attention was assumed to control the filtering device. This filter explains why multiple arrows can go between the outside world and sensory storage, whereas a much smaller set of arrows can go between the sensory store and the limited-capacity store.

A source of potential confusion in this model is that the unlimited sensory store was originally called a *short-term store*, whereas Atkinson and

Modal Model (after Broadbent, 1958)

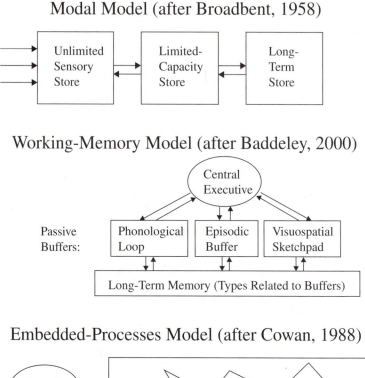

Working-Memory Model (after Baddeley, 2000)

Embedded-Processes Model (after Cowan, 1988)

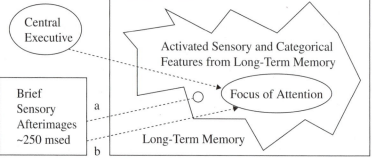

FIGURE 1.2 Schematic representations of the information-processing theoretical frameworks of Broadbent (1958), top; Baddeley (2000), middle; and Cowan (1988, 1999), bottom.

Shiffrin (1968) and others subsequently used the term short-term store to refer to the limited-capacity storage system.

There is a possible issue with the logical sequence of events in the functioning of the model (Cowan, 1988). First, it may be that sensory memory has to make contact with the information in long-term storage before information can be placed in the limited-capacity store; one needs to come up with the categories of sensory information before it can be coded as a finite number of objects. Second, because people easily seem to notice an abrupt change in an unattended spoken message from one voice to another (Cherry, 1953), it does not seem possible that information in unattended channels, after entering sensory memory, is simply thrown away entirely. It must be available for comparison with recent stimulation.

Working Memory and Long-term Memory

It is not clear where the term *working memory* came from, but it was used already in an important, forward-looking book by Miller, Galanter, and Pribram (1960), *Plans and the structure of behavior*. In place of the older conception that behavior results from associations flowing from stimuli to responses, Miller et al. suggested that behavior is governed by concepts serving the function of goals and plans, against which actions are judged and modified until a goal is reached. Within that context, it was clear that there had to be a working memory that was used to maintain the plans in an effective state and make comparisons between plans and actions.

The concept of working memory was brought to the forefront of the field with the publication of an influential chapter by that name by Baddeley and Hitch (1974), and later publications such as the book by Baddeley (1986) also titled *Working Memory*. By the time of the 1974 work, a number of competing models of human information processing had been proposed by various researchers that typically included a mechanism that was much like a unitary short-term memory in the modal model. The main message of Baddeley's work has been that the modal model is overly simplistic, in that the data provide support for a multifaceted holding mechanism in place of short-term memory. This multifaceted mechanism is what was termed working memory. It was said to include two separate, passive holding devices—the phonological store and the visuospatial sketchpad, processes that are capable of recycling information into these stores to keep it active so that it cannot fade (namely, rehearsal processes) and a set of central executive processes that carry out the active work in which information is shuttled in and out of these stores and to other aspects of the processing system.

The middle panel of Figure 1.2 shows the working memory model of Baddeley (2000), amended from earlier depictions (Baddeley, 1986) by the presence of an episodic buffer. Unlike the early renditions of this model, the relation between the buffer stores and long-term memory is explicitly shown. Information from long-term memory presumably helps to determine the form of the representation in the buffer stores.

As mentioned previously, the addition of an episodic buffer greatly increases the scope of information that can be stored in the model. It can include information that is not exclusively phonological or visuospatial in nature. However, this model still does not really address the question of how sensory memory is processed. It was probably the finding that printed words are remembered phonologically that pushed Baddeley away from an explicit representation of sensory memory; the sensory modality of the stimulus did not seem important for the phonological similarity effect or for the other effects that were the hallmark of the phonological loop, for example. Yet, other evidence shows that auditory sensory and phonological information are not interchangeable. For example, in the immediate recall of lists, there is an auditory modality superiority effect (Penney, 1989) that originates during encoding of the list and is easier to observe after several items have already been recalled, degrading the memory representations (Cowan, Saults, & Brown, 2004). Also, in the suffix effect (Crowder & Morton, 1969; Morton, Crowder, & Prussin, 1971) a list final item, or suffix, that does not have to be recalled interferes with memory for the end of a spoken list. A suffix word (such as the word *recall*) interferes more than a suffix tone, and a word in the same voice as the list items interferes more than a word in a different speaker's voice. It appears, therefore, that the suffix interferes with both sensory and phonological information. The interference with those two types of information seems to have different time courses, inasmuch as a silent distracting task interposed between the list and the suffix does not eliminate the suffix effect, but does make it no longer voice-specific (Balota & Duchek, 1986). The distracting task seems to remove the sensory information without removing the phonological information. Other research shows that mental imagery of a tone cannot completely preserve the information in an actual tone presentation (Keller, Cowan, & Saults, 1995). So, there is likely to be sensory information that must be saved in a way that is not phonological or spatiotemporal in nature, and an episodic buffer would not be the appropriate storage medium either.

Also, the model does not fully distinguish between information that is attended versus ignored at the time of its presentation. That distinction is clear in Broadbent's model because unattended information is not transferred from sensory memory to the capacity-limited store. In Baddeley's modeling framework, it is true that a case has been made that acoustic verbal information automatically enters the phonological buffer without a necessary role for attention, whereas printed information must be transformed through a process that presumably does require attention. The evidence for this distinction (Salamé & Baddeley, 1982) is that irrelevant speech interfered with memory of printed lists of words, presumably because the irrelevant speech cannot be kept out of the phonological buffer that is used for recall of the printed lists. The need for active processes for the printed lists is shown by the finding that articulatory suppression abolished the irrelevant-speech effect, just as it abolishes word-length and phonological-similarity effects for those items (Baddeley, Lewis, & Vallar, 1984). However, some cracks have appeared in that explanation. For example, Jones and Macken (1995) showed that the phonological similarity between the spoken and printed verbal items does not matter for recall, as Salamé and Baddeley originally thought (also see LeCompte & Shaibe, 1997). Cowan, Lichty, and Grove (1990, Experiment 4) found that even the perception of spoken consonants is considerably poorer when attention is directed away from the speech than it is when attention is directed toward it, so phonological information does not appear to enter working memory in full force without the help of attention to the stimuli.

In sum, the working memory model of Baddeley and colleagues has stood as the industry standard for many years, and for a reason. It is easy to grasp and serves to explain many important phenomena. It is a basis on which many predictions have been made and tested. It does, however, leave other phenomena unresolved or unexplained. Now we turn more specifically to the history of scientific exploration of a capacity of a holding mechanism that is limited in the number of units held.

☐ HISTORY OF RESEARCH ON IMMEDIATE-MEMORY CAPACITY

Some early studies investigated various issues related to capacity limits that are still important today. We already discussed Jevons' (1871) groundbreaking investigation in which he hurled groups of beans and tried to estimate their number without counting. More objective methods have been used in other studies of enumeration. In these studies, the presentation has been mechanized or computerized and the timing of presentation has been controlled (e.g., Kaufman, Lord, Reese, & Volkmann, 1949; Mandler & Shebo, 1982). Yet, the results have been similar to what Jevons (1871) obtained.

It is often said that the first true experimental psychology laboratory was established by Wilhelm Wundt. In some of his work, Wundt (1894/ 1998) also addressed capacity limits. For example, in one series of studies (pp. 260–265), he carried out a task in which a rapid series of metronome ticks was to be compared with a second series, the task being to determine whether the series were of equal length. This is like a sequential and acoustic version of the enumeration task of Jevons. However, the role of grouping of ticks together to form larger units also was considered.

The person who is known for initiating the field of memory is Hermann Ebbinghaus (1885/1913). In his work, also, one can see the involvement of immediate-memory limits. His method was to invent a large number of nonsense syllables so that he could arrange them into lists to be learned in order to study learning across various conditions without the very real but unwieldy-to-control contributions of semantic associations between items. In discussing the method, he remarks (1885/1913 translation), "As a general thing the capacity for voluntary reproduction persists after it has once been reached. In numerous cases, however, it disappears immediately after its first appearance, and is regained only after several further repetitions" (p. 27). This shows that the original recall may have been the result of a moment of special attention to the stimuli, resulting in some sort of temporary representation that does not give rise to an adequate permanent representation. Confirming that Ebbinghaus adopts this interpretation, he subsequently adds that precautions must be taken "In the case of the tests of the first period, in order to limit the significance of the first fleeting grasp ... of the series in moments of special concentration ..." (p. 33). In other words, what happens in immediate memory is important in understanding the formation of memories in general. This is a theme that was later emphasized by Broadbent (1958) in his book that helped to launch the field of cognitive psychology. Whatever is to be securely stored in long-term memory must pass through working memory, so the capacity of working memory is one limitation to the encoding of memories in general (Cowan, 1995).

Raffel (1937) examined the factor of grouping in the span of apprehension as an extension of work on a similar topic published by Cattell (1885). Raffel presented elements as organized line drawings of faces or as spatial rearrangements of these same line elements. With a short presentation, individuals reported that the details were not remembered any better in the case of organized faces than in the case of disorganized elements. Yet, the subjects "were often able to report certain aspects of the faces ... but unable to recall the details which gave rise to the impression" (p. 104). The conclusion drawn by the author was that "grouping of units increases the span of apprehension only if the units can be inferred from surrogates" (p. 104). In other words, the rapidly presented faces could be perceived on two levels: the level of detailed features and the level of an overall facial impression. Yet, these two levels remained separate. For example, a subject reported that the face had a scowl but was unable to recall how it was represented in terms of lines, so that this facial information did not assist in recalling the details. When the presentation time was long enough for the relationships between the line elements and the overall impression to be apprehended, then the overall impression did help in the recall of the elements. This relation between elements and overall impression is closely related to what Miller (1956) later termed *chunk formation*.

Dosajh (1959) examined the relation between the span of apprehension and intelligence in 50 children in India between 13 and 15 years of age. Span of apprehension was measured using 5 to 15 dots (arranged as 2, 3, or 4 groups with 3, 4, or 5 dots per group) presented for 200 ms using a tachistoscope; the subject was to indicate the number of dots. Intelligence was measured by the Madras Test for General Intelligence. A correlation of .45 was obtained. (Also, a pilot study using Ravens Progressive Matrices with 20 children resulted in a correlation with the span of apprehension that was not reported but was described as quite high.) Amazingly, there has been little subsequent work on this topic; the relation of subitizing (possibly a simple capacity measure) to intelligence apparently has not been studied much.

It is striking that evidence suggesting the possibility of a capacity-limited, active, and attention-related portion of the mind occurred so early in the history of experimental psychology. Still, it is not clear from this literature what the result means theoretically. The issues raised in the early literature still appear to be unsettled and will be revisited many times in this book.

Miller's Review of Capacity Limits

Miller's (1956) article on "The magical number seven plus or minus two" has been one of the most widely cited articles in the entire field of psychology. What it did was to bring up the possibility of measuring clear, fundamental limits of the human mind at a time when the cognitive revolution in experimental psychology was just beginning (e.g., Gardner, 1985). Miller tied together three phenomena. First, the number of items that could be repeated verbatim in immediate-recall procedures is about seven. Second, the limit in the span of apprehension (discussed previously) was said to be about seven. Third, in absolute judgment tasks, in which a single item is presented on each trial and has to be placed into one of several categories, the number of categories along a single dimension (e.g., categories of loudness, pitch, or brightness) that can be used reliably approximates seven. Early on, the article drew in readers with the facetious, yet intriguing complaint that "My problem is that I have been persecuted by an integer." However, it ended with a note of discouragement to the intrigued:

> What about the seven-point rating scale, the seven categories for absolute judgment, the seven objects in the span of attention, and

the seven digits in the span of immediate memory? ... Perhaps there is something deep and profound behind all of these sevens, something just calling out for us to discover it. But I suspect that it is only a pernicious, Pythagorean coincidence.

Miller (1989) cleared up some of the mystery about his intentions. He related the story of how he was asked to give an invited address but, in the current state of his career, had only two unrelated research topics that could not easily be combined into a coherent hour-long presentation. He at first declined the invitation in a long note, but was asked to reconsider on the grounds that "anyone who needed two pages to say no obviously wanted to say yes." He then did accept the invitation, based on the following thoughts. He asked himself if there was anything in common to his work on absolute judgments and on immediate recall. He reported that he came up with the following:

> The only thing I could think of was a numerical similarity. The span of immediate memory for digits is about seven. The channel capacities that had been coming out of the studies of absolute judgments ran around 2.5 to 3 bits of information. When I suddenly realized that 2.5 bits is six alternatives, I saw how the two might be linked together. It was a superficial similarity, but it enabled me to accept the EPA's[Eastern Psychological Association's] invitation. I chose a humorous title for the talk ... thinking to make it obvious that I knew this shotgun wedding of absolute judgment and immediate memory was little more than a joke. To give it a little more legitimacy, however, I threw in a third instance, the experiments at Mount Holyoke College on the discrimination of number: when haphazard patterns of dots are flashed briefly on the screen, people can estimate the number accurately up to five or six dots. (pp. 400–402)

One important message of Miller (1956) in relation to immediate-memory procedures was that the amount of information that could be stored depended on how the information was grouped together, so that the limitation in memory occurred not necessarily for separate stimuli, but for mental groups or "chunks" of information. In this regard, the article was echoing themes that had occasionally been put forward earlier; for example, by Cattell (1885) and Raffel (1937).

What was unclear, though, is the theoretical message about the limitation in capacity. If people can recall about seven items, that does not necessarily mean that they can recall about seven chunks of information because the information may be grouped. For example, telephone numbers are typically presented in small groups of three and four digits because it is too difficult to recall the numbers without grouping them. Perhaps the common limit of about seven items reflects some combination of a limit in how many chunks can be recalled and a typical amount of chunking that can be accomplished. Judging from how telephone numbers are grouped, one might speculate that it is possible to recall two or three groups of two to four digits and that the practical limit of seven reflects this.

Another account of why the fundamental short-term capacity limit might have been overestimated was described by Mandler (1967):

> When a[n] S [subject] is required to memorize relatively large sets of words, the mechanism apparently involves two separate processes: Short-term, or primary, memory (Waugh & Norman, 1965), which produces recall of the words immediately preceding the output; and organized memory, which typically includes earlier words from the list (cf. Waugh, 1961). Thus the number of 7 ± 2 may be made up of two components: 4 ± 1 plus 3 ± 1. (p. 332)

The ambivalence in Miller (1956) toward the notion of a common capacity across procedures, along with the theoretical uncertainty of what seven means in the absence of knowledge about how many chunks that reflects, has led many researchers to take a pessimistic view toward the usefulness of searching for capacity limits. On one hand, as a rule of thumb the magical number 7 has been accepted as a short-term memory limit. On the other hand, many sophisticated readers instead have taken the view that the capacity "all depends" on many different factors and therefore that capacity limits are not likely to be a useful topic of study. I hope to show as a major theme of this book that these capacity limits are a useful topic of study and that it is possible to be optimistic about measuring capacity limits by using approaches in which the mental formation of groups or chunks is estimated in various ways.

Capacity Limits and the Neo-Piagetians

It is clear that researchers' interest in primary or short-term memory was not simply to understand performance on a narrow set of tasks in which several items are presented for immediate recall. If this sort of memory was an indication of what an individual had in his or her mind, then its capacity might be related to the capacity for thought in many more complex situations. This view was developed by researchers called *neo-Piagetian* based on the connection of their work to that of Jean Piaget. His work was in stark contrast to the psychometric perspective of intelligence in which there was a pragmatic interest in whatever tasks turned out to discriminate between individuals with better versus poorer ability in school, work, or military settings. Piaget instead was interested in the structures of thoughts and the complexity that they encompass and how the permissible complexity evolves and develops. He examined this with respect to cognitive improvements with development in childhood, and to a lesser extent in other domains such as the history of science.

Piaget's theory was expressed in terms of the competence of an individual to understand certain rules. For example, the concept of reversible operations mandates that certain acts can be undone. If one pours water from a tall beaker to a wide one and then back again, the amount of water remains the same throughout (assuming none is spilled in transition); the operation is a reversible one. Children can be too young to comprehend such rules of nature. As an early neo-Piagetian, Juan Pascual-Leone (1970) sought to understand how limitations in the child's working memory are involved in understanding and expressing such a rule. In his own words:

> ... it has already been shown (Vernon, 1965) that Piagetian tasks constitute good measures of G [the general factor in intelligence]. ... It is well known that this heuristically powerful notion of general stages offers the possibility of constructing a natural ordinal scale of intellectual development. The dimension on which this scale is located appears to the present writer to be the informational complexity of the task considered from the *subject's point of view* ... an important corollary of this view is that any general stage of cognitive development could in principle have one numerical characteristic: the number of separate schemes (i.e., separate chunks of information) on which the subject can operate simultaneously using his mental structures. (p. 302)

Pascual-Leone developed a mathematical theory that incorporated a parameter M, the number of schemes that could be activated concurrently. He trained children of various ages to link certain stimuli to responses (e.g., raise your hand to a square, clap your hands to a red object, and close your eyes if there are open spaces in the contour of the figure) and then examined their responses in situations in which compound cues (such as a red square) were presented and should lead to multiple actions if the stimulus-response links were activated concurrently. The distribution of the capability M was said to depend on the "content of attention ... span of attention" and "intensity of attention." With the assumption that the children in the study understood and remembered the task instructions equally well, but had not learned to carry out multiple behaviors automatically, the number of schemes that could be carried out could then be assumed to reflect the use of capability M to attend to the stimulus-response links or schemes present in the stimulus. In a sample of children ranging in age from 5 to 12 years, the number of schemes that could be concurrently activated seemed to range from a typical value of one to three in the youngest group to a typical value of two to six in the oldest group. There was, however, a restriction placed on the selection of children: they were "all field-independent subjects preselected according to their performances on one test measuring Witkin's cognitive-style variable." Other children apparently would not be so analytically inclined in the compound task.

It is worth considering briefly how the M space was supposed to be applied to explain performance in a Piagetian task. Pascual-Leone and Smith (1969) explained it with reference to a class inclusion task. A young child is presented with some objects and is asked whether there are more of one kind or another. In a typical situation leading to errors in young children, the display might include three goats and two cows. The question presented to the child would be whether there are more goats or more animals. The incorrect answer is often given, that there are more goats. Now, there is ample evidence indicating that children who give the wrong answer actually would know that both goats and cows are animals (and the equivalent knowledge for other such questions). There also are control experiments that were mentioned, making sure that the problem is not simply a misinterpretation of the question. To solve the problem, though, all of the appropriate schemes have to be activated in the attention system at the same time so that they can be integrated to yield the correct response. If the scheme saying that goats are animals does not get activated as the child listens to the question because too many other schemes are directly activated, then the inference mechanism will discount the goats when counting animals. In general, the idea is that only a certain number of schemes can be activated at once and that a limitation in how many can be activated can result in incorrect logical inferences.

The baton of neo-Piagetianism was carried after that primarily by Robbie Case, who published part of his doctoral dissertation research in 1972, acknowledging Pascual-Leone as a member of his doctoral committee. Case developed another task to examine the increase in M space with age in childhood. In his task, each number within a spatially ordered series of numbers was uncovered and then covered up again. Then, a test number was presented and the child had to indicate where in the series (now covered) it would go. For example, in one trial, the series included the numbers 3, 9, and 18, and the test number was 11. It also was revealed and then covered so that four numbers had to be kept in mind, along with the task procedure. The results seemed broadly consistent with Pascual-Leone; 6-, 8-, and 10-year-old children were able to keep in mind two, three, and four numbers, respectively.

In Case's (1972) discussion of his results, he gave expression to what had to be a major controversy. He noted that performance depended on keeping in mind not only the numbers to be recalled, but also the procedure to be carried out. If the procedure took up less memory in older children, this would leave room for more numbers. So, it was unclear whether the change with age was a change in the amount that could be stored or in the efficiency with which that storage took place. In either case, as he noted, "whether or not the use of the phrase 'capacity construct' is justified, it is clear that the construct of Mental Space, as defined by Pascual-Leone, has cross-task validity" (p. 301).

Case, Kurland, and Goldberg (1982) appeared to resolve this issue with a striking outcome. They tested memory for sets of words in children 3 to 6 years old and found that word span (repetition of a list of spoken words) was linearly related to the speed at which words could be repeated. A single word was spoken via a tape recorder, and the time between the word and the child's response was measured. There was a linear relation between the speed of word repetition and the word span, a theme that reflected what also had been done in the adult span (Baddeley, Thomson, & Buchanan, 1975), which we will soon discuss. In another experiment (this time using children 6 to 12 years old), Case et al. developed a task that was intended to prevent rehearsal and grouping. It combined storage and processing, as had also been done in an adult study (Daneman & Carpenter, 1980). Case et al. used a "counting span" procedure that was described originally in an oral presentation by Case, Kurland, and Daneman (1979). In that procedure, each card in a set contained an array of colored dots to be counted. After several cards were presented, the sums of all of the cards had to be repeated. The number of cards that could be counted with correct recall of the sums was taken as the counting span. Again, similar to the word-span study, counting span was found to be linearly related to a processing speed; this time, it was counting speed. The implication that was drawn was that the age difference occurred because older children processed the items more efficiently and therefore left more of their working memory space free to retain the items to be recalled.

For both word span and counting span, Case et al. (1982) also reasoned that if adults were given materials that lowered their processing efficiencies, they might show commensurately less recall. That is, in fact, what happened. For adults, real words or digits were replaced with nonsense words such as *rab*, *slif*, and so on. Most impressively, in counting span, adults using nonsense words that they had been taught as substitutes to numbers displayed a counting rate and a counting span approximately the same as first-grade children.

Case (1995) reconsidered what this result actually meant. Originally, it had been taken to suggest that the developmental difference in memory span is the result of developmental differences in the efficiency of mnemonic operations that have to be carried out while items are held in mind (such as linguistic encoding and counting). However, an equally plausible explanation of the span–speed correlation was that a third factor such as neural maturation accounted for both of the changes: it could cause changes in both operational efficiency and storage capability. Indeed, that interpretation would be compatible not only with Case et al. (1982), but also with Case (1972), in which it seemed that only part of the developmental change could be attributed to the efficiency of operations. He appealed especially to the unpublished data of S. A. Griffin. He trained children on number concepts and found a considerable improvement on them, but no concomitant improvement in counting span or counting speed. This seemed to suggest that neither span nor speed could be attributed directly to the conceptual understanding in the processing domain, but rather to maturation. Of course, this sort of result does not clear up the path of causation between speed and span. An improvement in either one theoretically might help the other, or they both could benefit from the same maturational change without any causal path between them.

One still might be impressed that, in adults, Case et al. (1982) found that slowing down subjects by using nonsense words as stimuli reduced span, in both the word-span and counting-span tasks. However, another possibility that must be considered is that speed is still not the causal factor. An alternative possibility, for example, is that nonsense words are not a single chunk each. If given nonsense words such as *bif*, *sil*, and *pom*, it is quite possible to mix up the phonemes to produce *bil*, *sof*, *pim*, for example (Drewnowski & Murdock, 1980). Then, it might be that the effective units were smaller and the effective numbers of chunks were greater for nonsense words than for words. Such an increase in effective list length of the nonsense materials (measured in chunks) could have caused the slowdown in pronunciation or counting in adults. So the question of whether operational efficiency or capacity changes with maturation is not resolved by this line of research.

Another interesting variety of neo-Piagetian account of the role of working memory in cognitive development has been described by Graeme Halford and colleagues (e.g., Andrews & Halford, 2002; Halford, Wilson, & Phillips, 1998). This work expounds a theory of processing complexity that is a direct descendent of the thoughts by Pascual-Leone (1970) and by Piaget in references cited by Pascual-Leone, in which it was suggested that working memory serves as an integrating mechanism. Halford and colleagues suggest more specifically that the limit in cognitive performance of any particular child or adult is a limit in how many dimensions of concepts can be combined. For example, Andrews and Halford state:

> Relational complexity, henceforth RC, theory … refers to the arity of relations, that is, the number of arguments or entities related. Unary relations have a single argument as in class membership, dog (Fido). Binary relations have two arguments as in larger (elephant, mouse). Ternary relations have three arguments as in addition (2, 3, 5). Quaternary relations such as proportion have four interacting components, as in $2/3 = 6/9$ and so on. Each argument corresponds to a slot. For example, a binary relation has two arguments or two slots, each of which can be filled in a number of ways, such as larger (horse, dog) or larger (mountain, molehill). Thus each argument corresponds to a variable or dimension and a N-ary relation is a set of points in N-dimensional space. Halford et al. … proposed that number of related dimensions is a good measure of cognitive complexity. … Where overload occurs, it does not terminate processing. One effect is to cause strategies to be used that are less complex than the optimal ones. For example, if a ternary-relation task overloads a person, who consequently defaults to a binary-relational strategy, the probability of a correct response will be reduced but in most cases it will be greater than zero. (pp. 154–155)

Analyses of many cognitive tasks based on the concept of processing complexity as described by Halford and his colleagues has appeared to provide accurate predictions of what ages of children will tend to succeed at what tasks. An example is transitive inference. If a child understands that Jane is taller than Sue and that Sue is taller than Linda, that child still may not be able to draw the inference that Jane is taller than Linda because the cognitive complexity of that inference is higher, requiring both inequalities to be considered jointly as something like *tallness hierarchy* (Jane, Sue, Linda), changing a binary relation into a ternary one.

Although this model seems to work very successfully, over a broad range of cognitive tasks, some researchers remain apprehensive about the possibility that the logical analyses of specific tasks and the levels of complexity they impose are uncertain and perhaps are susceptible to post hoc rationalization. Also, it has been difficult for these investigators to demonstrate that the complexity limits are not caused by limits in the data that can be held to support processing at a particular level of complexity (though see Halford et al., 2001; Halford, Baker, McCredden, & Bain, in press).

One interesting question that arises is whether the level of complexity of the processing that has to be completed makes a difference for how much data can be held. Are storage and processing dependent on the same resource? For example, if one has to understand a ternary relation, does that reduce the number of unrelated items that can be retained in working memory at the same time compared with a situation in which one has to keep in mind only a unary relation? Conversely, does holding in mind several unrelated items reduce the likelihood of understanding higher level relations? One would think so. It may be that holding in mind an N-ary relation requires holding each of the elements involved plus each of the links between them. Two elements have a single link, three elements have three links, and four elements have six links between them. Perhaps there are intermediate levels of understanding if, for example, four elements are held, but only five of the six links between them are activated. That might result in a level of performance in which the quaternary response could be given only if the problem happens to rely on the particular links that are activated. Perhaps, through this type of mechanism, it is more than coincidence that the number of chunks that can be held and the number of dimensions that can be considered at once are both limited to about four in normal adults.

Regardless of whether such a clear link can be made between these distinct information-processing limits, the neo-Piagetian research has introduced some important phenomena to ponder. It has highlighted a possible tension between investigators wishing to use three different working memory mechanisms to help account for intellectual ability: (1) storage capacity, (2) efficiency and speed of operations, and (3) the complexity of processing that can be accommodated. The power of these cognitive complexity approaches will be validated to the extent that it is possible to do a priori task analyses and make correct predictions, based on an analysis of the complexity structure of each task.

This last mechanism, the complexity of processing, has been the focus not only of Halford's model discussed previously, but also of the model termed *cognitive complexity and control* (Frye, Zelazo, & Burack, 1998; Zelazo & Frye, 1998). The latter approach emphasizes that young children have difficulty using a condition-specific rule, such as sorting the same picture into one pile when the game is to sort by color, and into another pile when the game is to sort by shape. Andrews, Halford, Bunch, Bowden, and Jones (2003) compared the two complexity-based theories as they apply to the theory of mind: the acquisition of sophisticated concepts in which it is realized that another person does not necessarily have the same knowledge as the participant has. This, too, involves a contingent rule (e.g., if a person was in the room when a toy was hidden, that person may know where the toy was hidden; if a person was not in the room when it was hidden, that person probably does not know where it was hidden). The difficulty comes in both knowing the information and understanding that not everyone else knows the same information. It still seems unclear which neo-Piagetian model is preferable to account for extant data.

A Shift of Emphasis from Capacity to Time

The idea of a magical number may have been proposed only facetiously by Miller (1956), but it had the virtue of being easily testable. During the period of the modal model's success, in the late 1960s and early 1970s, it was supposed that there are about seven fixed "slots" in short-term memory. This supposition may have been made for the sake of simplicity rather than out of strong conviction. Nevertheless, it was overturned when Baddeley et al. (1975) found that memory for lists comprising short words were recalled more successfully than lists comprising an equal number of longer, multisyllabic words (i.e., a word-length effect).

Given just that result, it might have been possible to suppose that a single, long word sometimes might function as multiple chunks rather than as a single chunk. However, other experiments carried out by Baddeley et al. (1975) compared performance on short and long word sets that were equated on the number of phonemes and syllables in the sets and nevertheless differed in the duration it takes to speak the words. Still, a word-length effect was obtained. Baddeley et al. (1975) also obtained other results that seemed to link short-term memory to a time limit rather than an item limit. They found that individuals could recall about as much as they could repeat in about 2 s. This finding led to a simple theory of how memory was limited. The theory was that phonological information in verbal short-term memory persisted only for about 2 s unless it was refreshed through covert verbal rehearsal. The rate at which an individual could recite the words aloud was taken as an estimate of the rate at which they could recite the words silently. The reason that people could recall about as much as they could recite in 2 s was hypothesized to be that the rate of covert verbal rehearsal determined how many items could be kept active through rehearsal in a repeating loop. That was a stunningly simple hypothesis and it accounted for other evidence, such as the finding that the addition of articulatory suppression (repetition of a simple word during the memory task to block covert rehearsal) abolished the word-length effect, at least for printed lists.

The assumptions underlying the theoretical interpretation of Baddeley et al. (1975) were not new. There has been for many years an interest in the effects of time on immediate memory and the notion of decay (e.g.,

Baddeley et al., 1975; Baddeley, 1986; Broadbent, 1958; Brown, 1958, 1959; Peterson & Peterson, 1959). The idea that there may be a time limit in immediate recall was investigated using the word-length effect—informally by Simon (1974), more rigorously by Baddeley et al. (1975), and then by a number of other researchers, including those who examined age differences in children (e.g., Hulme, Thomson, Muir, & Lawrence, 1984) or the elderly (e.g., Kynette, Kemper, Norman, & Cheung, 1990) compared with a young-adult standard, and those who examined cross-linguistic differences in pronunciation rates (e.g., Ellis & Hennelly, 1980; Naveh-Benjamin & Ayres, 1986; Stigler, Lee, & Stevenson, 1986).

Evidence on the similarity between the rates of covert and overt rehearsal was presented by Landauer (1962). However, the article by Baddeley et al. may have been the first one in direct conflict with Miller's (1956) capacity notion inasmuch as it appeared to show that, as Schweickert and Boruff (1986) later put it, the limitation in immediate recall was not a "magic number" but rather a "magic spell" or period. After that work, there were many additional studies of the word-length effect and of the tendency for individual and cultural differences in speaking rate for a particular set of materials to be correlated with memory span. Some of them suggested modifications that were still in the spirit of "magic spell" interpretations, such as studies suggesting that much of the word-length effect occurred because of memory loss during overt recall rather than during covert rehearsal (Cowan et al., 1992; Dosher & Ma, 1998; Henry, 1991).

Other research, however, indicated that the magic spell could not be the entire explanation of immediate memory. Hulme, Maughan, and Brown (1991) showed that memory for nonwords was poorer than memory for words in a way that was not reflected in the rates at which items could be pronounced. Also, whereas Baddeley et al. (1975) and Cowan et al. (1992) found the word-length effect using word sets in which the short and long words were matched for the number of syllables and phonemes and differed only in spoken duration, other researchers found that, with other stimulus sets, that kind of stimulus matching eliminated or greatly diminished the word-length effect (Caplan, Rochon, & Waters, 1992; Lovatt, Avons, & Masterson, 2000, 2002; Service, 1998). There still appears to be an effect of spoken duration when the manipulation is large enough, as when Cowan, Wood et al. (1997) and Cowan, Nugent, Elliott, and Geer (2000) used the same word set for short and long words: the difference being in the instructed rate of pronunciation by the subject. However, it no longer can be maintained that the main factor in forgetting is in the amount of time that has elapsed between presentation and rehearsal of an item. Indeed, some authors, such as Lewandowsky, Duncan, and Brown (in press) deny that there is any effect of time on forgetting. They varied the recall speed in the presence of articulatory suppression of rehearsal and claimed to find no effect of recall speed, though I see what appears to be a small effect of time in their data. A general critique of the time-based theory of short-term memory can be found in Nairne (2002). In contrast, others argue that the time factor as reflected in the effect of word length still does a good job of accounting for serial recall after phonological characteristics of the words are adequately controlled (Mueller, Seymour, Kieras, & Meyer, 2003).

One fact that seems incontrovertible, though one might not realize it from some of the recent debate, is that the word-length effect is robust. In particular, if one compares recall of lists of monosyllabic words with recall of lists of the same number of multisyllabic words with the list types matched as carefully as possible on other qualities such as word frequency and imagery, one still obtains a clear advantage for recall of the lists of short words. The question is what factor accounts for that word-length effect. Investigators differ on the question of whether a word-length effect occurs for sets of short and long words equated for the amount of phonological material and differing only in the pronunciation times needed for words in each set.

Can Time Limits and Capacity Limits Be Reconciled?

I believe that the system that yields the word length effect probably is a phonological system, as Baddeley et al. (1975) and others have believed, but that it serves a backup role to a system that operates on the basis of distinctive cues fed into a capacity-limited store (Chen & Cowan, submitted; Cowan, Chen, & Rouder, 2004). Word-length effects predominate only when the stimuli in a list are homogeneous enough in length to minimize cues to the structure of the list (Cowan, Baddeley et al., 2003; Hulme, Surprenant, Bireta, Stuart, & Neath, 2004).

As often happens in the history of psychology and other sciences, what looked strong and certain turned out to be less so. Several studies suggested that the effects on the word-length effects that were obtained with phonemes and syllables equated between word lengths (that is, the time-based word length effect) could not be replicated with a wide range of materials. The problem originated largely in the method of using a small number of words over and over again (Baddeley et al., 1975; Cowan et al., 1992). This had been done to place an emphasis on serial order and because it is not easy to find sets equated for various factors such as word frequency as well as the number of phonemes and syllables. However, other studies suggested that there were subtle confounding factors in these small word sets, and that other word sets did not replicate the time-based word length effect (Caplan et al., 1992; Lovatt et al., 2000, 2002; Neath, Bireta, & Surprenant, 2003; Service, 1998). For example, Lovatt et al. (2002) were able to replicate Cowan et al. (1992) very closely using their word sets, but found different results with different word sets. They also found that the loss of information over recall time in the procedure of Cowan et al. (1992) occurred not because of time per se, but because an error made early on in recall tended to affect all subsequent phases of recall on that trial.

Against this trend, two studies found word length effects using the same words sets to represent the short and long sets, but with fast-versus-slow instructed rates of pronunciation at presentation and recall (Cowan, Nugent, Elliott, & Geer, 2000; Cowan, Wood et al., 1997). Often, these results have been dismissed as being caused by other factors that are introduced by the pronunciation-rate instructions. It should not be overlooked, though, that the percentage difference between the durations of short- and long-word pronunciations in these experiments was much larger than in the other studies examining time-based word-length effects. Very large time differences also exist when one compares monosyllabic and multi-syllabic words, for which the existence of a word-length effect is not in dispute. It remains possible, then, that there is a time-based component to the word-length effect in such cases, even though it might be difficult to confirm or disconfirm.

If the loss of information over time per se is not as extreme as the theoretical frameworks of Baddeley (1986) and Cowan (1988) supposed, then that opens the door to at least two other possibilities. First, it opens the door to a type of theoretical view in which there is no special mechanism for short-term memory as opposed to long-term memory (to cite two researchers at the University of Missouri from former years: McGeoch, 1932; Melton, 1963; to cite much more recent sources: Crowder, 1993; Nairne, 2002; Neath & Surprenant, 2003). However, a compendium of differences between immediate-test and delayed-test results (Cowan, 1995, pp. 118–134; Cowan, Wood et al., 1997; Davelaar et al., 2005) argues against this view. The issue will be addressed in Chapter 5.

Second, if there is a distinction between short- and long-term memory, the results seem favorable to the possibility that the special short-term limit is a magic number of some sort instead of, or in addition to, a magic spell. From that point of view, the difference between the recall of lists of shorter words (e.g., monosyllables) versus longer words (e.g., multisyllables) may occur because the latter are represented as more than one chunk each within a phonological representation.

A recent study on the word-length effect (Cowan, Baddeley et al., 2003) seems consistent with this interpretation. It compared short and long words, represented by monosyllables (*birch, clam, hoof, myth, pest,* and *trait*) and fairly long multisyllabic words (*administration, criminology, enthusiasm, hypochondriac, photosynthesis,* and *undergraduate*) matched for word frequency. Unlike other studies of the word-length effect, the short and long words were mixed together in various proportions. Of six words, zero, one, two, three, four, five, or six of them were short and the remaining words were long. The short and long words were randomly ordered. The predominant finding with mixed lists (that is, lists with one to five short words out of six) is that performance tended to be much better on whichever word length was less frequent in the list. It seemed, therefore, that the predominant factor was the formation of conceptual subgroups of short and long words, even though these subgroups had to be coordinated with one another in terms of the relative serial positions. When there were three short and three long words, there was still a fairly small advantage for short words.

Most important, when an articulatory suppression task was added, there was never an advantage for the long words no matter how many or few of them were in the list. The results are reproduced in Figure 1.3. They show that articulatory suppression appears to have hurt performance on the long words a great deal, while leaving performance on the short words nearly untouched. This suggests that the rehearsal process may be used to maintain only the long words within these mixed lists.

An overall interpretation of the results shown in the figure may be as follows. When there are cues that can be used to make some subsets of the words stand out against the others, then the words that stand out

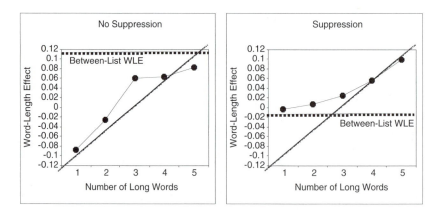

FIGURE 1.3 Results from a study of word length effects in homogeneous and mixed lists. Panels rearranged from Figure 2 of Cowan, Baddeley, Elliott, and Norris (2003). (A) No suppression; (B) articulatory suppression during stimulus presentation.

are remembered best. That happens with whichever word length is less frequent. However, a minority of long words cannot stand out against a majority of short words unless the long words are maintained as single units each. For that to happen, rehearsal processes are needed for the long words. When all words are of the same length, none of the words stand out against the others, so the phonological representation has to be held as a temporal sequence of phonemes rather than as a structured set. With articulatory suppression for homogeneous lists, this phonological representation cannot be used and nothing stands out within the list; perhaps it is an ordered list of semantic representations that is held, for which there is no word-length effect.

Although this interpretation is speculative, it illustrates that the word-length effect might well be explained with a processing system in which phonological representations and rehearsal play an important role, but in which it is capacity limits rather than time limits often play the dominant role, *if there is sufficient structure in the stimulus set*. In Chapter 3, I will make further suggestions as to how capacity and time-related limits may be combined.

I turn now to the present theoretical approach in which the capacity-limited system is assumed to play an important role in retention.

2 CHAPTER

The Present Theoretical Approach

In this chapter, I will highlight several characteristics of my own theoretical approach that distinguish it from the other approaches. Table 2.1 presents a summary of the information in this chapter and beyond by listing assumptions and themes important for the present, embedded-process theoretical framework for information processing. For each assumption, a source is offered to establish the "vintage" of the assumption. This will help to show not only where I stand on various issues, but also how my approach has evolved.

☐ A MORE GENERAL LEVEL OF ANALYSIS

Notice that there are two connotations of the term *working memory*. On one hand, there is its generic description as the set of processes that hold a limited amount of information in a readily accessible state for use in an active task. On the other hand, there is the explicit description of a multifaceted system by Baddeley (1986) and colleagues (for a more recent presentation, see Baddeley & Logie, 1999). Cowan (1988, 1995, 1999) sought to push the use more in the generic direction. That is basically because Baddeley's model, though quite useful, was not exhaustive.

Certainly, Baddeley had good reasons to posit the fractionation of the processing system that he did. Verbal and visual materials tend not to

TABLE 2.1. Some Key Assumptions of the Embedded-Processes Model and the Vintage of Each Assumption

1. A MORE GENERAL LEVEL OF ANALYSIS

It is clear that verbal and visuospatial forms of memory are very different, with more mutual interference between two tasks of the same sort than between one verbal and one visuospatial task. However, there may be other distinctions equally important, such as the auditory versus verbal versus tactile source of stimulation (Cowan, 1988). Therefore, it can be helpful to describe a processing model that is exhaustive, in that nothing is left out, even at the cost of the model being vague in places. Accordingly, the notion of temporarily activated portions of memory takes the place of discrete buffers. Activated memory can include both sensory and semantic features. Representations of two or more stimuli with similar features tend to interfere with one another within this activated portion of memory (Cowan, 1988).

2. EMBEDDED PROCESSES

The focus of attention is a subset of activated memory. When researchers discuss short-term or working memory they sometimes are referring to the entire activated area and sometimes are referring to the focus of attention. The focus is controlled by a combination of automatic orienting responses to changes in the environment and voluntary effort arising from central executive processes (Cowan, 1988). Many sensory features can be activated automatically, whereas the semantic features are more likely to be activated with the help of attention to the stimuli (Conway, Cowan, & Bunting, 2001).

3. FORMATION OF NEW LINKS IN WORKING MEMORY

Working memory goes beyond activated portions of long-term memory in that it also must include new episodic links between items presented concurrently. These new links presumably require attention to be formed and then are entered into long-term memory as new records, such as objects, chunks, or events (Cowan, 1995).

4. CAPACITY LIMIT OF THE ATTENTIONAL FOCUS

In situations in which stimuli are familiar and grouping and rehearsal of these stimuli is prevented, each stimulus can be assumed to be represented as a separate, single chunk in working memory. Many diverse examples converge on the estimate that adults typically can retain three to five chunks of information in working memory. My favored interpretation of this empirical limit is that it is the focus of attention that is so limited (Cowan, 1999, 2001; Verhaeghen, Cerella, & Basek, 2004). When the process of chunking is controlled through training rather than being prevented, a similar capacity limit of three to five chunks can be observed (Cowan, Chen, & Rouder, 2004). Activated memory has limits because of time and interference, but not capacity limits as such (Conway & Engle, 1994).

(Continued)

TABLE 2.1. Some Key Assumptions of the Embedded-Processes Model and the Vintage of Each Assumption (*Continued*)

5. RESOURCE-SHARING BETWEEN STORAGE AND PROCESSING

The focus of attention has a predominant representation in the parietal lobes of the brain, whereas the control of attention (central executive processing) has a predominant representation in the frontal lobes (Cowan, 1995). Given that the focus of attention is involved in both the retention of data and retention of the task goal and task processing (the latter with central executive direction from frontal structures), there can be a conflict between storage of information and processing of information (Morey & Cowan, 2004). That conflict need not be complete, inasmuch as processing sometimes becomes automatic with practice (Cowan, 2001), and some types of information can be stored within activated portions of long-term memory (Cowan, 1988).

6. FLEXIBILITY IN THE SCOPE OF ATTENTION

The scope of attention can be zoomed out to apprehend the maximal number of items (about four chunks), or zoomed in to hold on to a difficult task goal in the face of interference, plus any necessary data concurrently. Again, some information can be held in activated memory, alleviating the severe problem of data storage. Among individuals, good versus poor ability to control attention appears to be highly correlated with relatively large versus small capacities of the focus of attention (Cowan et al., in press-a; Vogel, McCollough, & Machizawa, 2004).

7. KEY UNRESOLVED ISSUES OF THE PRESENT APPROACH

The basis of individual differences related to intellectual aptitudes is still unclear. It is clear that the capacity and control of attention are related, but it is not clear why. It could be that the capacity of the focus of attention differs among individuals and that that capacity influences how well attention can be controlled. Alternatively, it could be that the ability to control attention influences how well the scope of attention can be adjusted to suit the needs of a particular task. A third possibility is that the capacity of attention and the control of attention are fully separable processes, but that they covary for neurobiological reasons (just as the arms and legs are separate modules, but covary in length). There also appear to be stimulus complexity–related limits for complex objects that are more strict than the limits on how many chunks can be represented concurrently (Alvarez & Cavanagh, 2004). Other unresolved issues have to do with the correct analysis of specific tasks.

interfere with each other very much in working memory tasks. The verbal materials did seem to be stored in a phonological form, as opposed to a sensory form, given that printed items were confused in working memory based on similarities in the sounds of their names, not based on the way they look (e.g., Conrad, 1964). For example, it is very difficult to recall, in the correct serial order, printed lists such as *b, p, d, t, c, g, v* because the names of these letters rhyme. Repeating a word or phrase interfered with verbal memory (e.g., Murray, 1966), whereas spatially arranged activities interfered with visual storage (e.g., Brooks, 1968). However, there were other types of storage that were not explicitly included in Baddeley's model, such as tactile storage, the storage of nonverbal and spatially arranged sounds, and so on. Perhaps more importantly, the concept of attention was used only to explain the processing of information held in passive buffers; there was no notion that attention itself, or the central executive, served any kind of storage function (at least, not by the time Baddeley's 1986 book was written). The strategy of calling certain types of storage explicit buffers was indirectly held up to scrutiny by Reisberg, Rappaport, and O'Shaughnessy (1984), who taught subjects to improve immediate memory for digits by using their fingers to hold some information and called it a new type of buffer (used to produce what was facetiously termed the *digit-digit span*). The implication seemed to be that there was practically no end to what new buffers could be identified.

In place of the discrete buffer–identification strategy, Cowan (1988) stepped back in search of a more general level of analysis. The aim was to see if the description of the processing structure could be exhaustive, even if not complete, in its detail. By analogy, consider two descriptions of a house that has not been explored completely. Perhaps it has only been examined from the outside. Baddeley's (1986) approach to modeling can be compared with hypothesizing that there is a kitchen, a bathroom, two equal-size square bedrooms, and a living room. That is not a bad guess, but it does not rule out the possibility that there actually are extra bedrooms or bathrooms, that the bedroom space is apportioned into two rooms very different in size, or that other rooms exist in the house. Cowan's (1988) approach, on the other hand, can be compared with hypothesizing that the house includes food preparation quarters, sleeping quarters, bathroom/toilet quarters, and other living quarters. It is meant to be exhaustive in that nothing was left out, even though it is noncommittal on the details of some of the rooms. The approach was later elaborated on in a book (Cowan, 1995) and a book chapter (Cowan, 1999).

Cowan's (1988, 1995) motivation to move toward an exhaustive approach was to avoid the risk of noting some important distinctions while omitting equally important ones. Baddeley (1986) and Baddeley and Logie (1999) may well be correct that phonological and visuospatial processing is separate, but that distinction appears to leave out other configurations of processing. Is memory for perceived sensations (e.g., just what something looks or sounds like) distinct from memory for information about the categories of stimuli (e.g., that the perceived objects were the letters *c, a, t,* forming a word meaning a small, furry, domestic feline)? If Baddeley's (1986) model were taken to be complete, it is not clear how these two types of information would be represented. How do we process the timbre of musical notes or the spatial arrangement of tones? How do we process the intensity of tactile sensations? How are verbal and visuospatial elements combined, as when one reads a map? Cowan (1988) acknowledged that an answer to many such questions was difficult to come by, and therefore put all of these types of processing under a common label of *activated memory*, the collection of features that are in an especially accessible state for a limited time. Activated memory was meant to serve the same purpose as Baddeley's two buffer stores together (phonological and visuospatial), plus any other buffer stores that might be posited in the future. The evidence on the separation between phonological and visuospatial storage was explained with the principle that interference occurs between stimuli with similar features. It was suggested that verbal items interfere more with other verbal items, spatial arrangements interfere more with other spatial arrangements, and so on. Taking this further, the notion was that the similarity between the physical and semantic features of stimuli plays a role in one stimulus overwriting another in activated memory.

Baddeley (2000, 2001a, 2003; Baddeley & Wilson, 2002) proposed a new buffer, the *episodic buffer*, that addresses some of these concerns and will be discussed in greater detail later. It seems to be based more on categorical, semantic information as opposed to phonological or spatial information, and it seems to be responsible for linking together information of a spatial and phonological nature. However, it still appears that the system with such a buffer is not exhaustive—for example, not providing a representation for tactile sensory information.

Practically, there may be only subtle (though potentially important) differences between a distinct-buffers view and a more integrated approach. An illustration of how data should be interpreted according to these two views is found in the case of object identity versus object location. Postle and D'Esposito (1999) found that these types of information have separate representations in posterior regions of the cortex, but that they are represented similarly, and together, in the frontal areas. Logie (1995) suggested that there are separate buffers for identity and location, controlled by common central executive processes. According to this distinct-buffers view, the frontal activation presumably is central executive activity and the posterior activities reflect buffer storage. In my more integrated conception, similarly, the frontal areas presumably reflect attentive processes with pointers to the information in the posterior regions. These pointers are the attended portion of working memory, and the posterior areas of activity reflect activation of the memory system, with the contrast between spatial versus identity information reflecting just one of many ways in which the posterior cortex is differentiated (see Postle, Druzgal, & D'Esposito, 2003). The views, however, appear to lead to slightly different expectations that can be examined in further work. According to the distinct-buffer view, for posterior information to be maintained, it presumably should not be necessary for the central executive (frontal) activation to continue throughout the maintenance period (as it appears to do in the study of Postle and D'Esposito). According to the integrated conception, that probably is necessary to maintain the activation in the face of interference (see also Awh & Jonides, 2001). One should also be able to find areas of integrated activity in the posterior inferior parietal areas, related to the seat of attention as opposed to the control of it (Cowan, 1995).

☐ EMBEDDED PROCESSES

Cowan (1988) distinguished between two special components of the processing system: (1) the subset of elements represented in memory that are in an activated state and (2) a smaller subset of activated memory that is in the focus of attention. Cowan (1999) later termed this an *embedded processes* model. A precursor to the first of these concepts can be found in the work of Donald Hebb (1949), who established the notion of working memory as a set of active, reverberating circuits of a neural cell assembly that carry the representation of a currently active concept in the brain. The precursor to the second concept can be found in the work of William James (1890), who introduced a distinction between secondary memory, the storehouse of information in the brain, and primary memory, the subset of information that is currently in conscious awareness. It seemed to me (Cowan, 1988) that the field of working memory was confused in its use of terminology because individuals sometimes were identifying the concept with activation and other times were identifying it with the attended, consciously available portion of memory and thought. James' attention-related component can be considered to be embedded within Hebb's activation component.

It seemed that these two facets of working memory could not be coextensive, inasmuch as there were studies of the activation of information outside of conscious awareness, as in the case in which a stimulus is presented very rapidly and followed by a mask. For example, one can present the word "dog" followed by a meaningless pattern so quickly that no word is detected before the pattern, and yet find that this severely masked word allows a semantically related word such as "cat" to be named more quickly than would be the case if "dog" had not been presented. This "unconscious priming" (e.g., Balota, 1983; Marcel, 1983) shows that not all of the activated memory is in the focus of attention. There are more obviously practical examples, as well. Thus one can surmise that the topic of a conversation that ended some seconds previously also slides out of the focus of attention at a time in which it is still active; for a short while, one can be reminded of the topic easily even though one is not currently talking about it or consciously considering it anymore (Cowan, 1988).

Cowan (1988, 1995, 1999) also delineated differences between the operation of activated memory and the focus of attention based on the extant literature. On the presentation of stimuli, some features in long-term memory are automatically activated. However, other features cannot easily be activated in this way and are activated only if the focus of attention is turned to the particular stimuli in question. As described at length in these literature reviews, abrupt changes in the environment attract attention and, to some extent, there also is voluntary control over the attentional focus.

The model as stated in these reviews left open the question of just how much information can be processed automatically, but recent evidence tends to suggest that, much as Broadbent (1958) originally thought, it is only physical features that are automatically processed, whereas semantic features can be processed only with the contribution of attention (e.g., Conway et al., 2001; Wood, Stadler, & Cowan, 1997). For example, Conway et al. reexamined the cocktail party phenomenon as investigated by Moray (1959). It had been known since the earlier research of Cherry (1953) and Broadbent (1958) that people hearing two different messages at once (in different voices or different ears to help distinguish them) typically find it impossible to comprehend more than one channel at a time. They are asked to repeat the message in one channel and, on doing so, miss the message in the other channel. Moray found that, nevertheless, some individuals notice their own names when these are presented in the channel that is not being attended (as measured by a post-listening questionnaire). However, the results of Conway et al. suggest that this occurs only when attention is not strongly riveted to the assigned task. Of individuals in the lowest quartile of working memory, who are least adept at keeping attention focused on an assigned task, 65% noticed their names; whereas, of individuals in the highest quartile of working memory, who are most adept at focusing attention, only 20% noticed their names. So, with attention firmly fixed to the task-relevant acoustic channel, physical features of stimuli in the irrelevant channel are still activated in the brain, but features detailed or abstract enough to detect one's name may not be activated in that case. This seems consistent with the early-filter idea of Broadbent (1958).

☐ FORMATION OF NEW LINKS IN WORKING MEMORY

Cowan (1988, 1995, 1999) thus proposed a structure with the focus of attention embedded within activated memory, in place of the multiple, separate storage devices and central executive of Baddeley (1986). Although this was a simple idea and not entirely new in the literature (e.g., Norman, 1968; Shiffrin & Geisler, 1973), perhaps it had an effect on the way people thought of working memory. One possible indication of this is that Baddeley (2000, 2001a, 2003) expressed an appreciation of some of the limitations in what could be explained with the structure of the working memory system as he had described earlier (1986). The solution, according to these more recent publications, was to add the component to the processing system termed the episodic buffer. This was conceived as a short-term parallel to episodic memory, holding new information of various sorts in a contextually rich record.

Two reasons for the episodic buffer were described by Baddeley (2003) as follows:

> The first was a need for a system that would allow visual and verbal codes to be combined and linked to multidimensional representations in LTM [long-term memory]. The second comprised the need for the temporary storage of material in quantities that seemed clearly to exceed the capacity of either the verbal or visuospatial peripheral subsystems. This shows up particularly clearly in the retention of prose passages. Immediate recall of prose was initially attributed to LTM, but this interpretation was challenged by a small number of densely amnesic patients who, despite grossly impaired LTM, nevertheless could perform at a normal level on immediate recall of a prose passage containing some 20 or more idea units, and hence considerably beyond verbal or spatial span. (p. 202)

The addition of an episodic buffer greatly reduces the differences between the predictions that might be made on the basis of the theoretical frameworks of Cowan (1988) and Baddeley (1986). For example, when one reads a map, how does working memory retain the links between particular spatial locations and the names that go with them? This could be accomplished in the focus of attention or in Baddeley's episodic buffer. Of course, to understand a prose passage with 20 or more idea units, as in the Baddeley passage, the view from Cowan (2001) would suggest that there has been a new structure rapidly formed in long-term memory, so that one does not actually need to keep in mind all 20 idea units at once, but only a few more thematic ideas at a time. Underscoring a similarity between views, Baddeley and Wilson (2002) suggested that the process of active binding "is assumed to be highly demanding of the limited capacity attentional system that constitutes the central executive" (p. 1738).

Baddeley (2000, 2003) also relied on the episodic buffer to help explain aspects of memory responses that are not explained by other portions of his working memory system. To understand this, it is helpful to review (briefly) the basic evidence for phonological storage reviewed by Baddeley (1986). In memory for a list of verbal items, one finds a complex of effects that Baddeley has taken to reflect the involvement of a phonological buffer. There is (1) the phonological similarity effect, the finding that lists of items that sound similar are difficult to recall in their correct order even if they are visually presented (e.g., the letters *b, v, t, c, d, p, g*); (2) the word length effect, the finding that lists of items that take longer to pronounce (e.g., *hippopotamus, encyclopedia*) are more difficult to recall than lists of items that are shorter (e.g., *duck, graph*); (3) the irrelevant speech effect, the finding that hearing irrelevant spoken items impedes performance on memory for printed verbal items; and (4) the articulatory suppression effect, the finding that repetition of a simple word or phrase (e.g., *the, the, the…*) lowers performance and reduces or abolishes the word length and phonological similarity effects. These effects are all understandable if printed items are converted to a phonological form and stored, along with spoken items, in a phonological storage mechanism, and if information is lost from phonological storage unless it is covertly refreshed through rehearsal. Similar-sounding items are easily confused during retrieval from phonological storage, lists of longer words are more likely to be lost before they can be refreshed through rehearsal, irrelevant items contaminate the mental record of the verbal items, and articulatory suppression prevents the conversion of print to a phonological form and also prevents covert rehearsal. Some of these phenomena have since been questioned and modified (e.g., the word-length effect: Lovatt, Avons, & Masterson, 2000, 2002; Service, 1998; the irrelevant speech effect: Jones & Macken, 1993; Macken & Jones, 1995). A discussion of these phenomena within the framework of Cowan (1995, 1999) was similar to that of Baddeley (1986) in principle, except that activated memory substituted for discrete buffers and the effects of irrelevant speech and nonspeech sounds were ascribed not entirely to interference, but at least partly to orienting responses to changes in sounds.

What is critical is that, even with the original phenomena as Baddeley (1986) understood them, there was not a good explanation for the residual amount of memory that remained when covert articulation (and hence verbal rehearsal) had been suppressed. Typically, under articulatory suppression throughout the presentation of items (and in some studies, during the recall portion of the trial as well), adults still typically recall three or four items. The episodic buffer is a mechanism whereby this could take place.

Baddeley (2000, 2001a) pointed to another feature of the working memory model, amended by the episodic buffer, that was thought to differ from the Cowan (1995, 1999) model. In particular, a key feature of the episodic buffer is that it is said to link together new elements from long-term memory. For example, if one tries to retain a telephone number long enough to key it in (or dial it, in oldspeak), it is not enough to have the digits of the number activated in memory. One must also link each digit to the appropriate serial position within the telephone number or the wrong number will be dialed. Thus the episodic buffer, and working memory more generally, must hold more than just an activated portion of long-term memory; it must hold new links between concurrently activated items and between these items and elements of the current context.

A closer look shows that Cowan (1995, 1999) also considered this need and thought of it as one function of the focus of attention. For example, Cowan (1995) stated:

> The information that is in an activated state must include new information as well as the activated set of previously learned information. Links between items and/or between each item and its serial position context must be generated and preserved as additional activated information. The new links comprise an episodic record that will become part of long-term memory. (p. 101)

Thus the difference between the working memory model of Baddeley (2000) and the embedded-processes model is not very large and is probably best viewed as one of the level of analysis: a level of specific phonological, visuospatial, and episodic storage properties versus a level of general principles of activated memory and attentional focus.

☐ CAPACITY LIMIT OF THE ATTENTIONAL FOCUS

This brings us to a key point that has been developing since the review of Cowan (1995). A key working memory mechanism appears to have a capacity of about three or four chunks in the average young adult, and that capacity is less in children (and presumably in the elderly). The capacity appears to vary from about two to six chunks in various young adults and varies also among children and the elderly. Cowan (2001) documented that capacity limit and tentatively suggested that the mechanism that is so limited is the focus of attention. The limit appears to be related to scholastic and intellectual abilities. The capacity limit occurs in situations in which the information cannot be stored effectively in long-term memory because there is a high degree of proactive interference from previous stimuli. It can be seen clearly only in conditions in which the formation of chunks can be controlled or measured, neither of which is usually the case in most tasks. These points are central to the book and therefore will only be stated here; much of the rest of the book serves to provide support for these statements.

The embedded-processes model of Cowan (1988, 1995, 1999) is depicted in the bottom panel of Figure 1.2. It provides explanations for some of the questions that can be raised in the context of the previous two models. In the model, information first gives rise to a brief sensory afterimage. It then excites relevant features in long-term memory, including sensory features and categorical features. Some of this information is in the focus of attention, which is dually controlled.

Dual Control of Attention

In part, the focus of attention is controlled by central executive processes. Additionally, abrupt changes in the environment, such as the change of an unattended message from one voice to another, recruit attention (Cherry, 1953). These changes presumably do this when a discrepancy is detected between the neural representation of ongoing stimulation and the new input, giving rise to an orienting response (Näätänen, 1992; Sokolov, 1963). These orienting responses can either assist the central executive, as when one listens to a lecturer using a lively intonation that attracts attention, or they can counteract the central executive, as when the lecturer speaks in a monotone during a thunderstorm.

Processing In and Out of the Focus

Information entering the focus of attention gives rise to a further activation of features. For example, in line with Broadbent's *early filter* model, it may be that ignored items only activate the relevant sensory features such as pitch and voice quality, or color and shape in the case of visual stimuli. It may be that stimuli must enter the focus of attention before the appropriate semantic categories can be activated. Alternatively, in line with what is termed a *late filter* theory (e.g., Deutsch & Deutsch, 1963), it may be that there is automatic activation of semantic features also; Cowan (1988, 1995, 1999) left that question unresolved. However, recent work shows that the role of automatic semantic activation is at best limited in that it does not seem to enter awareness automatically (Conway et al., 2001; Cowan & Wood, 1997; Wood et al., 1997). It may be automatically activated only if attention is directed to the locus at which a subliminal stimulus is presented (e.g., Marcel, 1983), and not necessarily if attention is strongly directed away from the locus at which a stimulus is presented.

This embedded-processes model addresses the problem in Broadbent's (1958) model that sensory information is somehow processed to allow a detection of abrupt changes in sensory features even for ignored stimuli; sensory information directly makes contact with long-term memory. That also addresses the problem that information from long-term memory must be used to create the units to enter into the limited-capacity system, which Cowan (1999) took to be the same as the focus of attention. The model also allows for a distinction between sensory and phonological features, although that is not explicitly shown in detail within the model. (Sensory and phonological features are different sorts of features in long-term memory that can be activated; they may differ in several ways. For example, some sensory features are available from birth, so that the long-term memory box must include these along with learned features.) A principle that must be added to the model is that stimuli encoded with certain types of features interfere with memory for other stimuli with similar types of features.

A main criticism that can be lodged against the embedded-processes model is that so much is left unspecified. It has advantages, though, that make it suitable to use as a launching point to investigate the question of working memory capacity. For example, it has sensory memory that can be used to hold information supplementary to the focus of attention, so that the role of sensory memory storage (and other forms of feature activation) must be explored before the capacity of the focus of attention can be investigated.

It should be emphasized that the embedded-processes model makes a strong distinction between the kinds of limitations that occur in activated memory, on one hand, and the focus of attention, on the other hand. This should be critical to understanding how the theoretical approach analyzes capacity limits. The focus of attention is suspected of having a limit in terms of the number of separate chunks of information that can be held at one time. However, activated memory as a whole is suspected of having no such limit; it is limited only by interference effects and possibly by the passage of time.

Cantor and Engle (1989) tested the assumption that fan effects are related to working memory capacity limits by how much information can be active at one time. Fan effects result in situations in which an item takes longer to retrieve from memory on the basis of an associated cue when other concepts have the same associates. For example, if one is asked to judge whether the sentence, "The banker is in the park" had occurred, it might involve having to suppress the urge to respond given the familiarity of the terms from other sentences that had been presented (e.g., "The banker is in the store," and "The plumber is in the park"). Cantor and Engle found that individuals with relatively small working memory capacities had relatively large fan effects. However, Conway and Engle (1994) revisited the interpretation. What was critical in the study of Cantor and Engle in producing span differences may not have been the total amount of material that had to be activated at the same time, but rather the need to suppress nontarget sentences. Conway and Engle used a procedure in which subjects simply had to search through sets of items that had been memorized to determine if a single probe item was a member or not. However, in two of their experiments, each item was used only in a single set, whereas in two other experiments, each item was a member of two different sets, so that it was necessary to suppress nontarget occurrences of the item. Differences between low- and high-span individuals in search rates occurred only in the latter circumstance. The theoretical implication was that, in these experiments and in those conducted previously by Cantor and Engle, there is not necessarily any limit in how much information can be activated at the same time, only a limit in how well conflicting information can be suppressed.

In a structural equation model, Schweizer and Moosbrugger (2004) found that sustained-attention and working memory tasks made contributions to the general factor in intelligence that were partly in common and partly separate, a finding that they interpreted as consistent with the Cowan (1988, 1995) approach in which attention accounts for some, but not all, working memory processes.

In sum, it seems to make sense to entertain the hypothesis that there are two fundamentally different types of working memory mechanisms with very different properties: a focus of attention with a limit in capacity per se and a broader activated portion of long-term memory with limitations caused solely by interference from incoming similar items (and possibly from memory decay over time).

☐ RESOURCE SHARING BETWEEN STORAGE AND PROCESSING

In a complex working memory task, I agree with some suggestions that resources are not always shared between tasks (e.g., Cowan et al., 2003; Hitch, Towse, & Hutton, 2001). However, if there is a focus of attention that sometimes plays a role in both storage and processing, then there should be instances in which resource sharing can be observed. This issue can be addressed using evidence from dual tasks and evidence from individual-differences research, which will be examined here.

Evidence from Dual Tasks

In the popular model of Baddeley (1986), as in the modal model, storage of information takes place in passive buffers, whereas processing takes place in separate mechanisms that control the movement of information from one storage component to another, termed *central executive processes*. Interference with these central executive processes would not be expected to damage storage per se, or at least not directly.

There is one fundamental way in which the model of Cowan (1995, 1999, 2001) differs from this logic. It holds that the focus of attention serves as one of several storage devices; in which case, making the central executive processing task more difficult might well interfere with storage (in particular, by pushing stored information out of the focus of attention). It is not clear whether the same thing characterizes the episodic buffer (Baddeley, 2000, 2001a, 2002, 2003), though it certainly could.

What would help to assess this view of shared resources is an examination of performance on two tasks, at least one of which is taken to indicate a capacity limit free of rehearsal and grouping effects. Studies have been conducted in which a short-term memory set is presented in the presence of another memory load, and tradeoffs are found (e.g., Roeber & Kaernbach, 2004; Sanders & Schroots, 1969). However, in most such experiments, neither task is one that was designed to measure the basic capacity limit in chunks as explained by Cowan (2001).

Cocchini, Logie, Della Sala, MacPherson, and Baddeley (2002) carried out studies in which a spoken digit sequence was combined with a spatial pattern, with one memory task embedded within the other. In the condition that is most relevant to the capacity issue, subjects heard a digit sequence, examined a spatial pattern, recalled the spatial pattern, and then recalled the digit sequence. This condition can be considered relevant if memory for the spatial pattern is nonverbal in nature and therefore shares nothing with the digit-span task, except for a central mnemonic resource. Small effects of a dual-task load on the spatial pattern were obtained, but it was argued that much larger effects would be expected if the two tasks relied on a common resource. However, it would be premature to conclude on the basis of this study that there is no common resource. Responses to the outer task (the digit task in this case) were correct 80% to 90% of the time and therefore may not have been difficult enough to tax a common resource much.

Morey and Cowan (2004) tried something similar in an examination of the effects of a verbal short-term memory task, as the outer task, on the visual-array procedure of Luck and Vogel (1997), as the embedded task, to determine the effects of a verbal memory load on visual-array performance. Control conditions ensured that the effects of the load could be distinguished from any effects of the articulatory suppression of rehearsal. The spoken stimuli in four conditions were (1) the phrase "nothing to say," (2) two digits to be repeated over and over at a rate of three digits per second, (3) seven digits to be repeated at that same rate, or (4) the phrase "your phone number," which always was a known seven-digit sequence; the subject recited his or her own phone number repeatedly. When vocalization was required (Conditions 2–4), a voice key was used to ensure that it began within 1 s of the end of the verbal list or instructions; if not, the trial was aborted and a new one began. That way, we knew that there would not be a long time to memorize the seven-digit lists.

The visual task involved two arrays of color squares presented in succession. The second array was identical to the first or differed in the color of one square. On each trial, one of the squares of the second array was encircled, indicating that this was the square that may or may not have changed. The number of squares varied from trial to trial (four, six, or eight squares). Recitation of the digits continued up until the point at which a response to the visual arrays was to be made (a key press indicating that the arrays were "the same" or "different"). The key press was to be made quickly, and then the memory load was to be repeated in the two- and seven-digit load conditions.

The results of the visual-array task condition are reproduced in Figure 2.1. As Luck and Vogel (1997) found, there was no difference between a two-digit load and no load. There was, however, a large effect of the seven-digit load. The phone number condition serves as a control for the articulatory and interference features of the seven-digit load, inasmuch as the articulatory requirements involved seven digits in both of these conditions. Performance in that condition, however, appears similar to the no-load and two digit–load conditions. It can be concluded,

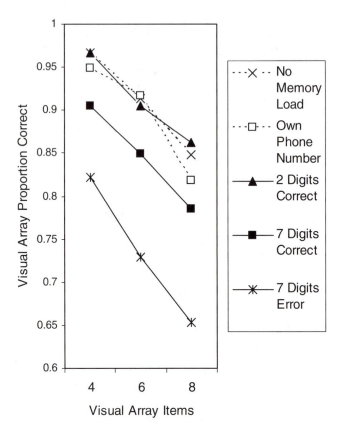

FIGURE 2.1 Reproduced from Morey and Cowan (2004, Figure 2). Visual array comparison proportion correct as a function of the visual array size (x axis) and the type of concurrent secondary task (graph parameter). The seven-digit load condition is shown separately for trials in which the load was reproduced correctly versus incorrectly.

therefore, that there was a substantial effect of verbal memory load on visual-array performance, which cannot be attributed to verbal rehearsal.

Whereas the two-digit load was almost never forgotten, the seven-digit load was recited and recalled without error on only 45% of the trials. Figure 2.1 shows that the effect of the seven-digit load was much larger on the trials in which the digits were recalled erroneously than it was on trials in which the load was recalled correctly. One explanation for this pattern of results is that the seven-digit load sometimes can be offloaded to the phonological loop and then retained without much demand for attention (Baddeley, 1986). However, when the seven-digit load is difficult, perhaps containing numerical repetitions and no obvious sequence of digits, it requires more attention; or perhaps the act of detecting one's mistake recruits attention. In either case, it is the need for attention that appears to conflict with performance on the visual-array task.

A different interpretation would be that the spoken-digit task, and the visual task, drew on visual memory in times of need. If that were the case, though, it might be expected that successful performance on the digit task would be found to correspond more often to unsuccessful performance on the visual-array task. Instead, subjects tended to be successful or unsuccessful on both tasks together.

This study, by itself, does not definitively prove that the storage of visual items requires a central resource such as attention. Instead, it could be the encoding or retrieval phases of the task that require the central resource. However, several recent studies suggest that, indeed, the central resource is needed for storage, as opposed to just encoding or retrieval of the visual items. First, Morey and Cowan (in press) presented the verbal memory load before the first visual array, but began the overt articulation of that verbal load either before or after the presentation of the first visual array. Interference was somewhat larger when the verbal load was articulated beginning after the presentation of the first visual array, i.e., during the beginning of the retention interval for that array. This showed that the articulation of the memory load had its effect primarily on maintenance, as opposed to encoding, of the visual array. Given that the first few rehearsals of a verbal load are probably the most attention-demanding (Naveh-Benjamin & Jonides, 1984), the indication is that splitting attention during the maintenance period is what damages visual-array comparisons. Moreover, helping to resolve the discrepancy between Morey and Cowan (2004) and Cocchini et al. (2002), Morey and Cowan found that it was primarily the retrieval of the verbal list that interfered with visual storage. When the list was held silently (as in Cocchini et al.), it still could be recalled about as well, but it had much less of an interfering effect on the visual memory task.

It could be argued that free time after the presentation of the first array was needed for consolidation of the array. However, the amount of time allowed before interference from speaking began in the late-articulation condition of Morey and Cowan (in press) was safely beyond the consolidation period that has been measured in other studies (Vogel, Woodman, & Luck, in press; Woodman & Vogel, in press).

Stevanovski and Jolicoeur (2003) showed that even simple retrievals interfere with maintenance of visual arrays in another task similar to that of Luck and Vogel (1997) and Morey and Cowan (2004). A simple, speeded tone-identification task interpolated between the array to be retained and the probe array had a large effect on array comparisons. The same type of interference occurred no matter whether testing included only one type of feature per object or two.

Woodman, Vogel, and Luck (2001) found that an array-comparison task with four items per array was not impeded by a visual search task interpolated between the two arrays, except for interference resulting from the presentation of the intervening stimuli even in a control condition in which no search task was carried out. Although there are several differences between this study and those in which an interpolated task did have an effect (Morey & Cowan, 2004; Stevanovski & Jolicoeur, 2003), a salient one is that the visual search task may not be the same as a task requiring retrievals. Recall an experiment earlier in which it was found that the degrading effect of an interpolated task on working memory depended on the rate at which retrievals had to be carried out in the processing task (Barrouillet, Bernardin, & Camos, 2004). If the visual search task of Woodman et al. was not sufficiently attention demanding (and did not require retrieval), there would be no reason to expect it to interfere with a central capacity.

The studies described here show that attention is needed for visual retention. A study by Jefferies, Lambon Ralph, and Baddeley (2004) shows that it is sometimes needed for verbal working memory as well. Unconnected words, unrelated sentences, or a coherent story, often considerably above span lengths, were encoded for immediate recall either alone or with a concurrent four-choice visual reaction-time task. This secondary task impaired memory for unconnected words and for unrelated sentences, but not for a coherent story. In accord with suggestions by Cowan (1995) and Baddeley (2000), entering unrelated chunks into working memory requires attention. Apparently, the coherent story structure makes the process of building up the representation more dependent on long-term memory (consistent with Ericsson & Kintsch, 1995) and less dependent on attention-related working memory.

In sum, the existing evidence on dual-task performance is promising in pointing to a central capacity that is needed for various types of working memory task.

Ultimately, though, using dual tasks to distinguish between types of theories is not as straightforward as it might seem because executive processes might be used to maintain memory. For example, if a memory load has an affect on the ability to carry out a separate attention-related process, that could be either because storage and processing both directly use attention, as Cowan (2001) suggested, or because a central executive process is used to carry out some sort of rehearsal-related activities that indirectly support storage, so that the effect of a dual task on storage is itself an indirect one (Baddeley, 1986). The latter is how Hester and Garavan (in press) recently explained the finding that two central executive functions, task-switching and inhibition of responses, are impaired when the memory load is increased. The literature offers no full resolution.

Evidence from Individual and Group Differences

Another method to determine which functions rely on the same cognitive mechanisms is to examine which ones are related to each other among individuals. In the approach of Baddeley (1986), it is possible for individual differences to occur—either because of a problem with a particular storage buffer or a problem with central executive processes that control the flow of information between buffers. For example, the integrity of phonological storage is said to underlie individual differences in vocabulary learning in children (Baddeley, Gathercole, & Papagno, 1998), whereas the efficiency of rehearsal processes is said to underlie normal age differences in immediate verbal recall and frontal lobe damage is said to cause a dysexecutive syndrome that hinders performance in complex tasks, such as producing a string of random numbers without too many predictable sequences (Baddeley, 1986; Baddeley & Logie, 1999). In principle, buffer-storage and central executive processing capabilities need not be related according to this approach.

A different logic came from seminal articles on group and individual differences by Daneman and Carpenter (1980) and Case, Kurland, and Goldberg (1982). These articles promoted the argument that a common set of resources is used within working memory to store and process information. The more efficiently the processing system works, the more resources are left for temporary storage. Therefore, working memory is measured in tasks in which processing must be carried out in a manner interleaved with items to be stored. The amount that can be stored in the presence of processing is said to be the total measure of the working memory system. This approach seems fundamentally akin to the one in which the focus of attention is involved in both storage and processing (Cowan, 1999, 2001; see also Lovett, Reder, & Lebière, 1999). Storage and processing capabilities necessarily correlate when they involve attention.

Combined Storage and Processing Tasks

Because Daneman and Carpenter (1980) decided that a good test of working memory must engage both storage and processing, they invented the *sentence span* task in which an individual must comprehend a sentence and try to retain the last word of the sentence; comprehend another sentence and try to retain its last word; and, after a certain small number of such sentences (almost always in the range of two to six), recall all final words of the sentences. The number of sentences that can be presented without failure in comprehension or recall is taken as the sentence span. It can be presented in written form (in *reading span*) or spoken form (in *listening span*). Similarly, Case et al. (1982) developed the *counting span* task, in which a series of screens each has a number of dots that have to be counted, and the sums of all the screens then are to be recalled in order. Turner and Engle (1989) developed the *operation span* task in which a series of arithmetic problems is presented, each followed by a word to be recalled later. Different types of working memory span in which a processing task and a storage task are combined yield similar results are reliable (Klein & Fiss, 1999), yield similar results (Daneman & Merikle, 1996; Engle, Cantor, & Carullo, 1992), and correlate with one another, and with intellectual aptitude tasks, well (Conway, Cowan, Bunting, Therriault, & Minkoff, 2002; Engle, Tuholski, Laughlin, & Conway, 1999; Kyllonen & Christal, 1990). So, if it is a process that is critical for the correlations with intellectual abilities, it is a rather general process, though there of course are likely to be domain-specific skills involved also, such as the distinction between verbal and spatial abilities (e.g., Shah & Miyake, 1996).

Nevertheless, there is an ambiguity as to why these correlations are obtained. Subjects could differ in how much working memory capacity is available for both processing and recall. Alternatively, they could differ in how much effort and attention had to be shifted away from the retention of the memoranda to process the sentences, math, or items to be counted. An individual yielding a superior span might excel in storage capability, processing capability, or both. Finally, it is possible that, in some circumstances at least, storage and processing do not actually draw on a common resource at the same time. There may be attention-switching from one task to the other (Hitch et al., 2001), allowing forgetting of the memoranda if it occurs too slowly (Towse, Hitch, & Hutton, 1998, 2000), or there may be retrieval of the memoranda from long-term memory, using aspects of the processing episodes to provide a context (Cowan et al., 2003).

So, why should such a task be considered useful despite the ambiguity about its interpretation? It has opened up the possibility that what differs between individuals with better versus poorer intellectual abilities is, to a large extent, working memory abilities broadly defined as including storage and processing abilities together.

Moreover, there are new leads suggesting what is happening in tasks that combine storage and processing. Barrouillet and Camos (2001) have argued that when time is kept constant, there is indeed a remaining effect of the difficulty of the processing task on storage. Saito and Miyake (2004) argued the same thing for the extensiveness of the processing task.

However, that does not indicate that selection of exactly the correct processing task is necessary for the working memory task to do its job; Conway and Engle (1996) found that adjusting an arithmetic task to equalize performance across individuals did not statistically diminish the relation between the operation span task and reading comprehension.

Results of Barrouillet et al. (2004, Experiment 7) suggest that what is important is not the difficulty of the task per se, but the proportion of time during which rehearsal is preempted; indirectly, this can depend on the difficulty of the processing task. Barrouillet et al. examined the recall of consonants while either printed numerals from 1 to 12 were named or a meaningless syllable *ba* was repeated over and over. In the numeral condition, there were either 6, 8, or 10 s between successive letters, a period that was filled with 4, 8, or 10 numerals in each case. A subset of three of these nine conditions was used in the *ba*-repetition condition. The result showed that the main determiner of performance in the numeral-reading condition was the density of numerals; performance dropped linearly from a span of about 5.5 consonants with a secondary task density of 0.5 numerals per second, to a span of about 2.5 consonants with a secondary task density of 2.0 numerals per second. The drop was roughly half as steep in the *ba* condition. It was suggested that attention is used to reactivate items (Anderson & Lebière, 1998; Cowan, Wood, et al., 1998; Lovett et al., 1999) during the breaks between the processes necessary for the secondary task, and that the necessary breaks were longer for the numeral-reading task than for the *ba*-repetition task because multiple memory retrievals were not needed for the more automated *ba*-repetition task (Barrouillet & Fayol, 1998; Logan, 1988).

Gavens and Barrouillet (2004) used a computer-controlled operation span and showed that, even with both the difficulty of the intervening task and the delay that it causes controlled for across age groups in children, there was still a developmental difference in span. This they attributed to a developmental increase in a basic capacity, as in that of Cowan et al. (1999; see also Swanson, 1999). Lépine, Barrouillet, and Camos (in press) showed that, in sixth-grade children, cognitive performance was accounted for well by a span task that included a simple but computer-controlled processing component: reading letters aloud.

The most basic uncertainty regarding storage and processing together is the extent to which a common resource is actually shared between storage and processing in the reading, listening, and counting-span tasks. At least in some situations, it seems clear that storage and processing can share resources. For example, Logan (1979) examined two-, four-, and eight-choice reaction time tasks with a concurrent eight-digit memory load or no load. Early on in the task, the effect of memory load was large and interacted with the number of reaction time choices, producing a larger effect with more choices. After extensive practice, the small effect of digit load that remained did not interact with the number of choices.

Circumventing Shared Resources

In some other studies with different methods, the expected effects of memory load on processing have not emerged (e.g., Klapp, Marshburn, & Lester, 1983; Oberauer, Demmrich, Mayr, & Kliegl, 2001), except when access to the memory load is required as part of the processing task (Oberauer et al., 2001). Klapp et al. found this for up to nine memory items, provided that there was a period during which the items could be consolidated. A set of memory letters did not interfere with several processing tasks if there were a consolidation period. Their last experiment showed that it could not simply be that the memory load was memorized. Memory for a list of six letters was interfered with by the need to receive and recall three digits while the letters were retained. Therefore, it could not be said that the letter list following a consolidation delay was simply held in long-term memory.

How is this result of Klapp et al. (1983) to be reconciled with studies showing that there is interference between storage and processing? It still might be said that the consolidation delay that they provided was used to set up a rehearsal loop, which could take the pressure off of capacity-limited aspects of working memory. Performance on the six letters was correct in 47% of the trials in which immediate recall of three digits was embedded between letter presentation and recall, in 68% of trials in which the embedded digits were pronounced but without the need to be recalled, and in 94% of trials in which there were no embedded digits. Pronouncing the embedded digits could interfere with the phonological loop representation of the letters, but perhaps not as much when the digits only had to be pronounced but not remembered. In the study of Oberauer et al. (2001), a phonological loop might have been used for the memory load, taking the pressure off of capacity-limited aspects of working memory except when the memory load had to be retrieved as part of the processing task.

Processes that Aid Storage

Much current work in the field of working memory emphasizes that effortful processing may be the most important aspect of working memory resulting in individual differences and in age differences. The view is that the difficulty in keeping items in working memory is not so much in activating them, but in deactivating the items or ideas that are not really relevant to the task at hand, thereby allowing working memory to focus on the items and ideas that are actually relevant. This hypothesis has been stated with respect to deficits in children or older adults in comparison with young adults (Bjorklund & Harnishfeger 1990; Hasher, Stoltzfus, Zacks, & Rypma, 1991; Hasher & Zacks, 1988; Spieler, Balota, & Faust, 1996). Part of the reason why inhibition is said to be critical is that tests of working memory use similar material on every trial. In *proactive interference*, items that were presented on previous trials interfere with the recall of items from the present trial. The hypothesis is that the inability to use inhibitory processes to overcome proactive interference is the reason why elderly adults have lower working memory spans than do young adults. When the long lists are presented before the shorter lists, proactive interference with performance on the long lists is minimized and so is the age difference in working memory span (Lustig, May, & Hasher 2001; May, Hasher, & Kane, 1999). Older adults remember less of the information that was supposed to be recalled, but the deficit on recall of incidental information is smaller or nonexistent

Stoltzfus, Hasher, and Zacks (1996) acknowledged the need to address capacity limits in a way that reconciles them with findings regarding inhibition. Hedden and Park (2003) offer results that suggest an interpretation in which inhibition may sometimes be a product of memory storage rather than a fundamental process. Working memory tasks require the use of long-term memory processes. To do well, one must not only remember the various items, but also which ones occurred in the present trial and are task-relevant and which ones occurred in previous trials or are task-irrelevant. It is possible to ask participants not only about the task-relevant items, but also about the task-irrelevant items. People seemed able to recall the task-irrelevant items when asked, suggesting that these items were not so much inhibited, but tagged as irrelevant. Young adults surpassed older adults in this regard.

Although repeatedly inhibiting an item can make it harder to recall when one is later asked to do so (Anderson & Green, 2001), Carretti, Cornoldi, De Beni, and Palladino (2004) showed that high- and low-span individuals were equivalent in recalling information that previously had had to be inhibited. Yet, in shorter term tests, the information was more easily recognized by low-span individuals (see also Gernsbacher, 1993). This supports the view that information is inhibited by high-span individuals only in a context-specific manner, seemingly consistent with the interpretation of Hedden and Park (2003).

We still have a lot to learn about the extent of involvement of actual inhibition in working memory tasks and, assuming that inhibition does play a role, how it works. It could work in conjunction with a storage limit by allowing the limited space to be cleared of "dead wood" or, instead, it could work independent of any limit by removing the activation of irrelevant concepts

Control of Attention and Resource Sharing

A wealth of studies using a variety of techniques has now shown that individual differences in working memory capacity (whether because of age differences, within-age individual differences, or various pathologies), measured using both storage and processing, relate to how well the individuals carry out various central executive processes such as updating information, inhibiting incorrect but natural responses, and filtering out irrelevant information (e.g., Bjorklund & Harnishfeger, 1990; Conway et al., 2001; Conway et al., 2002; Engle et al., 1999; Friedman & Miyake, 2004; Hasher et al., 1991; Hasher & Zacks, 1988; Kane, Bleckley, Conway, & Engle, 2001; Kane & Engle, 2003; Lustig et al., 2001; May et al., 1999; Miyake, Friedman, Emerson, Witzki, & Howerter, 2000; Oberauer, Süβ, Wilhelm, & Wittmann, 2003; Spieler et al., 1996). At first glance, this might be taken as support for the common-resources view of Daneman and Carpenter (1980), Case et al. (1982), and Cowan (2001). However, most of it actually has been interpreted more in line with the modular approach of Baddeley (1986) and colleagues. In particular, it has been suggested that individual differences in the ability to store information depends primarily on central executive processes for purposes of maintenance and exclusion of irrelevant information from the storage buffers, rather than interfering with storage directly—the same processes used to maintain a goal under interference and carry out other control of processing (e.g., Engle et al., 1999; Kane et al., 2004).

Engle and colleagues have amassed a varied set of findings leading to the conclusion that the difference between individuals with good versus poor working memory is in the ability to control attention. The control of attention could be used to achieve inhibition of irrelevant information, but that is not its only mission. The work of Engle et al. has been based on the measures of working memory in which storage is combined with processing and the key dependent measure is related to storage, so the implication is that the control of attention is important for storage and processing.

Reviews of his work have tended to emphasize either an earlier phase of the research (e.g., Engle, 1996) or on a more recent phase (e.g., Conway, Kane, & Engle, 2003; Engle, 2002). The major thrusts of the research appear to be as follows:

1. The relation between working memory span and other intellectual skills does not seem to be entirely specific to a processing domain.

Reviews by Engle (1996, 2002) cite studies indicating correlations between working memory span and performance in many other domains, including reading and listening comprehension, learning to spell, following directions, vocabulary learning, note-taking, writing, language comprehension, bridge-playing, and learning to write computer programs. The extant work may not completely resolve the question of how big the differences are between a verbal/arithmetic domain on one hand and the spatial domain on the other hand (see Shah & Miyake, 1996), but recent work indicates that there is a fair amount of commonality between working memory tasks in these two domains (e.g., Kane et al., 2004; also see Süß, Oberauer, Wittmann, Wilhelm, & Schulze, 2002). Most important, perhaps, working memory capacity has been found to be an excellent predictor of the general or *g* factor in intelligence (Conway et al., 2002; Engle et al., 1999), which has a heavy correlation with a broad array of intellectual aptitude tasks. (For the related argument that complex spans involve processing efficiency that cuts across domains but domain-specific storage capabilities, see Bayliss, Jarrold, Gunn, & Baddeley, 2003.)

2. The relation between working memory span and other intellectual skills does not occur because of knowledge or expertise in the processing task. Engle et al. (1992) found that reading or arithmetic expertise can be controlled without reducing the relation between span and reading comprehension. Hambrick and Engle (2001) looked at memory for baseball games and found a strong influence of baseball knowledge, but there was also an effect of working memory (or, at least, some more general domain of knowledge associated with it) that was independent of the specific baseball knowledge effect.

3. The relation between working memory span and other intellectual skills depends on the availability of concentrated attention in the high-span individuals. Rosen and Engle (1994) had individuals in the upper and lower quartiles of working memory span retrieve exemplars of semantic categories (e.g., name fruits). In one condition, they had to carry out a concurrent secondary task, reading digits that appeared on the computer screen, while generating the category exemplars. The secondary task made little difference for the low-span individuals, but it reduced the performance of high-span individuals to the point where they did not differ from low-spans. Further analyses indicated that the most attention-demanding aspect of the task was not generating responses, but inhibiting responses that had already been used. Thus only the higher span individuals had enough free attention to keep track of which words they had

already produced. Attention could be needed either to encode the memory of responses or to repress responses that might seem appropriate before they can be checked against memory of having already generated that response. (See also Conway & Engle, 1994; but cf. Jenkins, Myerson, Hale, & Fry, 1999).

4. The type of task in which storage and processing must be carried out together goes well beyond ordinary, simple memory span in correlating with intellectual skills. Engle et al. (1999) collected information from both sorts of working memory task, those in which there was a separate processing task and those such as digit span, in which simple lists of items are presented for recall and the span is estimated by the longest list that can be repeated. Several measures of intelligence were obtained, measures that heavily reflect the g factor in intelligence (Ravens Standard Progressive Matrices; the Cattell Culture-Fair Test of Intelligence). The assumption was made that no single task is a pure measure of what it purports to measure; therefore, latent variables were constructed that reflected the common variance among several measures of each type. There were latent variables for storage plus processing types of memory span, for simple span, and for the g factor in intelligence. (Such an approach requires a large subject sample.) A structural equation model was used to determine the relations between latent variables. The finding was that there was little unique in the simple spans that correlated with g. Even the common variance between the simple and complex spans had only a modest (.29) significant relation to the g factor of intelligence. However, the relation between the variance unique to the storage plus processing types of span and the g factor was considerably higher (.49). Conway et al. (2002) found similar results and further found that another commonly discussed variable, *processing speed*, was related to the variance in common to both types of working memory span task but not to the variance unique to the storage-plus-processing tasks or to g.

5. Tasks that require attention but not memory (other than holding in mind the goal of the task) are carried out better by high-span individuals than by low-span individuals. One such task is the *Stroop* task (Stroop, 1935). In the critical condition, a word is presented in a conflicting color that is to be named. For example, the word *red* presented in blue ink should lead to the response *blue*. This often leads to errors and slower reaction time than is found in control conditions (in which the color of ink to be named does not form a color word). The reason is presumably that word-reading is a faster, more automatic response than color-naming. The amount of interference can be increased by presenting trials in which the color and word

match and by minimizing the proportion of trials in which there is a conflict between the color and the word. In that way, the task conditions encourage subjects to rely on the words even more than they otherwise would. Under such conditions, Kane and Engle (2003) found that high-span individuals outperformed low-span individuals.

Another relevant task is the *antisaccade* task examined by Kane et al. (2001). When an object appears on a computer screen, a natural tendency is to make a saccade, or movement of one's eyes toward the object. In an antisaccade task, the instructions are to move one's eyes in the opposite direction. That, however, is a difficult thing to do. It requires constantly keeping in mind the task instruction and applying it at the right moment. Although low- and high-span participants do not differ in saccades, the high-span participants perform more reliably in the antisaccade task. Importantly, even though the task appears to involve mainly inhibition, individual differences in this task related to working memory come from aspects of executive control beyond just inhibition (Unsworth, Schrock, & Engle, 2004), such as generation of a voluntary eye movement.

Conway et al. (2001) examined performance in the old task of *selective listening with shadowing* (repetition of speech). Different monosyllabic words were presented to the two ears through headphones simultaneously, in different voices, at a steady rate of one word per second. The task was to repeat the words presented to the right ear and ignore those presented to the left ear. Actually, the right-ear words had a 30-s head start to allow practice in shadowing. After 4 min of shadowing and again after 5 min, a name was presented among the words to be ignored. One of these was the subject's own first name, whereas the other was the name of a yoked control subject who participated in the experiment at a different time. (Only subjects with monosyllabic names were used!) Later, a recording of shadowing responses was examined for errors and hesitations just after the presentation of a name and a postshadowing questionnaire was used to determine if the name was noticed and remembered. In this test situation modeled after a classic study of Cherry (1953) and refined by Wood and Cowan (1995), about one third of subjects notice and remember their names, but rarely notice the control names or almost anything else in the irrelevant channel, the well-known *cocktail party phenomenon*. Those who did remember hearing their names did so at a cost, producing a spurt of errors and hesitations shortly after their names were presented. Conway et al. found that 65% of low-span individuals noticed and remembered their own names, whereas only 20% of high-spans did. The implication is that attention is more tightly focused on the shadowing task in higher span subjects.

6. Superior working memory performance depends on the involvement of brain mechanisms that help to carry out central executive processes. This argument is based on a large and varied brain research literature indicating that frontal lobe areas (and the cingulate gyrus) are involved in working memory tasks and other tasks involving central executive processes and the control of attention and intelligence (Kane & Engle, 2002). Damage to these areas impairs working memory; the areas are seen to be active using neuroimaging methods during tasks with a high working memory load.

There are some studies that appear to disconfirm this general approach by showing that processing and storage do not conflict. For example, Logan (2004) found little or no conflict between storing a series of task names to be carried out and switching attention between one task and another to maintain a mixed set (as opposed to simply recalling the task names). However, if storage occurred by means of phonological rehearsal or retrieval from long-term memory, no conflict with task-switching would be expected. For that reason, a carefully defined set of circumstances must hold for task interference to be expected; it must be circumstances in which one expects that the focus of attention has to be used to retrieve and hold items.

☐ FLEXIBILITY IN THE SCOPE OF ATTENTION

Evidence from Cowan et al. (in press-a) and Converging Sources

One limitation with the popular approach of Engle and colleagues is that it has no built-in method of explaining the capacity limit of about four chunks in working memory observed in so many circumstances (Cowan, 2001; Cowan, Chen, & Rouder, 2004). One way to account for it is to suggest that individuals differ in the ability either to expand the focus of attention to its maximal scope, taking as many chunks of information into the focus of attention at once as the system will allow, or to narrow the focus of attention to intensify its effort to hold on to a goal in the face of distraction or prepotent responses, in which case its ability to hold other information at the same time is compromised (Cowan, 2004, 2005;

Cowan et al., in press-a). Such a conception owes a debt to other researchers, including the zoom lens model of attention of Eriksen and St. James (1986) and the narrow versus wide gradient of processing of LaBerge and Brown (1989). However, unlike these previous sources, my concept is not specific to visual processing or the spatial aspects of processing. Whereas individual differences in the spatial extent of a visual attention spotlight could be due to perceptual factors (for a review of the effects of aging, for example, see Kosslyn, Brown, & Dror, 1999), that is not the case for the more abstract scope-of-attention notion referred to here.

The notion that a flexible focus of attention is an important source of individual differences in working memory was addressed empirically by Cowan et al. (in press-a). It included a critique of the use of storage and processing tasks as the gold standard for testing individual differences in working memory. Such tasks are often contaminated by possibilities, such as the use of methods other than sharing resources between the two tasks; for example, switching attention from the storage task to the processing task (Hitch et al., 2001) or storing items in long-term memory when details of the processing task permit that (Cowan, Towse et al., 2003). It was suggested the task that measures the capacity of the focus of attention in its zoomed-out state can provide simpler measures of the relevant qualities. To measure the capacity of the focus of attention per se, one presumably needs only to prevent rehearsal of the presented memoranda or grouping them to form larger chunks, processes that can mask the individual's underlying central storage capacity. Tasks in which grouping and rehearsal presumably could not occur are those with fast presentation times or simultaneous arrays. For example, in a running memory span task, digits were presented acoustically at a very rapid, 4/s rate and stopped at an unpredictable point (after 12 to 20 digits), after which the digits at the end of the list were to be recalled (after Cohen & Heath, 1990). In a visual-array comparison task, an array of colored squares was followed by an identical array or one in which a single square had changed color (after Luck & Vogel, 1997). It was found that such tasks correlated well with the counting and listening span (dual-task, storage and processing) measures of working memory. Like them, it picked up a relatively large portion of the variance on verbal and nonverbal intelligence measures. The suggestion was made that the key aspect of the storage and processing measures is not necessarily that they tie up both storage and processing, but rather that the processing task prevents the rehearsal and chunking that can take place in an ordinary memory span task, obscuring a more fundamental capacity limit (see also Barrouillet et al., 2004).

To gain more insight into the task analysis motivating Cowan et al. (in press-a), consider the task they used that has been most widely researched: the running memory span task, which has been in use for many years

(Pollack, Johnson, & Knaff, 1959). In that sort of procedure, an unpredictable number of items is presented, and then the presentation suddenly stops. At that point, the task is to recall as many items as possible from the end of the list or, in some varieties of the task, to recall a certain fixed number of items from the end of the list. This unpredictability works against the ability to rehearse and group the items. When the items to be recalled are spoken quickly, it becomes nearly impossible to rehearse, update, or group the items. Still, it is possible to draw items from an auditory sensory memory representation of the end of the list into working memory. Hockey (1973) most convincingly demonstrated this. He used running memory span with a rate of one, two, or three spoken digits per second and instructed subjects in one of two ways. Some subjects were to sit passively while listening to the digits, whereas others were to "concentrate on the items as they arrive, trying to form them into groups of three" using a rhythmic rehearsal method. There was a crossover interaction between the presentation rate and the instructions such that, at slower presentation rates, the active rehearsal strategy was advantageous, whereas, at the fastest presentation rate, there was actually an advantage for listening passively. Adults typically can recall about three or four items in their correct serial positions from the end of the list in this sort of task with rapid presentation (a finding we have verified in several studies not yet published), presumably by pulling information from auditory sensory memory or phonological storage into a limited-capacity working memory.

To examine the question of whether running span requires the same attentional resource as processing tasks, Bunting and Cowan (2004) made use of the running memory span task of Cowan et al. (in press a), with a rapid (four items per second) presentation. The running span task was modified to include a visual target on one side of the screen, before the digits could be recalled. In the "propress" condition, a button was to be pressed on the same side as the target, but in the "antipress" condition, the button was to be pressed on the opposite side, a difficult task. Then the digits were to be recalled. When the visual target task had to be carried out in a speeded manner, a larger running memory span was obtained in the propress condition compared with the antipress condition, even though there was no longer delay in response. The difference was about one half of an item in running span. A comparable finding was obtained in a condition in which the lists were always six digits long and were presented at a standard one item per second rate, if the subject had to carry out articulatory suppression (repeating a word over and over) to block the use of verbal rehearsal during the trial. Our tentative interpretation is that a method of retrieval of information into the focus of attention, as a temporary storage device, was required in the case of either (1) rapid and unpredictable presentation of digits or (2) slower, predictable presentation of digits with rehearsal blocked. Therefore, a distracting goal-maintenance task was detrimental to performance in those cases.

Children in the earlier elementary school years are typically too young to benefit from rehearsal (Flavell, Beach, & Chinsky, 1966; Ornstein, Naus, & Liberty, 1975). Unlike adults, children rarely mention grouping when asked how they recalled the items in a list (Cowan et al., in press-b). For such young children, even a simple memory-span task should pick up the basic capacity limit unclouded by grouping or rehearsal contributions. Cowan et al. (in press-a) obtained large correlations between intelligence measures and digit-span performance for second- and fourth-grade children, but not for sixth-grade children or college students.

Colom, Rebollo, Abad, and Shih (in press) reanalyzed several correlational data sets that have played an important role in the recent literature (Bayliss et al., 2003; Conway et al., 2002; Engle et al., 1999; Kane et al., 2004; Miyake, Friedman, Rettinger, Shah, & Hegarty, 2001) in a way that warrants scrutiny here. They used a uniform model and found that the major part of the variance in common between working memory and aptitudes was the variance that was shared between both simple span tasks and tasks that included concurrent storage and processing. A second part of the variance in aptitudes, uniquely predicted by the storage and processing tasks, was generally smaller. This fits the possibility that the common variance included the capacity of the focus of attention. The reason that the variance unique to storage and processing tasks did not generally play a more important role could be that it reflected primarily learned skills, as opposed to the use of attention. The contribution of attention could have been present in both factors to some extent, and it is not clear how much of it is unique to storage and processing tasks.

Contradictory Evidence?

There is an enigma in the literature that has yet to be resolved, however. As mentioned previously, ordinary memory span in adults does not correlate well with intellectual aptitude tests, unlike complex storage-plus-processing spans. If that is the case because of the obscuring effects of verbal rehearsal in memory span, then removing the contribution of verbal rehearsal should increase the correlations between span and aptitude tests. Results of two studies bear on that point. First, Engle et al. (1999) found that memory for lists of phonologically similar words (that cannot be rehearsed to good advantage; see Baddeley, 1986) did not correlate with two measures of intelligence, the Cattell Culture-Fair Test and Ravens

Progressive Matrices. I corrected the correlations for attenuation of the list-recall measure because of its only moderate reliability, though I assumed of necessity that the Cattell and Ravens' tests were perfectly reliable (because no reliability measures were available). The corrected correlations for dissimilar word lists with these aptitude tests were .06 and .22, respectively. For lists of similar words, the correlations rose to .26 and .28. These were still not as high as the corrected reading span correlations with these aptitude measures, which were .33 and .38. (There are no significance tests available for these corrected measures.) Of course, reading span may include skills and abilities other than working memory, such as linguistic ability. Operation and counting spans had slightly higher correlations, but they are in a nonverbal domain so that the comparison with verbal span would seem less fair.

Conway et al. (2002) did a similar experiment, but used a slightly different pair of manipulations. All word lists were phonologically dissimilar, but they were either composed of an unlimited set of words that changed from trial to trial or a fixed set of words that repeated, in a different order, from trial to trial; and on some trials, concurrent articulatory suppression was required. According to a great deal of previous research, verbal rehearsal is needed to maintain order for a fixed set of words, but articulatory suppression prevents that process (Baddeley, 1986). Examining correlations comparable to those that I calculated previously for Engle et al. (1999), with an unlimited set there was no change with suppression, in line with expectations from previous work. The correlations with a fixed set with no suppression were .08 for both the Cattell and Ravens' tests. With suppression, those correlations rose to .27 and .13, respectively, though they were still somewhat below those for reading span, which were .35 and .18, respectively.

Overall, then, the phonological similarity and articulatory suppression manipulations might be considered to be moderately successful in that the correlations of intelligence tests with span in the presence of those two characteristics are closer to the correlations with reading span than they are to the correlations with ordinary span (i.e., dissimilar lists with no suppression). Nevertheless, more evidence on these points is needed.

In another study seeming to contradict the approach of Cowan et al. (in press-a), Tuholski, Engle, and Baylis (2001) found no correlation between one potential measure of the capacity of attention, the number of items that can be subitized, and working memory defined by an operation-span task (arithmetic processing along with lexical storage). However, Basak and Verhaeghen (2003) did find such a difference between younger and older adults and it is not yet clear why these findings are inconsistent (e.g., sample differences versus methodological differences).

Convergent Evidence on Storage and Executive Processing

The next important step to establish the view that working memory capacity depends on the ability of the focus of attention might be to correlate its abilities in a zoomed-in state and a zoomed-out state. We do not yet have, for example, direct confirmation of a prediction that the ability to inhibit irrelevant information will be correlated with the ability to perform on tests such as running span and memory for visual arrays. However, Vogel et al. (2004) recently found that individuals who have a higher working memory storage capacity for items in a visual array also have a better ability to filter out irrelevant items.

☐ SOME UNRESOLVED ISSUES OF THE PRESENT APPROACH

Last, an examination of my theoretical approach would be enriched by a brief discussion of some of the issues that remain outstanding for this approach.

Basis of Resource Sharing Between Storage and Processing

Suppose one accepts, for the sake of argument, the premise that a core storage function and central executive processing do share an attentional resource, at least in some tasks. Suppose one accepts also that this shared resource is an important source of individual differences in aptitude, in line with the result from Vogel et al. (2004) previously described and with the theoretical position of Cowan et al. (in press-a). Then there are still at least three ways in which this state of affairs could come about. First, it might be that what differs from one individual to the next is basically the scope of attention. A relatively large scope of attention in an individual could be helpful for difficult processing tasks if it means that there is less chance that the task goal slips out of mind while other data are being held and processed in the task. Second, it might be that what differs is basically the control of attention. Individuals might not differ in the maximal scope of attention, but rather in how quickly and appropriately the scope of attention can be adjusted to the needs of the task. Third, it might be that attention-related storage and attention-related processing rely on separate neural systems, but are correlated only because individuals with neurally better scope-of-attention systems are also more likely to have better control-of-attention systems also. This could occur either because the result of general properties of the nervous system that vary among individuals or because storage and processing rely on systems that happen to prosper (or not) together as neural neighbors. This is an important question that, at present, I cannot answer.

Varieties of Central Executive Functions

A second unresolved issue is why not all tasks that appear to require attentional control correlate with working memory tasks. In particular, Miyake et al. (2000) found that, although three varieties of central executive function shared some variance (among the functions of the updating of working memory, inhibition of prepotent responses, and set shifting), each one also reflected some unique components of variance. Friedman and Miyake (2004) found, perhaps more impressively, that types of inhibition and interference can be strongly dissociated. Prepotent response inhibition and resistance to distractor interference correlated highly with one another, but were not significantly correlated with resistance to proactive interference. Perhaps some central executive tasks make more of a demand on the focus of attention than others do.

Hidden Role of Other Functions of Working Memory

A third issue is whether the emphasis on the control of attention can mask or obscure other important factors in working memory. For example, in a neuroimaging study using positron emission tomography, Reuter-Lorenz et al. (2000) found that the elderly displayed bilateral recruitment of frontal areas of the brain for verbal and spatial working memory tasks that produced one-sided activation in young adults. The initial interpretation might be that the elderly make less efficient use of controlled attention. However, it also was found that the neural response to stimuli was degraded in areas other than the frontal lobes. Reuter-Lorenz et al. raised the possibility that the more extensive frontal lobe activity in the elderly results from extra effort that they exert in an attempt to compensate for a general neural decline, which would affect processes such as perception and rehearsal. (For comparable findings as a function of intelligence in normal young adults, see Neubauer, Grabner, Freudenthaler, Beckmann, & Guthke, 2004). Note that the explanation of age effects on the basis of neural decline and an attempt at compensation would appear to be discrepant from the explanation of individual differences in young adults. For young adults, it has been shown that divided attention impairs performance in high-span individuals but not in low-span individuals (e.g., Rosen & Engle, 1994), suggesting that the low-span group does not compensate through greater effort. What would be helpful is an application of the methodology of Reuter-Lorenz et al. (2000) to individual differences and an application of the methodology of Rosen and Engle to aging.

It is not yet entirely clear what motivational, emotional, and state factors come into play in influencing the scope or control of attention. For relevant articles, see Ashcraft and Kirk (2001); Gray (2001); Klein and Boals (2001); Linnenbrink, Ryan, and Pintrich (1999); May et al. (1993); and Wegge, Kleinbeck, and Schmidt (2001).

In Chapter 6, the question of just why capacity limits occur will be considered in light of recent evidence on cognitive, neural, and teleological or evolutionary bases. The chapters before that help to expand and refine the data base relevant to the present theoretical approach that has been expounded in this chapter and summarized in Figure 1.2 (bottom) and Table 2.1.

CHAPTER

Capacity Limits and the Measurement of Chunking

☐ PAST APPROACHES TO THE MEASUREMENT OF CHUNKING

It appears that progress in understanding chunking emerged sooner in nonverbal domains than in the verbal domain in which Miller (1956) worked. Accordingly, nonverbal and verbal literature will be examined in turn. After evidence is presented and some theoretical issues are explored, a recent study by Cowan, Chen, and Rouder (2004) will be used to examine the hypothesis that there is a fixed capacity limit in terms of chunks recalled.

Nonverbal Studies

De Groot (1965) and others carried out work summarized in Chase and Simon (1973) on how chess masters, experts, and novices operate when they have to reproduce a chess arrangement from memory onto an empty chess board. Chess masters can reproduce the positions of about 20 to 25 pieces, whereas ordinary players can reproduce only at best, in their words, "a half dozen" (6) pieces correctly. By examining the recall times, it was found that the masters recall a group of pieces and then pause before the next group. The theoretical explanation is that masters have chunks of multiple pieces and recall an entire chunk, then pause, then recall the next one, and so on until they can recall no more. In support of this interpretation, if the placement of pieces on the chess board to be recalled is random rather than reflecting real chess positions, the masters do little better than the ordinary players. Formation of chunks requires that the board conform to the structures that they have stored in long-term memory.

Gobet (2001), who replicated the findings of Chase and Simon (1973), described in somewhat more detail how chunks could be identified:

> In the *recall task*, based on de Groot's (1965) method, a chess posi-tion was presented for five seconds, and players had to reconstruct as many pieces as possible. In the *copy task*, the stimulus board remained in view, and the goal was to reconstruct it onto a second, empty board. As the stimulus and the reconstruction boards could not be fixated simultaneously, Chase and Simon used the glances between the boards to detect memory chunks. Comparing the laten-cies between successive pieces in the copy and recall tasks, they inferred that pieces re-placed with less than 2 seconds' interval belonged to the same chunk, and that pieces placed with an inter-val of more than 2 seconds belonged to different chunks. Finally, they showed that the chunk definition based upon the latencies between two successive pieces was consistent with a definition based upon the pattern of semantic relations (attack, defence, prox-imity, colour, and type of piece) shared by these two pieces. This converging evidence was used to infer the chunks used to mediate superior performance, and to explore how they allowed masters to find good moves despite their highly selective search. A number of other experimental tasks (reviewed in Gobet & Simon, 1998) have brought converging evidence for the psychological reality of chunks, as defined either by latency in placement or by number of relations between pieces. (p. 337)

This type of evidence has been collected as novices and experts in chess learn to memorize positions (Gobet & Jackson, 2002; Gobet & Simon, 2000). The finding is that the size of chunks increased with training but that the number of chunks remains constant at around three or four. Gobet and Simon (2000) also explained why older studies sometimes inflated the number of chunks recalled:

> ... the apparent number of chunks in experiments using physical chess boards instead of computer displays was inflated and their

average size reduced by physical limits (subjects' inability to grasp more than about a half dozen pieces in the hand at once). In replacing large chunks, subjects had to pause within the chunk for more than 2 s to pick up additional pieces, and single chunks were thus counted as two or more. Chase and Simon's players sometimes placed as many as 7 or more chunks, while in our current experiment we have seen that the usual limit was 3 or 4, consistent with other evidence on limits of STM visual memory. (p. 668)

The computer-controlled method was also used by Gobet and Simon (1998), who found that with that method, masters, experts, and ordinary chess players differed significantly in the size of chunks recalled, but not in the number of chunks recalled.

Verbal Studies

Keeping in mind the many different kinds of limits to immediate memory that have been explored, let us return to the concept of capacity as it relates to serial recall and the work of Miller (1956). Miller's famous article established two points regarding serial recall: first, that people could recall about seven items and, second, that the number of items that could be recalled could be increased through a process of "chunking," in which items were mentally grouped together. The prime example Miller gave was the process of combining series of 1s and 0s into higher order digits. However, Miller did not really provide a road map to combine these two points. The seven or so items seemed like some sort of natural limit. However, were we to assume that the seven items that people could recall reflected seven separate chunks? Or could it be that seven items were typically grouped to form a smaller number of chunks? If so, could we find out whether there was a natural limit in recall expressed in terms of chunks? The difficulty was in determining how the material is chunked.

In the late 1960s and early 1970s, there were some studies that tried to resolve this issue, most of which are not very well recalled today. Perhaps the reason for this is that the outcome of these studies was ambiguous. I will mention just a few representative studies here (their literature reviews discuss some others).

Slak (1970) had himself and a paid participant spend many hours learning to recode digit triplets into syllables. The first digit became an opening consonant, the second digit became a vowel, and the third digit became a closing consonant or cluster. Thirty transformation rules were learned. When the stimuli were to be presented, they were to be read aloud either in their original form or as a series of syllables (because the lists always occurred in multiples of three digits in this condition). Then they were to be reproduced in a digital form. Such coding did increase the number of digits that could be retained and recalled, but not as dramatically as one might expect. These two subjects apparently became somewhat expert at recalling digits in the control condition, producing spans of more than nine items. Using the recoding method, they produced spans of 13 and 14 digits, whereas perfect use of the code would predict that 27 digits would be recalled. It is unclear how many chunks actually were recalled in either condition. For example, nine digits might reflect only three or four chunks, or it might reflect heavy use of a phonological loop. Performance after recoding might involve three times the number of digits per chunk, but probably less because it may prevent some of the chunking together of digits that ordinarily might take place without the learned recoding.

A second study illustrates the range of possible materials. Kleinberg and Kaufman (1971) had a few participants learn patterns, each composed of an array of dots within an 8×8 grid. They learned to give different letter names to different dot-pattern series. For some participants, there were only two distinct dot patterns, and they appeared in series of four dot patterns in a row (with repetition); each possible four-pattern sequence was given a different letter name. For other participants, there were four distinct dot patterns and they appeared in series of two dot patterns in a row (sometimes with repetition); each possible two-pattern sequence was given a different letter name. Still other subjects had no such recoding experience. Then, in the test phase of the experiment, long series of dot patterns were presented and the participant had to reproduce as much of the series as possible. Those who had learned letter names for dot-pattern series could produce about three to five letters' worth (or chunks) before making an error.

The problem with most studies in this era is that they did not appear to have an independent indication of how chunking actually was taking place. In the case of the digit-to-syllable recoding of Slak (1970), it might have been the case that the individual nonsense syllables could not be considered single chunks in memory. Consider that you have to recall a set of similar syllables (e.g., *wil, jil, bem, gel, wem*); it is quite possible to recall something about a syllable without recalling all of it. In that case, the transformation of the syllable back into digits will be incorrect. In the case of dot patterns, the need to convert the retained pattern of letter codes back into dot patterns may be susceptible to some error. Also, it is possible that participants who are not taught to chunk sometimes develop a coding system on their own. All of this is likely to reduce the apparent effectiveness of chunking.

Simon (1974) pointed out that explanations of performance that include a limit in the number of chunks that can be recalled are untestable unless there is an independent source of evidence allowing the chunks to be identified. He suggested the time to learn a list as one such source of evidence. The example that was given was that it took about 2.5 times as long to learn a list of nonsense syllables as it did to learn a list of an equal number of simple (presumably monosyllabic) words. The ratio of memory span scores for nonsense syllables versus these words was similar at 2.1. These two findings together were taken to suggest that the nonsense syllables each comprised slightly less than three chunks on average, whereas the simple words each comprised a single chunk.

Zhang and Simon (1985) did not measure chunks with an independent source, but obtained results with Chinese speakers who could be interpreted with a simple model that took into account both chunks and phonological representation in short-term memory. *Radicals* are visual configurations with no pronunciation, *characters* are elaborations of the radicals that do have a pronunciation, and *words* are formed from two characters each. Zhang and Simon's Experiment 1 showed written recall of lists of the unpronounceable radicals was relatively poor: an average of 2.71 radicals was recalled in comparison with 6.38 characters or 3.83 words. It might be concluded from this experiment that the basic chunk actually was the character, which could be pronounced in a single syllable. Radicals might sometimes be encoded as multiple chunks, and words apparently are often encoded as multiple chunks as well; that two characters are bonded to form a word did not seem to increase very much the number of characters that could be recalled. However, the characters lent themselves to phonological rehearsal. Experiment 2 used characters that had large sets of homophones; each character was pronounced the same way as five or more other characters, so that the phonological representation was of little use. In this experiment, the memory for characters was no higher than the memory for radicals. Thus, with the phonological loop out of commission, the basic capacity appears to have been about three chunks.

Additional experiments carried out by Zhang and Simon (1985) led to a model to measure chunks recalled (C) for materials that were in phonological form. The model involved the rehearsal time for the list (T ms), the time to bring each new chunk into the articulatory mechanism (i ms), and the time to articulate each syllable in the chunk beyond the first (b ms). With S representing the average size of the chunk in syllables, the formula was:

$$T = C[i + b(S - 1)]$$

This formula could be rearranged to yield an estimate of the number of chunks recalled, C. The estimate was close to observed values in Experiment 6 of 6.58 characters recalled, 4.58 words recalled, and 3.00 idioms recalled. According to the authors' interpretations, the characters, words, and idioms each served as chunks when they were used as stimuli. However, the formula may succeed only in situations in which the phonological loop can be used. Also, the fit is not especially compelling given the use of two free parameters (*i* and *b*) to account for three data points. It thus remains possible that the chunks were not exactly as expected; for example, that not every idiom was a single chunk. There was no independent measure of chunking in this study. The next section considers further complications in the notion of chunks.

☐ CHUNKS, ASSOCIATIONS, TEMPLATES, AND RETRIEVAL STRUCTURES

Complications in the Chunking Concept

As useful as Miller's (1956) notion of chunking is, it has to be viewed as somewhat of an oversimplification of how knowledge helps working memory. Some of the possible ways in which the situation may be more complex are as follows:

1. *Chunks may have a hierarchical organization.* There are chunks within chunks. If you are asked to recall the written phrase, "first stop light past the school," you are able to group the letters together to form words. Then you are also able to group the words *stop* and *light* to form the well-known object and, perhaps, "past the school" as a familiar modifying phrase. It is probably because of the existence of chunking on multiple levels that you are able to keep this phrase in mind with little or no difficulty. The capacity limit is exceeded by shifting attention to higher and lower levels of organization, at different times.

   As another example, suppose you are asked to write down a line of poetry that has been spoken. The juxtaposition of the words is probably somewhat novel. If the line of poetry is not too long and complex, you may be able to keep it in memory. However, at some point your attention must shift to the word level to spell one word, and then the next, correctly. The line of poetry probably has to be committed to memory so that the limited-capacity store does not include the entire line of poetry at the same time that you are writing one of the words. The line of poetry then has to be shifted back into the capacity-limited store for you to determine which word to write next, and the process continues in that manner.

This sort of idea of a hierarchical organization of ideas in memory, and a shifting focus on one level and then another, is an old one. For example, Mandler (1967) wrote, "It might be noted that whereas Miller's early formulation advances the general notion of informationally rich chunks, later formulations discuss hierarchical systems similar to the one advocated here (Miller, 1962, p. 49; Miller, Galanter, & Pribram, 1960)" (p. 332).

Ericsson, Chase, and Falloon (1980) provided an especially interesting example of hierarchical chunking. Their subject (as with several others in more recent replications) was able to learn, over several months, to repeat longer and longer series of digits. This subject eventually could repeat up to about 80 digits. However, the learning process went in two phases. There was steady improvement, up to a temporary plateau of about 20 items. This increase could be attributed to a process in which the subject was able to group digits together on the basis of known information in long-term memory. In particular, the subject had memorized a large number of athletic records that could be used as a starting point so that digits could be grouped into chunks of three or four digits at a time.

However, this first type of chunking process only raised the digit span from about 7 items to about 20 items. Somehow, after that, the subject learned to combine chunks together to form superchunks, which led to the ability to recall about 80. Although it is not clear exactly how this was possible, it is worth contemplating the regularity that occurs within the process. It may be easiest to combine no more than about four items together at any one point to form a new chunk. The items (or chunks) may have to reside in working memory at the same time for a new chunk to be formed. Three or four items fuse together to form a chunk. Later, three or four chunks fuse together to form a superchunk.

2. *The working memory load may be reduced as working memory shifts between levels in the hierarchy.* The previous example illustrates this. The subject of Ericsson et al. (1980) probably did not have to think about the digits in a chunk and the chunks in a superchunk all at the same time. Instead, each new chunk probably was entered into long-term memory as a new episode. Then, after several chunks were entered in this way, the working memory system presumably could retrieve each one as a single item and fuse them together to form a superchunk.

This shifting between levels of a hierarchy no doubt takes place under less exotic circumstances, as well. Take, for example, the process of writing. One can imagine that the focus of attention zooms out to think of some ideas that are to be put down on paper. Then, after that structure is grasped, attention must zoom in a bit to allow thoughts about the wording of the sentence that is about to be written. Some attention may also have to zoom in further to permit the correct spelling of some of the more difficult words.

3. *Chunks may be the endpoints of a continuum of associations.* A chunk is a set of active memory elements strongly related to one another and weakly related or unrelated to other active memory elements. In ordinary life, though, there must be cases in which the degree of association between elements is intermediate in strength. For example, if you are asked to remember the words, *bath, paint*, you may find that the words are not closely associated. They do allow an association to be made, though. You can imagine a bathtub that needs painting. It is not a very common association and, faced with the task of remembering other words (e.g., *chair, hallway, peanut, tree, box*), you may tend to forget which word went with paint. A weakly associated pair such as *bath, paint* might have the effect of less than two chunks in memory, but more than a single chunk.

4. *Chunks may include asymmetrical information.* If I give you the word *air*, you may well think of the associate *conditioning*. In contrast, if I give you the word *conditioning*, it seems less likely that you will think of the word *air*. Asymmetries in associations may mean that a set of linked ideas is cued more easily by some elements, such as the beginning words, than it is by other elements, such as the ending words. When we use the term *chunk*, we at least need to specify whether we are talking about an association that includes or excludes serial-order or serial-position information.

5. *There may be a complex network of associations.* Assuming that there is a complex set of links between ideas, people may well be able to tap into this knowledge to assist working memory. Suppose I ask you to list similarities and differences between schools and factories. You can easily come up with similarities (e.g., that they both involve large buildings and may have public address systems and computers) and differences (e.g., that schools are for children, are for teaching, and are mandatory), whereas factories are to manufacture things, are typically for adults, are to produce goods, and are voluntary (so that workers, unlike students, must be paid for their participation). To make that comparison, it would appear that you have to place in working memory pointers to the two concepts (schools and factories). After that, you are able to wander among

the features of the two concepts. Surely, this is not done by holding all of those features in working memory, but rather by holding the pointers and the question in working memory while a complex network of associations is searched. The concept of a chunk is probably too simple to describe everything you know about a school or a factory. The concept coheres, but your full set of knowledge must be considered if we are to understand how working memory actually operates.

6. *Chunks may increase in size rapidly over time.* One function of the focus of attention may be to link together all of the items that are concurrently attended (Baars, 1988; Cowan, 2001). Therefore, what starts out as, say, three independent chunks in memory may soon be welded into a single chunk. Perhaps surprisingly after all these years, we really have very little information on how quickly chunks ordinarily form.

7. *Information in working memory may benefit from rapid storage in long-term memory.* The new chunks that form in working memory, just discussed, may be potent precisely because they are quickly stored in long-term memory. There has been an important change in the concept of how long-term memory is involved in working memory tasks. Miller (1956), in his seminal review, and Chase and Simon (1973), in their study of memory for chess boards, were thinking of a unidirectional transfer of information in which long-term memory was used to recode short-term memory information. For example, Miller discussed the possibility of recoding three binary digits into a single octal digit (e.g., binary 101 = decimal $1 \times 4 + 0 \times 2 + 1 \times 1 =$ octal 5). The octal digits would then be held in short-term memory. Chase and Simon similarly thought of a recoding process in which chess masters could look at a chess board and perceive a cluster of chess pieces as representing a single particular configuration familiar from previous games. The clusters would then be held in short-term memory.

This position was later reconsidered in the field, for several reasons. The most important basic reason is that information often proves to be more impervious to interference than one would expect if the information were being held in a short-term store or working memory. For example, Bjork and Whitten (1974) carried out an experiment showing that one can put long distracting tasks between pairs of words in a list to be recalled, and between the end of the list and the recall period, and still find a large advantage for the most recent items in the list. On the basis of many such findings, Cowan (1995) wrote a chapter on the existence of a virtual short-term store, after the term *virtual memory* in computer jargon, referring to a portion of the hard disk (the computer's long-term memory) that is set aside to function as an expansion of random access memory, the computer's short-term memory.

On a similar basis, rapid amendment of long-term memory has been proposed in the application of working memory to complex problem-solving. In the area of chess, it was found that masters could switch from one game board to another (Cooke, Atlas, Lane, & Berger, 1993), though apparently without interference only up to four or five boards (Gobet & Simon, 1996); the general suggestion was that the types of interference that would be expected to overwrite information in working memory did not eliminate memory for chess positions (Charness, 1976; Frey & Adesman, 1976). Ericsson and Kintsch (1995) advocated a *long-term working memory* process in which retrieval structures are formed that allow many of the specifics of the test situation to be saved in such a way that it links into the knowledge of the subject. Similarly, based on evidence on memory for chess arrangements specifically, Gobet and Simon (1996) proposed a *template* structure in which there is a core (related to prior knowledge) and a number of slots that can be filled (related to variable aspects of the specific situation). To be sure, there are remaining disagreements among these researchers as to the best way to represent information, such as how high level the learned structures are and how dependent they are on true expertise as opposed to shorter term, more superficial types of intensive learning (Ericsson & Kintsch, 2000; Gobet, 2000). There is at least good evidence that cue-dependent retrieval occurs in working memory tasks (Nelson & Goodman, 2003).

It is worth noting that although the concept of long-term working memory sounds quite different from the modal model of memory inspired by such writers as Broadbent (1958) and Atkinson and Shiffrin (1968), it actually fits into those models rather easily. Shiffrin and Geisler (1973) provided a processing diagram in which the long-term store was divided into a "long-term repository" and a "long-term working memory" and the short-term store was divided into an "icon" and a "short-term working memory," with an explanation of the long-term working memory component that seems very much in keeping with the further elaborations provided by Ericsson and Kintsch (1995). The long-term working memory was said to contain "a relatively small amount of information that is very easy to retrieve" (p. 55).

The Lasting Value of Simple Chunks and Chunk Equivalents

The cases we have just covered suggest that the notion of a "chunk" is a great oversimplification. There is no good reason to assume that the units of information in working memory are generally as simple and unconnected as chunks. Instead, people may recall a complex web of associated information with various strengths of connection and various types of connection. (Regarding types of connection, two sets of information, X and Y, the types of connection include many possibilities: that X is a subset of group Y, X usually precedes Y, Y is what usually follows X, X and Y are similar in kind, X typically causes Y.) Despite this potential complexity, I maintain that the notion of the chunk is an important one that serves a critical function in theories of working memory.

The critical function of simple chunks is to allow a unit of measurement. Discrete units can be used to measure nondiscrete things; if a container of liquid weighs the same as three 1-kg weights, then it weighs 3 kg even though the water is not discrete. Information in a complex data structure is like a liquid; it is not discrete, yet in principle it is possible to measure the load on working memory in terms of *chunk equivalents*. For a particular data structure, its chunk equivalent is the number of simple, separate chunks of information that would cause the same decrement in available, unoccupied working memory capacity as this information causes. However, this is a rather unexplored topic at present.

The notion of measuring working memory load may seem pointless if individuals can supplement their working memory with extensive long-term knowledge and with the storage of new episodes in long-term memory. However, I do not believe that to be the case. One ability that is highly developed in humans, importantly, is the ability to adapt to new situations in which one does *not have much expertise*. In such a situation, the basic working memory capacity should be of heightened importance.

Think, for example, of the feeling that occurs when one is surrounded by a new group of individuals one does not know (for example, on a job interview). One may feel that every word that is spoken has to be kept as available as possible, because it could indicate the personality or intentions of the individual speaking. One must not only retain a number of statements, but also attempt to think of them at the same time so as to make sense of them. For example, if George is heard making statements that frequently contradict what Bill said a little while earlier, it may be worth considering that George has some hostility toward Bill or disrespect of Bill. This hypothesis, in turn, may be worth keeping in mind (which can happen deliberately or otherwise) so that new information can be used to evaluate the hypothesis. The person on a job interview may be more likely to forget what the choices of salad dressing are if he or she is preoccupied by some sort of novel but important issue regarding the relationships between several of the people at the table. This is just one of countless possible scenarios illustrating how a high working memory load rather than a known, richly connected data structure is often the basis of behavior.

☐ DEMONSTRATIONS OF A CONSTANT CAPACITY IN VERBAL RECALL

There is a straightforward line of reasoning that can be drawn from Miller (1956) that was never fully followed up with verbal materials (though see Simon, 1974; Zhang & Simon, 1985). Items can be combined into multi-item chunks. If we could tell how items were combined into chunks, we would be able to tell whether there is a constant capacity limit in terms of chunks.

It can be argued that Miller (1956) "sort of" investigated this question and came up with the answer that the capacity limit is seven chunks. He discussed the notion of chunking at length, but the examples that he gave seemed to involve either preexisting associations between items (an example would be recall of the nine letters *IBM, CIA, FBI* chunked into three familiar acronyms) or types of recoding that can only be carried out quite deliberately and probably somewhat slowly (an example that Miller gave was recoding of binary numbers into a shorter, octal format). He does not seem to have considered explicitly that it might have been possible on the spot to convert seven digits into a smaller number of chunks, rapidly, as may be commonly done when telephone numbers are remembered long enough to be entered into the telephone. Such chunks could allow better immediate recall even if the associations within the chunk are not strong enough (or unique enough) to survive in long-term memory for later recall or even recognition. Then again, Miller did not explicitly state that the magical number seven referred to seven separate chunks recalled; as mentioned previously, he was basically using the magical number seven as a rhetorical device to tie together his talk (Miller, 1989).

There are several possible reasons why not much research was done after Miller (1956) to follow up on the hypothesis that there is a constant capacity stated in chunks. A more superficial reading of the article would make one believe that the capacity limit was seven, and many did (and still do) take that as the powerful rule. A more sophisticated reading might have focused on the point that we do not know how items are combined into chunks, leading to skepticism that the number seven is in any way magical; Miller ended his article with the suspicion that the different sevens that crop up in different procedures may be a coincidence. Neither stance would lead to an avid search for a constant capacity in chunks.

Tulving and Patkau (1962) did follow up on Miller's idea. In a free recall task, they used materials that included high-frequency words or both high- and low-frequency words and formed some order of approximation to English to vary the amount of association between words. In an nth-order approximation, every sequence of n words made sense in English.

For example, a third-order approximation might be, "Yesterday we went home today and thought over our message announcement was about things we said are important for health." Within this sequence, "Yesterday we went" is a meaningful sentence fragment, as is "we went home," "went home today," and so on, but the entire sequence is not a well-formed sentence. The sentences presented were first-, third-, fifth-, and seventh-order approximations and well-formed text. Tulving and Patkau looked at free recall of such sequences and discussed "adopted chunks" as sets of items that were presented together and also recalled together in order. They showed that recall of a list comprised a nearly constant number of adopted chunks, for different approximations to English, whereas the size of the adopted chunk increased across approximations to English. Subjects recalled between 4.6 and 6.0 chunks, with no systematic trend across approximations to English. McNulty (1966) carried out a similar study except that the stimuli in approximations to English were not even regular words; they were letter sequences with various levels of approximation to English. He found that subjects recalled about seven adopted chunks in every condition.

Studies by Johnson (1969, 1978) exploited several aspects of the recall protocol to show that the formation of chunks is important in recall. For example, he looked at transitional error probability—the probability that a word would be recalled correctly given that the previous word was recalled—and showed clear between-chunk boundaries at which the transitional error probabilities spiked. Reaction time analyses provided converging information in that regard, with faster reaction times within a chunk (see also Anderson & Matessa, 1997).

Other investigators have examined effects of associative links within words in serial recall. Baddeley and Levy (1971, Experiment III) examined serial recall of eight-word lists composed of noun adjective pairs that were compatible (e.g., *priest-religious*) or incompatible (e.g., *priest-delicious*). No effects of pair compatibility were observed in immediate recall, though small effects were observed in delayed recall. Apparently, semantics do not play a large role in serial recall. However, Stuart and Hulme (2000) found that new associations formed between low-frequency words improved recall of lists containing the associated word pairs. Hulme, Stuart, Brown, and Morin (2003) found that pairs of words alternating between high and low frequency within the language were recalled equally well, whereas among lists homogeneous in frequency, high-frequency word lists are recalled better. Therefore, it is clear that associative information between words provides a powerful cue to recall that is not necessarily semantic in its origin.

Recently, Cowan, Chen, & Rouder (2004) attempted to carry out a similar investigation in serial recall. We came up with a remarkably constant capacity across conditions in which the support for the formation of two-item chunks varied, but the familiarity with the items themselves was held constant. The observed capacity limit was close to the value to be expected on the basis of the literature review by Cowan (2001): between three and four chunks. First I will examine this new experiment. Then, in Chapter 4, I will describe converging results from the broader literature examined in the review of Cowan (2001).

Study of Cowan, Chen, and Rouder (2004)

In this experiment, there were three trial blocks per subject, each of which used different sets of monosyllabic words. Each trial block included three phases: training, list recall, and cued recall. The training phase was always first. For some subjects (Experiment 1, $N = 16$), list recall always preceded cued recall, whereas, for other subjects (Experiment 2, $N = 16$), cued recall always preceded list recall.

Training Phase

Table 3.1 illustrates key aspects of the methods. Each training session included 32 words that were each repeated four times in random order, but with words sometimes presented in pairs. The conditions varied in terms of how many times the words were presented paired as opposed to individually, but were equated for the total number of training presentations of each word. The conditions included in this phase were as follows:

The *zero-paired* condition, in which eight items were presented four times singly.
The *one-paired* condition, in which eight items were presented one time in pairs and three times singly.
The *two-paired* condition, in which eight items were presented two times in pairs and two times singly.
The *four-paired* condition, in which eight items were presented four times in pairs.

The words and word pairs from all of the conditions were randomly mixed together. The task was to pronounce each word or word pair aloud as it appeared on the computer screen. If one were to look through the presentation to identify items from one condition, skipping words that

TABLE 3.1 Method of Cowan, Chen, and Rouder (2004), $N = 32$

Training Phase

Stimuli

Words with 3–4 letters, 3–5 phonemes, 1 syllable, a Kucera and Francis (1967)
   written word frequency higher than 12, and a concreteness rating higher than
   500. Random presentation of words and word pairs.

Training Conditions (all intermixed)

0-paired condition: 8 items were presented 4 times singly.
1-paired condition: 8 items were presented 1 time in consistent pairs and 3
   times singly.
2-paired condition: 8 items were presented 2 times in consistent pairs and 2
   times singly.
4-paired condition: 8 items were presented 4 times in consistent pairs.

Procedure

The task is to read each word aloud as it appears.

**Serial-Recall Phase (Experiment 1, second phase;
Experiment 2, third phase)**

Stimuli

Lists of 8 words presented in the same pairs as were used in the training
   phase.
All 8 words in a list from a single training condition.
In the 0-paired condition, pairings were not previously known to the subject.
In a no-study condition, words in the list did not appear in the training phase.

Procedure

The task is to recall the 8 words in a list in order by typing them in to the
   keyboard.

**Cued-Recall Phase (Experiment 1, third phase;
Experiment 2, second phase)**

Stimuli

The first word in a pair is presented. The pairings are the same ones used in
   serial recall and, in the 1-, 2-, and 4-paired conditions, used previously in
   training. Words from all training conditions randomly intermixed.

Procedure

The task is to recall the second word in the pair by typing it into the computer.
   In Experiment 1, in the no-study and 0-paired conditions, the correct response
   was known only from the serial-recall phase. In Experiment 2, in the no-study
   and 0-paired conditions, the pairing had never yet been seen and a permitted
   response was *N* (word never yet seen) or *S* (word seen before but not in a
   pair).

came from the other conditions, an example for the two-paired condition would be as follows:

> *...brick...hat...fish...car-fish...shoe-dog...hat...hat-grass...shoe-dog...toe-brick...shoe...dog...toebrick...car...fish...car...grass...toe...car-fish...brick...toe...shoe...grass...dog...hat-grass*

This example includes four randomly determined pairs of items: *shoe-dog*, *toe-brick*, *hat-grass*, and *car-fish*. In this two-paired condition, each pair occurs twice, and each of the words in each pair occur twice singly. This arrangement ensures that the items from all of the conditions appear four times in the training phase, but differ in the number of times that they appear in pairs. In the zero-paired condition, there were designated pairings between the words, even though the subjects had no way to know about the pairings at this point in the experiment.

List-Recall Phase

Each trial in this phase included a to-be-recalled list comprising four pairs of words, all drawn from the same training condition and with word pairings the same as those designated in the training session. In the list-recall phase within each trial block, there was one list of word pairs drawn from each training condition. These included the zero-, one-, two-, and four-paired conditions. Another trial was drawn from words that were not included in training at all, the no-study condition. The task was to wait until the list ended and type in the eight words in the order they had appeared. The spelling could be corrected until the space bar was pressed. If the subject did not remember a word, it was possible to skip that word and go on to the next one.

Cued-Recall Phase

Recall that this phase occurred after list recall in Experiment 1 and before list recall in Experiment 2. In each trial, the first word of a pair was presented; the task was to type in the second word of a pair and press the space bar when satisfied with the spelling. In Experiment 1, if a pair was not presented within the training phase, it was still possible to remember it from the list-recall phase. However, in Experiment 2, in which cued recall preceded list recall, pairs in the no-study and zero-paired conditions never had been seen. In those conditions within Experiment 2, it was possible to respond with an *S* (indicating that the words within the pair had been seen before) or an *N* (indicating that the words within the pair never had been seen before).

Identification of Chunks

The initial plan for an independent measure of chunking in the results of Cowan et al. (2004) was to use the results of the cued-recall test. The notion was that if a word pair *A-B* was presented and formed a chunk in long-term memory, then presentation of *A* should result in the paired associate *B*. What we learned from the data, though, as will be shown, is that cued recall to some extent underestimated chunking in serial recall. During the list-recall presentation, it was possible for a pairing *A-B* to be formed that was adequate for the recall of *B* following *A* in list recall (an immediate-recall procedure), but not strong enough to produce a correct response in cued recall (a delayed-recall procedure). Specifically, consider the proportion of trials in which a word pair *A-B* that had been presented in the list was recalled in the order *A-B*, with no intervening items in the list response. This we termed an *intact pair*. In every training condition, the proportion of such intact pairs in serial recall slightly exceeded the proportion of cued-recall trials in which *B* was recalled successfully to the probe *A*. Therefore, to estimate more accurately the number of chunks recalled within a list, we had to look for other indications of chunking within the list-recall responses themselves.

There were two ways in which chunks were identified from list-recall responses. The first method was based on raw data. Every intact pair was counted as having been recalled as a single chunk. The reason for accepting only the *A-B* order and not the reversed order is an implicit assumption that the chunk included directional information. (The assumption was not very important, though, inasmuch as a contiguous *B-A* response was given for only 3% of the presented pairs.) Single words recalled anywhere in the list, but not recalled as part of an intact *A-B* pair, were counted as single one-word chunks. Both the one- and the two-word chunks contributed to the total chunk count even if they were not recalled in the correct serial positions in the response.

This measure of total chunks recalled, considered a priori, was rather weak because it was logically possible that words *A* and *B* would be recalled as two separate one-word chunks but, just by chance, would be recalled in contiguous positions in *A-B* order. Nevertheless, it was considered that, if this scoring method indicated a constant number of chunks recalled across conditions, the method would have some convergent validity. The simplest way to explain the constancy would seem to be that the scoring method approximated reality and that there was a constant limit to how many chunks could be recalled.

A second method took more seriously the possibility that *A-B* recall might not indicate that *A* and *B* together formed a single chunk. That possibility was evaluated using multinomial models of performance, one for each experiment. Each model portrayed the data for a particular word pair (*A-B*) in the order in which the experiment was conducted. The model for Experiment 1 is shown in Figure 3.1. Within the list-recall phase, with probability *r* it was possible that the chunk *A-B* would be retrieved. If that happened, *A* and *B* would be recalled contiguously in the response. In the subsequent cued-recall test, presentation of *A* would result in response *B* with probability c_1. With probability $(1 - c_1)$, it would not be recalled. That brings us through the top branch of the model.

List-Recall Result

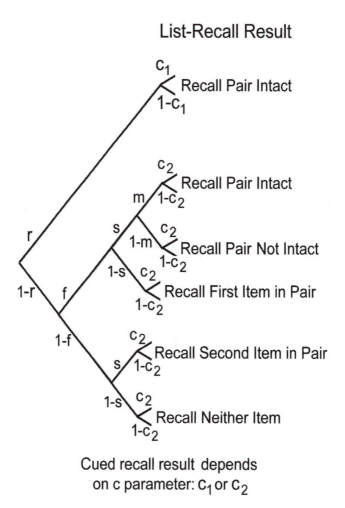

Cued recall result depends
on c parameter: c_1 or c_2

FIGURE 3.1 Multinomial model of performance in a task to examine chunking and capacity limits in serial recall. Reproduced from Figure 5 of Cowan, Chen, and Rouder (2004) (model is for Experiment 1; serial recall before cued recall).

With probability $(1 - r)$, the chunk is not retrieved. Then with probability f, the first word in the pair (A) is retrieved as a separate unit. Should that happen, with probability s, the second word in the pair (B) also is retrieved as a separate unit. Moreover, recall of both A and B separately leaves open the possibility that, with probability m, the two words are recalled contiguously in the order A-B. This occurrence is what we term a *counterfeit chunk*; it is the outcome that serves as the objection to the raw scoring method presented above.

There is still the question of whether the cued-recall probe A is correctly answered with B. However, it cannot be assumed that this probability is the same as it was when the chunk A-B was retrieved in serial recall; it should be lower. Therefore, in the model, the parameter c_2 is presented to reflect this possibility.

That covers all the parameters in the model. The other branches of the model consist of failings of one type of retrieval or another. If A and B are not both recalled, the parameter m for contiguous, in-order recall is, of course, not applicable. The parameter s is assumed not to depend on whether the first word in the pair was recalled. The parameter c_2 is assumed to apply for all of the branches falling under $(1 - r)$, no retrieval of the chunk within the list. After all, separate recall of A, B, or both would not be sufficient to mediate cued recall.

For Experiment 2, the model is shown as Figure 3.2. It is similar to the model for Experiment 1 except that the first branch of the model was the outcome of cued recall, c versus $(1 - c)$, because cued recall was presented before list recall in that experiment. When cued recall was successful (c), the probability of retrieving A-B as a single chunk was said to be r_1. Within the $(1 - r_1)$ branch, the probability of retrieving the first and second words (A, B) separately were said to be f and s_1, respectively. When cued recall was unsuccessful $(1 - c)$, this was assumed to lower the probability of retrieving either the A-B chunk or the second word in a pair, given the absence of practice from a prior cued recall. It was assumed not to influence the probability of recalling the first word in a pair, because there was no obvious reason why it should. Therefore, the parameters used in this part of the model were r_2, f (as previously), and s_2. As Cowan et al. (2004, Footnote 1) described, both models fit the data well.

Results

Figure 3.3 is a scatter plot of the proportion of correct cued recall as a function of the proportion of pairs that were recalled intact (either in the correct two serial positions or shifted in the list), according to the raw scoring method. Each data point is a different training condition in Experiment 1 (solid points) or Experiment 2 (open points). If the recall of

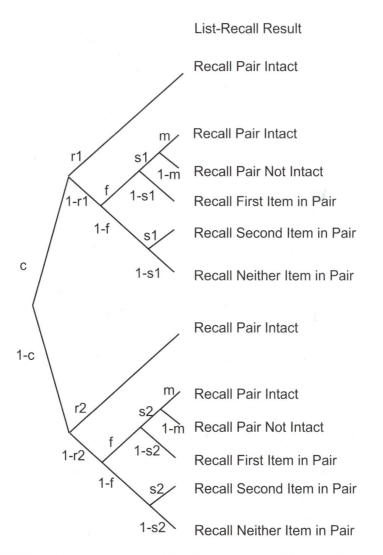

FIGURE 3.2 Multinomial model for Experiment 2 of Cowan, Chen, and Rouder (2004), in which the cued-recall task was presented before serial recall.

intact pairs were based on chunks in long-term memory as judged according to cued-recall success, the points should have fallen on the diagonal line. That the points are mostly above the line illustrates that there was some information available in list recall that was not available in cued

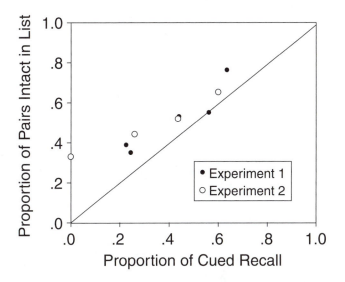

FIGURE 3.3   Scatter plot of the proportion correct in cued recall by the proportion of intact pairs in each condition of two experiments. Notice that the proportion of intact pairs was always at least as high as cued recall. Reproduced from Figure 3 of Cowan, Chen, and Rouder (2004).

recall. An open question not answered by this figure is whether the excess performance in list recall reflects real chunks or counterfeit chunks.

The top panel of Figure 3.4 helps to answer this question. It shows the mean number of two-word chunks that were formed, from four possible in a list, according to the raw scoring method (bars) and according to the multinomial models (lines). The error markers are standard errors according to the raw scoring method; the multinomial model was based on group data, so error markers cannot be constructed. It can be seen that the two methods agree almost perfectly. The figure shows that the proportion of trials in which the words in a pair were combined to form a single chunk increased markedly as a function of pairings within the training condition, from about 1.5 of 4 or 38% of the time in the zero-paired condition, to about 3 of 4 or 75% of the time in the four-paired condition.

The reason that the raw and multinomial modeling methods of identifying chunks agreed with one another is that the probability of a counterfeit chunk was very low. It was calculated from the models as $[(1 - r)fsm]$ in Experiment 1 and as $[c(1 - r_1)fs_1\,m + (1 - c)(1 - r_2)fs_2\,m]$ in Experiment 2. This proportion turned out to be only 2% of all of the intact pairs overall, and 9% or lower in every condition of each experiment. The vast majority of intact pairs were instead judged to be true two-item chunks. This

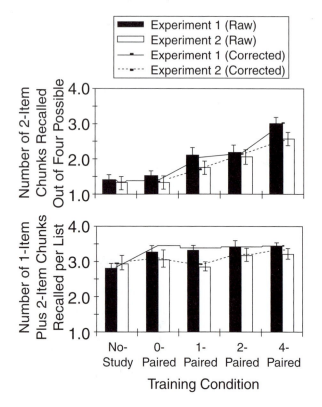

FIGURE 3.4 (Top) Mean number of two-word chunks recalled per trial in every training condition in two experiments (black bars, Experiment 1; white bars, Experiment 2). (Bottom) Mean number of one- plus two-word chunks recalled. The lines reflect the results of mathematical models to take into account the possibility of counterfeit chunks, as explained in the text. Notice that, according to either the bars or the lines, the number of one- plus two-word chunks remained constant (bottom) across the zero-, one-, two-, and four-paired training conditions despite an increase in two-word chunks (top). Reproduced from Figure 4 of Cowan, Chen, and Rouder (2004).

implies that the main reason that the recall of intact pairs in list recall surpassed what would be expected in cued recall was because temporary chunks formed in list recall.

Bowles and Healy (2003) showed that there is not much effect of grouping on the long-term learning of temporal sequence. This validates the notion that temporary chunks could form, but it also leaves open the exact nature of long-term sequential learning. Instead of grouping, phonological rehearsal may take the leading role for that kind of learning, as discussed later with the results of Chen and Cowan (in press).

TABLE 3.2 Modeling-Parameter Values from Cowan, Chen, and Rouder (2004)

Training	Condition Parameter						
	Experiment 1 (serial recall, then cued recall)						
	r	f	s	m	c1	c2	
No-study	0.34	0.25	0.33	0.24	0.51	0.11	
Zero-paired	0.35	0.40	0.40	0.35	0.51	0.08	
One-paired	0.51	0.32	0.41	0.35	0.66	0.22	
Two-paired	0.55	0.36	0.35	0.00	0.72	0.37	
Four-paired	0.76	0.16	0.33	0.20	0.73	0.35	
	Experiment 2 (cued recall, then serial recall)						
	c	r1	r2	f	s1	s2	m
No-study	0.00	0.00	0.33	0.35	0.00	0.27	0.00
Zero-paired	0.00	0.00	0.33	0.34	0.00	0.32	0.00
One-paired	0.26	0.69	0.33	0.26	0.24	0.29	0.37
Two-paired	0.44	0.60	0.47	0.30	0.20	0.35	0.02
Four-paired	0.60	0.71	0.52	0.27	0.31	0.28	0.69

The parameters resulting from the multinomial model for each condition in each experiment are presented in Table 3.2 to allow any other calculations to be carried out.

The bottom panel of Figure 3.4 is the key figure for assessing the constant-capacity hypothesis. It plots the total number of chunks recalled in each training condition. Within this panel of the figure, there were two possible types of chunks: (1) two-word chunks and (2) single words that were taken to reflect separate one-word chunks. These two types of chunks were added together. This was done either with the raw method, using intact *A-B* pairs as indications of a two-item chunk (bars), or according to the multinomial model, using the estimate of counterfeit chunks to correct the raw measure (lines). The figure shows that the total number of chunks recalled (two-item chunks plus singletons) remained approximately constant across the zero-, one-, two-, and four-paired conditions, consistent with a constant-capacity hypothesis.

It is worth noting that the model counts chunks only for pairs that were recalled in the presented order. In contrast, Kahana and Caplan (2002) showed that association strengths for words within studied pairs are rather similar for forward and backward associations. However, they also showed that the forward associations are much stronger than the backward ones in serial lists. Moreover, in the training method of Cowan,

Chen, and Rouder (2004), the stimulus in cued recall was always the first item in a pair and the response was always the second item, strengthening the forward association. There were very few pairs recalled backward, so the capacity estimates do not change substantially if backward-recalled pairs are counted as single chunks.

The lower number of chunks recalled in the no-study condition is understandable. When a word has not been studied, its appearance in list recall may result in a memory trace that can be easily confused with other words. For example, the subject who saw the word *trail* within a list may not recall whether it was that word, a semantic associate such as *route*, a phonological associate such as *kale*, or an orthographic associate such as *trial*. These kinds of confusions are much less likely after a word has been presented four times within the training phase. In essence, a word that has not been made familiar within the experiment does not always serve as a good chunk.

Perhaps some will be skeptical regarding the means that Cowan, Chen, and Rouder (2004) used to identify chunks. It is possible to ignore the problems with using cued recall as the measure of chunking and to reanalyze the data in that manner. Then, for every subject and in each condition, the estimate of the number of two-word chunks recalled is the number of correct responses on cued recall (of four possible). The estimate of the total number of chunks recalled is the number of words recalled from the list (out of eight possible) minus the number of two-word chunks recalled. The reason is that, for each two-word chunk recalled, two words that were recalled in the list belong to the same chunk and should count only once in this estimate of chunks recalled. The result of this new analysis is shown in Figure 3.5.

In an analysis of the number of two-item chunks with the two experiments combined (for simplicity), the effect of training condition was highly significant, $F(4, 120) = 71.41$, $MSE = 0.36$, $p < .001$, as were the effects involving the experiment as a factor (as shown in the top panel of Figure 3.5). Even with only the one-, two-, and four-paired conditions in the analysis, the training effect remained highly significant, $F(2, 60) = 26.78$, $MSE = 0.34$, $p < .001$. In an analysis of the total number of chunks recalled, there again was a significant effect of training condition but only because the estimate of two-item chunks recalled in the no-study and zero-paired conditions was zero, which ignored the possibility of chunks being formed during the list presentation and therefore inflated the estimate of total chunks recalled in those conditions. In an analysis of total chunks recalled that included only the one-, two-, and four-paired conditions, the training effect did not approach significance, $F < 1$, $MSE = 0.56$, and none of the other effects approached significance either (as shown in the bottom panel

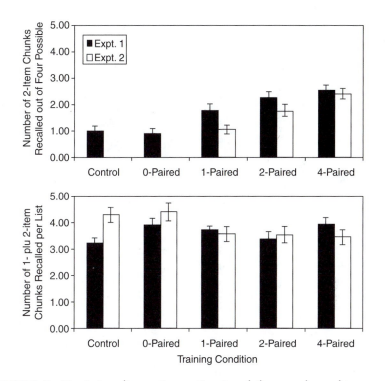

FIGURE 3.5 (Top) An alternative estimate of the number of two-word chunks recalled in every training condition of two experiments from Cowan, Chen, and Rouder (2004), using cued recall as the estimate of chunking. (Bottom) An alternative estimate of the number of one- plus two-word chunks recalled in every condition of these two experiments. Once again, the number of one- plus two-word chunks (bottom) is approximately constant across the zero-, one-, two-, and four-paired training conditions.

of Figure 3.5). So this new analysis provides further evidence in favor of a constant-capacity hypothesis in serial recall.

Last, recall that this constant capacity was observed using a scoring method that did not take into account mistakes in the serial order of chunks (although it did require the correct serial order of words within a chunk). Cowan, Chen, and Rouder (2004) also addressed the question of serial order information briefly, but here I will address it in a more straightforward manner. Figure 3.6 shows the proportion of words recalled in the correct serial position in the response and the proportion of words recalled out of position, in each training condition. It is clear from the figure that the effect of training was to increase the number of in-position responses without any change in the number of out-of-position responses. Indeed,

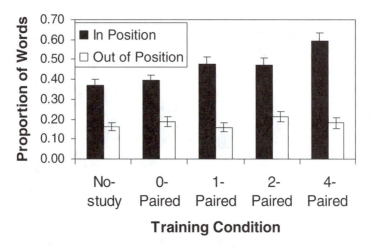

FIGURE 3.6 Correctly and incorrectly placed words in every training condition of two experiments in Cowan, Chen, and Rouder (2004).

the training condition main effect was highly significant for items in position, $F(4, 120) = 12.83$, $MSE = 0.15$, $p < .001$, but not for items out of position, $F(4, 120) = 1.19$, $MSE = 0.10$ (not significant). Thus it appears as if training on an association between words was accompanied by excellent serial position information. All of the effects of training can be attributed to an increase in items recalled in the correct serial positions. This is especially noteworthy inasmuch as the training regimen itself focused on associations within a pair, but not on the order of pairs in the list. Learning the pairing and thus having a two-item chunk available makes it much more likely that the words in the chunk, when recalled within the list, will be recalled in the correct serial positions. It makes sense that larger chunks are less likely to be relocated, but the details of this process still are worthy of investigation in future studies.

There is more to the serial position story. Although paired-associate training did not increase the raw number of out-of-position items, it did increase the number of out-of-position contiguous (intact) pairs. The total number of such pairs in the no-study, zero-, one-, two-, and four-paired conditions was 29, 26, 41, 53, and 69, respectively. However, these intact pairs tended to replace an equivalent number of other out-of-position responses (those in which the two words were recalled out of order or noncontiguously, and those in which separate, unpaired words were recalled). Therefore, it cannot be said that all learned pairs are accompanied by correct serial position information. Instead, it appears to be simply that larger chunks are harder to misplace.

In sum, the data of Cowan, Chen, and Rouder (2004) demonstrate that in a verbal, immediate serial recall task, it is reasonable to believe that the capacity of recall is typically limited to about three to four chunks. This, in fact, may be a simple psychological constant (Cowan, 2001). Yet, there are many unknowns remaining. It seems likely that there will be boundary conditions to these findings, and it is important in future research to identify and understand these boundary conditions. It also is not clear why such a limit occurs.

The results of Cowan, Chen, and Rouder (2004) also have been put to use to examine the question of how aging affects working memory. Previous studies (Allen & Coyne, 1989; Allen & Crozier, 1992) reached the conclusion that elderly adults chunk lists into the same-size chunks that young adults do. However, they used only short lists. Using the method of Cowan et al., in collaboration with our laboratory, Moshe Naveh-Benjamin and Angela Kilb found in unpublished work that elderly adults recall fewer chunks, and smaller chunks, than young adults do. Similar effects seem likely in children (Cowan et al., in press-b; Towse, Hitch, & Skeates, 1999).

☐ THE DOMAINS OF CAPACITY AND OF TIME

One conundrum resulting from the data of Cowan, Chen, and Rouder (2004) can immediately be observed. A learned two-word chunk, formed from monosyllabic words, seems formally analogous to a bisyllabic word. It is clear that immediate recall of lists of bisyllabic words is inferior to recall of lists of monosyllabic words, an example of the word-length effect discovered by Baddeley, Thomson, and Buchanan (1975) and since replicated by many other investigators. (It is only the *time-based* word-length effect that has been questioned by others such as Lovatt et al., 2002). By analogy, it should be possible to recall more chunks from lists that include more one-word chunks and fewer two-word chunks because the smaller, one-word chunks are like shorter words in studies of the word-length effect. Yet, we find a constant capacity in chunks no matter whether that capacity comprises mostly smaller chunks (in the zero-paired condition) or mostly larger chunks (in the four-paired condition).

There are many ways in which the procedure of Cowan, Chen, and Rouder (2004) differed from what has been used in word-length effect studies. Some progress in resolving the apparent contradiction can be made by considering what those differences are and what implications they have. One difference between these studies is the use of a small set of words and strict serial-order scoring in most studies of the word-length effect. However, a few studies have obtained word-length effects using a large set of words (Hulme, Surprenant, Bireta, Stuart, & Neath, 2004; LaPointe & Engle, 1990), even with free recall (LaPointe & Engle, 1990), so that is not likely to be the critical difference.

Most studies of word length have used homogeneous lists of short and long words, whereas Cowan, Chen, and Rouder (2004) presumably were dealing with situations in which the one- and two-word chunks were mixed together. Also, word-length effects typically have been examined in terms of the number of items recalled in lists of a fixed length. Although Cowan et al. always used eight-word lists, these lists presumably contained far fewer chunks in the training conditions that included stronger word-pair associations. We did not compare, for example, lists of eight words comprising four well-learned, two-item chunks with lists of four separate, unassociated words.

Comparisons between paradigms can be made by reexamining word-length studies in terms of capacity and reexamining the capacity data in terms of analogies to word length. First, consider the word-length data of Cowan, Baddeley, Elliott, and Norris (2003). They studied memory for lists of six words including six, five, four, three, two, one, or zero monosyllabic words and a complement of multisyllabic words, with monosyllabic and multisyllabic words in random order. The words always were drawn from the same small set. The proportion of words correct on lists of all short words (.61) was, as expected, considerably higher than the proportion correct on lists of all long words (.50). However, in mixed lists, categorical cues dominated. It was found that there was better performance for whatever length of word was less frequent in the list, making that type of word stand out. When there was only one long word, performance was at .58 for the short words and .66 for the long word, an 8% reversed word-length effect. Conversely, when there were five long words and only one short word, performance was at .61 for the short word and .52 for the long word, a 9% word-length effect. The situation was not completely symmetrical, however; when there were three words of each length, there was a 6% short word advantage.

In this study of Cowan et al. (2003), it can be calculated that the total numbers of words recalled in correct serial position was, in word-length mixtures with six to zero monosyllables, respectively, 3.7, 3.6, 3.3, 3.3, 3.0, 3.2, and 3.0 chunks. That is fairly close to a constant capacity in words. If we abandon the assumption that each item was recalled as a separate chunk and replace it with the assumption that short words are more likely than long words to be combined on line to form multi-item chunks, that factor would be expected to bring the data closer to a constant capacity of about three chunks per list. Given that this experiment required strict serial order scoring (inasmuch as a small set of items was used), it is not surprising that the observed capacity is slightly lower than was observed by Cowan, Chen, and Rouder (2004) using a free scoring.

Hulme et al. (2004) found a slightly larger word-length effect in a reconstruction-of-order task with three short and three long words mixed together randomly (2.6%) than with three short and three long words alternating (1.2%). One explanation of that larger effect (which is still non-significant, however) is that it reflects the possibility of joining together two adjacent short words in the random condition only. Thus the word length data are not highly inconsistent with the notion of a near-constant capacity.

The other way to compare the capacity findings with the word length effect would be to carry out a different type of experiment to observe capacity, which Chen and Cowan (in press) have done. A list of 8 words comprising 4 well-learned pairs can be compared with a list of 4 unpaired words or with a list of 8 unpaired words, and a list of 12 words comprising 6 well-learned pairs can be compared with a list of 6 unpaired words or with a list of 12 unpaired words. The 8-item lists in serial recall replicated Cowan, Chen, and Rouder (2004) closely when scored the same way. Regarding the proportion of words recalled, though, the results depended on the exact procedure. Lists of 6 learned pairs in free recall (or in serial recall with a lenient scoring of the results) were recalled about at the same proportion correct as lists of 6 singletons, providing evidence of a chunk-based capacity limit. Recall of lists of 12 singletons was at a much lower proportion correct despite a list length equivalent to 6 learned pairs. In contrast to this pattern of results, lists of 4 learned pairs in serial recall, examined with strict serial-position scoring, were recalled only as well as lists of 8 singletons, indicating a phonological-length-based limit, and much below lists of 4 singletons. Other combinations of list length and scoring method yielded intermediate results compatible with the idea that both limits may work together. According to one theoretical view that could account for this pattern of findings, there are two stages of representation involved in serial recall. In the first stage, some chunks of information are kept active in a capacity-limited form of storage (generally limited to three or four chunks). In a second stage, a phonological rehearsal process (perhaps limited to about 2 s of speech, as suggested by Baddeley, 1986) retains a much better memory for the serial order of chunks, but can only include chunks that are represented in the first stage.

This two-stage process may take place only for lists that have a uniform length of chunks in the list. When lists are composed of chunks or words of mixed lengths, the chunk lengths (or word lengths) may serve as potent cues to the list structure, perhaps replacing the phonological-rehearsal process (Cowan, Baddeley et al., 2003; Hulme et al., 2004).

The constant-capacity hypothesis seems like a natural one, but it has not been popular in the field of cognitive psychology. Researchers have been skeptical of it on the grounds that human cognition is too complex to result in such a simple limit, that the basis for such a limit is unknown, and that there rarely are independent indices of the chunks that have formed. Consequently, there has not been much research attempting to find a constant capacity. I hope to have shown in this chapter that a constant-capacity hypothesis is still viable, at least. That is especially the case for procedures in which rehearsal and grouping at the time of stimulus presentation are controlled. The next chapter will delve into a broader array of evidence that Broadbent (1975) and Cowan (2001) amassed in favor of this hypothesis, in situations specially restricted to allow the number of chunks to be estimated by the number of items presented. Some evidence that Cowan (2001) omitted also will be considered, as will some post-2001 discoveries. A discussion of arguments against this hypothesis that have been put forward by skeptics, and a discussion of why the capacity limit might occur, will be deferred until Chapter 6.

4

Capacity Limits for Unstructured Materials

The evidence that has been presented so far in this book shows that, in certain circumstances, one can begin to measure what appears to be chunks in memory. The various studies on memory for chess layouts (e.g., Chase & Simon, 1973; Gobet & Simon, 1996) and the recent work on serial recall by Cowan, Chen, & Rouder (2004), along with other works discussed in Chapter 3, suggests that there is a constant capacity. However, an important question is whether that capacity is limited to a few key situations or whether it is more general across various processing tasks. The message of this chapter is that the capacity limit of three to four chunks in the average adult (and less in children and probably in the elderly) is quite pervasive.

It is not always possible to measure intricacies of the processing task that indicate chunk boundaries. However, there is another tactic. One can identify situations in which (1) the stimulus items are familiar and are therefore unlikely to reflect more than a single chunk each, and (2) the demands of processing should make it difficult to group the stimulus items into chunks of more than one item. If both of these conditions are fulfilled, then each stimulus item should reflect a single chunk in memory. By counting how many items can be remembered, one is then, in effect, counting the chunks in memory.

The strength of this type of reasoning depends on how confident one is about the task analyses that recommend particular situations for inclusion as methods to examine capacity. However, this type of analysis may be strengthened by the striking similarity that emerges among very different test procedures when one does apply this sort of theoretical analysis. Of course, individuals will differ in how much stock they place in these analyses. The sources of these analyses begin with the book chapter by Broadbent (1975) and continue with the large-scale literature review of Cowan (2001). Along the way, they rely on support from a number of other authors, such as various studies and essays of George Mandler.

☐ THE REVIEW BY BROADBENT (1975)

If one is going to trace the origins of the cognitive revolution in experimental psychology, one major figure is George Miller, with his seminal 1956 article, among other important contributions. Another major figure is Donald Broadbent who, in his 1958 book and elsewhere, dealt with issues of perception, attention, and memory and presented a sketch of what the human information processing system's structure might look like. Among his lesser-known work, however, is a book chapter (Broadbent, 1975) that serves as a commentary on the capacity limits proposed by Miller (1956) within the domain of short-term memory.

Broadbent (1975) first set up the logic of how short-term memory and long-term memory were likely to interact. This involved a short-term memory that could include a limited number of units of one type and then could shift its scope to a different logical level to examine other units:

> The apparent size of the memory span thus depends on the complexity of the encoding processes which the individual has learned; so equally will his utilization of long-term memory. One would expect on this basis that long-term memory will be organized into hierarchical trees or clusters, in which each item at one level can be replaced by a number of alternatives (say, seven) at another level. (p. 3)

For example, imagine being asked to name as many living things as possible. One might first think of a handful of categories of living things. Then, retrieval is likely to proceed in terms of groups from one category (perhaps types of mammals) followed by another (insects?) and another (birds?), and so on. Some intrinsic limit is apparent in that, in order to think of as many types of mammals as possible, one must temporarily stop thinking about insects, birds, plants, and so on. Evidence on this sort of task (Mandler, 1967; Tulving and Pearlstone, 1966) was noted by Broadbent. He also noted Tulving and Patkau's (1962) examination of "adopted chunks," sets of items that were presented together and also recalled together. They showed that recall of a list comprised a nearly constant number of adopted chunks, for different approximations to English. Subjects recalled between 4.6 and 6.0 of these chunks in each condition.

For Broadbent (1975), this work on recall from categories or sequences was the point of departure. He summarized additional evidence from several domains indicating that the most basic capacity limit was more like three chunks, and that observations of higher numbers could be explained in terms of multiple chunks being grouped together. The basic evidence was of the following types:

1. *The limit of perfect performance.* Although normal adults often can repeat lists of seven items, it can be done on just a proportion of the trials. In contrast, lists of three items can be repeated almost 100% of the time. The notion here appears to be that there is some reliable mechanism usually supplemented by mnemonic strategies that require some amount of effort. This effort falters on some trials, but the reliable mechanism that is responsible for three items does not falter.

2. *Running performance.* There were experiments in which streams of items were presented and simple responses had to be made to every stimulus. For example, in the *eye-hand span* (Poulton, 1954), arrows might be presented, and, in response, a joystick would have to be manipulated. Performance could lag behind the presentations, but this could not be done reliably if the lag was more than two or three items.

   Why should the limit (two or three items) be so much smaller than what is obtained when one receives a discrete list and then must repeat it (five to nine items)? One obvious difference is that the encoding and responding must be accomplished during the same period in running performance. Another difference is that each item cannot be assigned to a fixed serial position. These factors may prevent the use of strategies to recode, rehearse, and group the incoming stimuli.

3. *Modal rather than average category size.* The size of semantic categories can be ascertained in various ways. One can ask individuals to recall lists of items or one can ask them to group sets of items together. Broadbent's contention was that, although some groups include up to about seven items, the modal value of categories is

about three items, and that larger numbers occur when two or three categories have been grouped together into a supercategory.

4. *Primary memory.* In the recall of a long list of words, activity interposed between the list and the response does not much hinder recall of most of the list, but it has a profound effect on recall of the last three or so serial positions. (The cited study was Postman & Phillips, 1965; further evidence comes from Glanzer & Cunitz, 1966.) Broadbent's explanation was that the last few items are still in primary memory and therefore are vulnerable to intervening activity.

5. *Effects of stimulus duration.* This topic concerned procedures in which a visual array of characters is presented for a brief time and items must be reported from it. The evidence was that as the array duration increases, recall quickly increases to about three items and then slowly increases beyond that. Based on the reasoning of Sperling (1967), it was suggested that a short period of parallel processing occurs, in which characters are apprehended, but that this early stage of processing only includes about three items. After that, an articulatory store must be used to encode additional items more slowly.

6. *Grouping.* This was perhaps the most direct evidence. It was pointed out that "the best performance [on memory tasks] is usually obtained with groups of three or four" (Ryan, 1969; Wickelgren, 1964). Broadbent summarized unpublished research by Clive Frankish in which the responses to lists presented in various ways were timed. The results (Broadbent, 1975) showed that "in almost every case the subject imposes on the material a grouping into sections no longer than three or four" (p. 7). A similar result was obtained in an experiment in which "subjects wrote down alpha-numeric lists on segmented paper" (Broadbent & Broadbent, 1973).

This topic was reinforced with new research in which individuals were to recall members of a category from long-term memory: the seven dwarfs, the seven colors of the rainbow, the countries of Europe, or the names of regular television programs. The recall timing was examined in various ways (Broadbent, 1975):

> ... the shortest interval for each subject was determined for each category, and all other intervals for that subject and category scaled in units of that shortest one. (It was normally either one or one-half seconds, except for the television programmes.) The data were then examined (1) for changes as recall proceeded, (2) for the number of items in the longest run separated by intervals of one unit,

and (3) for the number of items recalled before the first interval longer than the next successive interval. (pp. 8–9)

For all of the measures, it was found that the runs most often contained two or three items, though there was variance around that mode. One table of data from Broadbent's chapter is depicted in Figure 4.1. It shows the length of the first run of responses for three of the tasks, defined as the number of words that were produced until the postword interval, was longer than the one after it. Clearly, the limit of such a run was four items. This was presumably the number of items that was at first recalled, although in such a task, it must be cautioned that another limit might be the amount that can be spoken in a single breath (analogous to the limit in hand capacity noted for early studies of memory for chess boards; see Gobet & Simon, 2000).

Moreover, the general finding that output slows down as the task continues (Bousfield, Sedgewick, & Cohen, 1954) was found in the large, previously studied category (countries of Europe), but it had to be modified. Slowdown occurred not because of a general increase in the times between all words, but because of "pauses of increasing duration between runs of responses made with normal speed" (Broadbent, 1975, p. 9). In theoretical terms, the slowdown in recall as time went on was the result of a slower retrieval of additional clusters of information into a capacity-limited store, with no effect on recall from the store after it was refilled from long-term memory.

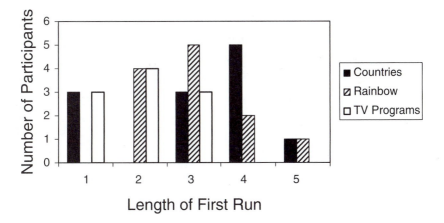

FIGURE 4.1 Data from Broadbent (1975). Number of subjects with each length of the first run (rapid burst of recall) in long-term recall from three semantic categories.

☐ THE REVIEW BY COWAN (2001)

My own literature review of capacity limits (Cowan, 2001), "The Magical Number 4 in Short-Term Memory: A Reconsideration of Mental Storage Capacity," picked up where Broadbent (1975) left off. Not much with a similar approach can be found in the literature in the intervening 26 years, so part of what I did was update the literature review. I also thought of research domains, both old and new, that Broadbent did not discuss.

Perhaps more importantly, I broke down the information into categories (coincidentally, four of them) and tried to establish general principles or guidelines to judge whether a particular type of data should or should not be counted as evidence for a fundamental storage capacity limit. The general logic is depicted in Figure 4.2 and the categories of evidence, with examples of each, are shown in Table 4.1, reproduced from Cowan (2001).

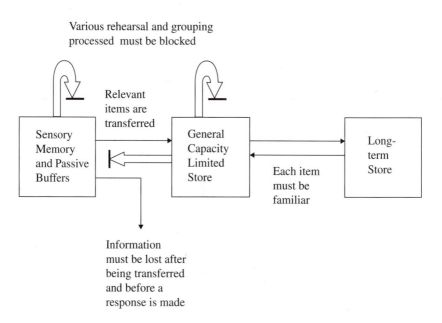

FIGURE 4.2 Illustration of the logic governing the literature review of Cowan (2001).

TABLE 4.1 Types of Evidence for a Four-Chunk Capacity Limit Discussed by Cowan (2001), with Representative Citations.

1. Imposing an information overload
   1.1. Visual whole report of spatial arrays (Sperling, 1960)
   1.2. Auditory whole report of spatiotemporal arrays (Darwin, Turvey, & Crowder, 1972)
   1.3. Whole report of unattended spoken lists (Cowan, Nugent, Elliott, & Saults, 1999)

2. Preventing long-term memory recoding, passive storage, and rehearsal
   2.1. Short-term, serial verbal retention with articulatory suppression (Pollack, Johnson, & Knaff, 1959; Waugh & Norman, 1965)
   2.2. Short-term retention of unrehearsable material (Glanzer & Razel, 1974; Jones, Farrand, Stuart, & Morris, 1995; Simon, 1974; Zhang & Simon, 1985)

3. Examining performance discontinuities
   3.1. Errorless performance in immediate recall (Broadbent, 1975)
   3.2. Enumeration reaction time (Mandler & Shebo, 1982; Trick & Pylyshyn, 1993)
   3.3. Multiobject tracking (Pylyshyn et al., 1994)
   3.4. Proactive interference in immediate memory (Halford, Wilson, & Phillips, 1988; Wicklegren, 1966)

4. Examining indirect effects of the limits
   4.1. Chunk size in immediate recall (Chase & Simon, 1973; Ericsson, 1985; Ericsson, Chase, & Faloon, 1980; Ryan, 1969; Wickelgren, 1964)
   4.2. Cluster size in long-term recall (Broadbent, 1975; Graesser & Mandler, 1978)
   4.3. Positional uncertainty in recall (Nairne, 1991)
   4.4. Analysis of the recency effect in recall (Watkins, 1974)
   4.5. Sequential effects in implicit learning and memory (Cleeremans & McClelland, 1991; McKone, 1995)
   4.6. Influence of capacity on properties of visual search (Fisher, 1984)
   4.7. Influence of capacity on mental addition reaction time (Logan, 1988; Logan & Klapp, 1991)
   4.8. Mathematical modeling parameters (Halford et al., 1998; Kintsch & van Dijk, 1978; Raaijmakers & Shiffrin, 1981)

Note. Adapted from Cowan (2001, Table 1).

Logic of Estimating Capacity Limits in Diverse Tasks

A general premise of the review of Cowan (2001) was that recall ordinarily is based on a combination of mechanisms. Just one of those mechanisms may be a capacity-limited store that is of particular interest as a fundamental limitation in cognition; it may be of interest philosophically, as well as practically, if it reflects a capacity limit of the focus of attention. However, other mechanisms contribute to recall, and they may obscure the role of the capacity limit by supplementing it. For example, sets of items presented for recall may be grouped together rapidly to form multi-item chunks, or may correspond to previously learned chunks; there may be sensory memory of a stimulus field; and there may be rehearsal of a series of verbal items in a repeating loop, or other types of rehearsal. If, however, one selects situations from the literature in which these supplementary memory mechanisms are likely to be suppressed, then one should find that each item presented for recall is retained separately using the limited capacity. If the items are familiar to begin with (e.g., known words rather than nonwords), then each item should be represented as no more than one chunk, whereas it is possible that an unfamiliar item such as a nonsense word would be represented by separate chunks for different portions of the stimulus. With both of these preconditions met (i.e., familiar items presented and supplementary memory mechanisms suppressed), the number of chunks in the mental representation should equal the number of items presented for recall.

In Figure 4.2, depicting this logic, there are several features that need to be discussed. First, for the sake of simplicity, sensory and passive storage buffers are all represented by a single box. The passive buffers would include Baddeley's (1986) phonological and visuospatial stores. There are three different instances of double arrows representing rehearsal and grouping processes in the model, all of which must be blocked. The presence of three such arrows reflects our uncertainty as to exactly how rehearsal takes place. According to Baddeley's theoretical view, subjects can rather automatically, covertly rehearse phonological information, and this is reflected in the recurrent arrow from the passive storage processes faculty to itself. It is also possible that the capacity-limited store can give rise to a different, attention-demanding sort of rehearsal, either by depositing information back into the passive stores (which may be the case when a visual image is mentally scanned) or through thoughts leading to a better grouping or analysis of the material to be recalled, as reflected by the recurrent arrow from capacity-limited processes to itself.

This sort of evidence relies on logical analyses of various tasks. There is not always a guarantee that a particular type of task suppresses supplementary mechanisms of memory (rehearsal, grouping, and sensory memory). However, if a good-faith effort to select tasks that qualify produces similar results across all such cases, the task analysis is strengthened. That is what Cowan (2001) claimed. Many such situations appeared to result in between three and five items recalled, on the average, by adults (and fewer by children).

The broader hypothesis is that this capacity limit of three to five chunks would be found not only when the situation is restricted so that each item is a separate chunk, but also in situations with larger chunks. Cowan, Chen, and Rouder (2004), discussed at length in Chapter 3, provided one form of support for that broader hypothesis.

Selected Evidence for the Capacity Limit

The general logic by which various types of data could provide more evidence of capacity limits was represented by four different types of evidence, as Table 4.1 shows. Many examples of each type were given by Cowan (2001). The logic will be illustrated by a few studies of each basic type. (For a more extensive description of relevant studies, contact me for a copy of the Cowan, 2001, article, or other related articles, by e-mail at CowanN@missouri.edu.)

Evidence Type 1: *Imposition of an information overload.* There is a limit to how much information humans can process at one time. If a stream of information comes in one simple stimulus at a time at a reasonably slow rate, there is the possibility of encoding that information in a sophisticated manner. One can find associations to the stimuli or between them and can group them together into larger chunks. However, there are various conditions that make this sophisticated type of processing impossible. One such condition is when many items are presented at the same time in a visual field and the amount of time allowed for encoding the items is short. Another such condition is when one item is presented at a time, but an attention-demanding, competing task is to be carried out simultaneously. When either of these conditions occur, items still are represented for a few seconds in sensory memory. Thus Cowan (1988, 1995) summarized considerable evidence from previous studies indicating that humans have a rich sensory memory of stimulation outlasting the actual stimuli for a number of seconds, which is perhaps unlimited in the number of stimuli that can be represented concurrently. However, this sensory memory does not include categorical information about the identities and meanings of the stimuli. Although many stimuli can be encoded in a sensory manner at one time, only a subset of them can be identified before the sensory memory becomes inadequate. Metaphorically, it is as if the spotlight of attention has to be shined on the various parts of the sensory memory field before it disintegrates. Some elements can be pulled into working memory under such circumstances, but (1) often not all of them and (2) typically without the benefit of the items being grouped together, which would have required a more leisurely application of attention.

The most famous example of the presentation of multiple items at once is probably the study by Sperling (1960). He wanted to determine how long information is held in a visual sensory form and how much of it can be converted to a more analyzed form. Multiple characters (in most experiments, letters) were presented in an array for a brief time, a fraction of a second. What happened next in the trial depended on the condition. In a *partial report* condition, there was a tone cue indicating that the characters in the top, middle, or bottom row should be recalled (indicated by a high, medium, or low tone). This reduced the difficulty of converting information from a sensory form to a categorical form. When the partial report cue (the tone) followed very closely after the onset of the array, it was possible to recall most of the items in the cued row (comprising at most four items). This finding suggested that visual sensory memory holds information about most or all of the sensory field for a short while. However, there was a stricter limit in how much information could be transferred to working memory. In a *whole-report* condition, all items in an array were to be recalled. Across variations in the number of items in the entire array, it was found that the number that could be recalled never exceeded an average of about four items.

As a function of increasing distance between the array and the following partial report cue, the usefulness of the cue diminished until, when it was presented about 1 s after the array, it was of almost no use and only a small portion of the characters in the cued row could be recalled. If one multiplies the amount recalled per row by the number of rows, one again finds that the total number in memory is about four characters. The interpretation is that most items are available in sensory memory, but only about four of them survive after sensory memory has faded.

Figure 4.3 shows the results of one of Sperling's studies, as redrawn by Bundesen (1990). The points represent the number of letters recalled in whole report as a function of the number of letters presented. Notice the limit of about four characters recalled, regardless of how many were in the array. The line represents Bundesen's mathematical model fitting the data, which will be described later. There are at least two possible explanations of the findings. It could be that there is a time limit; the sensory memory representation might fade before more than four characters can be transferred to working memory. Alternatively, there could be a capacity

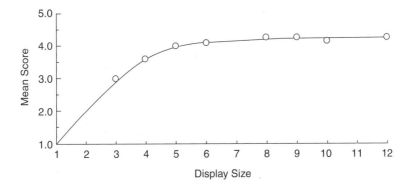

FIGURE 4.3 Reproduction of Figure 1 from Bundesen (1990). Data from Sperling (1960) on the number correct in whole recall for display sizes 3 through 12, fit to Bundesen's theoretical model.

limit; the working memory faculty might not be able to hold more than about four items. How to distinguish between these possibilities? Several factors point to the working memory capacity limit as the critical factor.

In one experiment, Sperling (1960) varied the time of presentation of the stimulus array from 15 ms to 500 ms, and there was very little effect of stimulus array duration on whole report. This suggests that it is not the rate of processing of items in the array that was important, but rather the storage limit of the working memory faculty to which information was transferred.

Bundesen's (1990) model also is in favor of the claim that the limit in whole report is in the capacity of working memory, as opposed to the speed of processing. The model includes parameters for the speed of processing in elements per second and includes a limit in the capacity of working memory. The model, which was fit to a wide variety of data, worked best for this data set with the processing speed allowing 9.85 characters to be processed before sensory memory faded, but with a working memory limit of only 4.34 characters. According to this model, the asymptotic limit or leveling off shown in Figure 4.3 occurs primarily because of the working memory limit, not because processing was too slow.

One would imagine that the processing time per item would be roughly comparable in the visual and auditory modalities. Darwin et al. (1972) carried out an experiment in adults that was similar to what Sperling did in the visual modality, except that the stimuli to be recalled were different three-character lists (comprising letters and numbers) spoken at left, right, and central locations simultaneously; that is, nine different spoken characters in a spatiotemporal array. The partial-report cue, when it was present, was visually presented and indicated that all three characters presented at the cued spatial location were to be recalled. The results were similar to those that Sperling (1960) obtained in the visual modality, except that the value of the partial-report cue was not lost until the cue followed the array by 4 s. This striking difference from the visual modality presumably reflects a longer persistence of usable sensory memory in the auditory modality, and it should allow much more time for the transfer of sensory information to working memory than what was found in the visual research by Sperling (about a 1-s persistence). Yet, the whole-report limit was very similar to what was found by Sperling using visual stimuli. To account for the results of the auditory and the visual modality without having to postulate very different processing rates for stimuli presented in those modalities, it seems simplest to assume that it is not the rate at which items can be processed that limits working memory in these procedures, but, rather, the holding capacity of working memory itself.

In these whole-report experiments, one may worry that the capacity is affected by output interference. The recall of each item may interfere with the recall of subsequent items. Indeed, it has been shown that output interference is an important factor, at least in serial recall (Cowan, Saults, Elliott, & Moreno, 2002). However, an alternative possibility is that there will be no substantial output interference provided that the number of stimuli (or chunks of information) do not exceed working memory capacity. One way to examine this question would be to examine performance on a version of the array task in which there is only one response to be made.

Luck and Vogel (1997) carried out the relevant study. Their stimulus fields were arrays of small, colored squares, which was possible because of the nature of the response. In each trial, the first array was followed shortly by a second array that was identical to the first or differed in the color of one square only. In the most relevant version of the task, one square in the second array was encircled so that the subject knew that, if anything changed between the arrays, it was the color of the encircled square. The task was simply to say whether the square had changed color or not. This is therefore a variety of partial-report task. Importantly, the same color could appear at more than one location in the array, so it was necessary to remember not only the colors present, but also the location of each color in the array. It was found that performance was excellent with up to four squares in each array and then decreased markedly as a function of the increasing number of squares.

One might wonder why a capacity-limited source of information has to be used in this task, as opposed to a mental image of the entire first array. The answer is that the mental image is a sensory memory that is vulnerable to overwriting from the second array before a comparison can be made. This point has been directly tested. If a cue, indicating which object may have changed, is given in the interval between the two arrays, this greatly increases accuracy in the task, but there is no such benefit if the cue is given simultaneous with the second array (Becker, Pashler, & Anstis, 2000; Landman, Spekreijse, & Lamme, 2003).

Lamme (2003) suggested that these findings have implications for the relation between attention and awareness. The argument was that the iconic representation was a short-lived type of awareness of the entire array but that only an attended portion of it could be reported. Instead, it might be said that the initial awareness was of a pattern without awareness of individual items making up that pattern.

Cowan (2001) described a simple model to estimate the working memory capacity limit in this type of task, a modification of a slightly different formula by Pashler (1988). (For details see Cowan et al., in press-a, Appendix A.) The method was described as follows (Cowan, 2001, Section R2.4):

> Upon examining a briefly presented array of N items, the subject is able to apprehend a certain fixed number of items, k. The apprehension of these items would allow a change to be detected if one of these k items should happen to be the changed item. Thus, with probability k/N, the change is detected. If the change is not detected, the subject guesses "yes, there was a change" with probability g. Thus, the formula for the hit rate H is: $H = k/N + [(N - k)/N]g$. If there is no change between the two arrays, and if the cued item happens to be an item that is included within the set k that the subject apprehended, then that knowledge will allow the subject to answer correctly that no change has occurred (and this is where our formula differs from Pashler's). If there is no such knowledge (for $N - k$ items), then the subject still will answer correctly with a probability $1 - g$, where g is again the probability of guessing "yes." Given that memory is used to respond in the no-change situation, it is useful to define performance in terms of the rate of correct rejections, CR. The assumptions just stated then lead to the following expression: $CR = k/N + [(N - k)/N](1 - g)$. Combining equations, $H + CR = 2k/N + (N - k)/N = (k + N)/N$. Rearranging terms, the capacity can be estimated as $k = (H + CR - 1)N$. (p. 166)

This equation also can be expressed as $k = N$ (hits – false alarms). It was found to be more suitable in estimating k than was the one offered earlier by Pashler because this equation generally yields estimates of capacity that are more nearly constant across set sizes. For the data presented by Luck and Vogel (1997), for example, the estimate of capacity comes out to around three squares, for every set size larger than three. There was very little effect of the array exposure duration within a broad range, similar to what Sperling (1960) found. The results of Luck and Vogel with only one response per trial provide some assurance that the capacity estimates obtained with whole-report methods are affected little, if at all, by output interference.

It may be that output interference is an important factor only for lists exceeding the working memory capacity limit of three or four items observed in these studies. For example, in the study of output interference by Cowan, Saults et al. (2002), lists of nine digits were presented, almost certainly exceeding the capacity limit.

Another way to impose an information overload is to present the items to be recalled one at a time but to distract the subject during the presentation of these items. Cowan, Nugent, Elliott, Ponomarev, and Saults (1999) did this in a developmental study with children in first grade (7- to 8-year-old children) and fourth grade (10- to 11-year-old children), and college students. The basic method was one in which the subject first was tested to determine his or her digit span. Later, a visual task was introduced in which the subject was to match a target picture with one of several other pictures on the basis of which one had a name that rhymed with the target picture's name. During the rhyming game in the main part of the experiment, lists of digits were presented through headphones, with the length of the lists equal to the longest list that the subject had been able to repeat (termed *span length*) or shorter than that length by one, two, or three digits. These spoken lists were presented frequently, but with varying amounts of time between them. Most lists were to be ignored. Occasionally, though, the rhyming task ceased and a visual cue indicated that the subject was then to use the number keypad to recall the last spoken list that had been presented, which had just ended, with the digits in order. The response display showed a space for each digit that was to be recalled. There also were other control conditions and safeguards, such as sessions in which the rhyming task was carried out with no sounds, and in which the subjects attended to the sounds instead of playing the rhyming task.

There are many potential pitfalls regarding the allocation of attention in such situations. I will not go into them here, but elsewhere have discussed the measures that indicated it was a safe assumption that the manipulation of attention was a very effective one for subjects in all groups, and that factors such as the familiarity of the items and the keyboard did not determine the developmental trends (for details see Cowan, Elliott, & Saults, 2002). Data from two main conditions of Cowan et al. (1999) are redrawn in Figure 4.4. The left-hand panel shows performance on lists that were attended when they were presented, as a function of the list length relative to span. The dependent measure is the

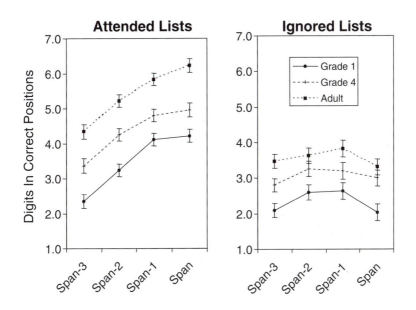

List Length (Relative to Span)

FIGURE 4.4   Data from Cowan, Nugent, Elliott, Ponomarev, and Saults (1999). (Left) For three different age-groups (graph parameter) attending to spoken digit lists, the number of digits recalled in the correct serial positions, as a function of the list length relative to the subject's span. (Right) The comparable data for spoken digit lists that were ignored during their presentation. Notice that the number of ignored digits recalled does not increase with the list length, unlike the number of attended digits recalled.

number of digits recalled in their correct serial positions. The use of this measure underscores an important point: that an "item" in a study such as this is actually the binding between the digit and the serial position. (We also scored the data according to the recall of the correct digits in any serial position and got somewhat comparable results but, as list length increases, the influence of guessing changes, making it difficult to interpret such a measure.)

The left-hand panel of Figure 4.4 shows that, for attended spoken digits, the number of items recalled increased monotonically with the list length. In striking contrast, the right-hand panel shows that the number of items recalled during sessions in which the lists were to be ignored during their presentation (while the rhyming task was carried out) remained fairly constant across list lengths.

The account of the data that Cowan et al. (1999) offered was basically as follows. When the digits are attended during their presentation, they can be rehearsed and perhaps converted into a smaller number of groups in working memory. For this reason, the number that can be recalled is not constant across list lengths. However, when they are ignored during their presentation, the information persists in sensory memory only. When the occasional cue to recall a list occurs, items must be transferred from sensory memory to working memory and there is no time to group or rehearse them. Therefore, each digit transferred to working memory remains a separate chunk of information for the subject. Given these assumptions, the relatively constant number correct shown in the right-hand panel of Figure 4.4 presumably reflects the capacity limit of working memory, for a reason similar to the whole-report conditions of Sperling (1960) using simultaneous, visual arrays, and Darwin et al. (1972) using spatiotemporally arranged, spoken character arrays.

More can be said about the data in the right-hand panel of Figure 4.4. First, the capacity limit observed in adults was similar to the limit observed by Sperling (1960), Darwin et al. (1972), and Luck and Vogel (1997), and in many other procedures discussed by Cowan (2001). Second, the observed capacity was smaller in children. Third, the age-group difference is almost as large for ignored lists as it is for attended lists (see Figure 4.4). This suggests that the age difference cannot be accounted for primarily by factors that involve the use of attention-demanding strategies at the time that the list is presented. Instead, the more important factor in the development of digit-span performance seems to be the basic capacity.

Results were similar, though somewhat more variable, when performance was examined on lists of four, five, and six digits, which were available in most subjects in all age groups, as opposed to relative list lengths as shown in the figure.

Similar results are obtained using a running memory span task in which 12 to 20 digits are presented on each trial (after Cohen & Heath, 1990), spoken at the rapid rate of four items per second. This unpredictability and rapid rate make it impossible to rehearse or group the items, so that the means of performing the task can only reasonably involve waiting passively for the list to end and then transferring items from a passive storage stream to the focus of attention. Previously, I discussed research of Hockey (1973) verifying that assumption; with a fast rate of presentation in a running-span task, rehearsal instructions actually were detrimental to performance compared with waiting passively for the list to end.

In short, the research strategy of imposing an information overload, either by simultaneously presenting items or by distracting items during their presentation, has produced a considerable amount of evidence favoring a constant capacity of about four chunks in adults, and fewer in children.

Wilken and Ma (2004) offered an alternative account of capacity limits for visual arrays, based on signal detection theory. According to their account, the capacity limit is not because of a fixed number of slots, but rather to neural noise that builds up as a function of the number of items in the array. They indicated though that "It remains an interesting empirical question whether the changes in noise associated with set size are due to factors prior to encoding (e.g., saliency and/or attentional effects ...) and/or caused by interference between items encoded within memory ..." (p. 1131). Until this question is answered, it is not clear if the signal detection account is a sophisticated version of a capacity-limit account or an alternative account. Another limitation for the time being is that they found certain signal-detection models to fit the data much better than the model of Pashler (1988), but did not compare these models with the formula discussed previously and by Cowan (2001) and Cowan et al. (in press-a).

Evidence Type 2: *Prevention of the use of long-term memory recoding, passive storage, and rehearsal through other means.* Dividing attention is a good way to ensure that items are not grouped together or memorized during their presentation, but it is not the only way. Another way, for example, is to repeat a single word over and over during presentation of stimuli, the type of task known as *articulatory suppression*. There is reason to believe that this repetition quickly becomes automatic and therefore does not tie up attention very well, at least in adults (Guttentag, 1984). Yet, it effectively blocks covert verbal rehearsal (Baddeley, 1986). Without such rehearsal, the verbal memoranda presumably become inactive in working memory and, moreover, memorizing them might be impossible to carry out.

Cowan (2001) also assumed that articulatory suppression also prevents grouping or chunking of the stimuli. In an apparent contradiction to that assumption, Klapp, Marshburn, and Lester (1983; Experiment 2) found grouping effects in a task in which digits to be recalled were visually presented and the subject was to say "la" every time a digit was presented. However, this sort of verbalization vocalizes the grouping itself and is slower than the usual articulatory suppression task. Hitch, Burgess, Towse, and Culpin (1996) found that articulatory suppression at a faster rate of two words per second eliminated grouping effects for printed lists, though not for spoken lists.

One problem with the use of articulatory suppression is that it also is thought to prevent the conversion of printed words to a phonological representation (Baddeley, Lewis, & Vallar, 1984). Under such circumstances, it is possible that a familiar printed word is represented as more than one chunk. In contrast, spoken words are thought to enter the phonological buffer rather automatically, even when there is an articulatory suppression task. (More pervasive effects of articulatory suppression on the recall of printed lists, as opposed to spoken lists, have reinforced that conclusion; see Baddeley et al., 1984).

Given such considerations, Cowan (2001) examined the literature to find experiments in which articulatory suppression was carried out along with spoken lists. Typically in such studies, the spoken stimuli are presented through headphones to minimize acoustic interference from the articulatory suppression task. If a phonological representation forms but cannot be used to achieve grouping and rehearsal processes during presentation of the list, then the situation is similar to the one that is encountered in memory for ignored speech or in running memory span with a fast presentation rate. Information must be pulled from phonological memory into the capacity-limited store one item at a time. (Theoretically that might be done either online, or after the list has ended, which was what was assumed by Cowan, 2001.) Cowan found 17 such experiments with English words. The results are summarized here in Figure 4.5, with the results from the 17 data sets reordered according to the resulting memory estimate. One can see that there was not much variation among the sets and that the memory estimate was similar to the other basic capacity estimates that have been offered, in the range of three to five items.

Presumably, the results shown in Figure 4.5 may be slightly depressed estimates of capacity because we cannot assume that grouping did not

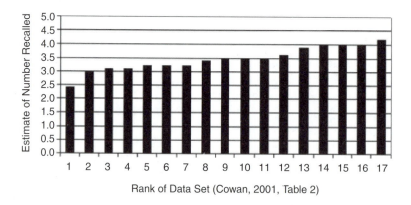

FIGURE 4.5 Data from Cowan (2001, Table 2) illustrating the number of items recalled in studies of immediate verbal memory with auditory presentation and articulatory suppression.

take place even in the presence of articulatory suppression, given the findings of Hitch et al. (1996), which indicated that articulatory suppression does not eliminate grouping for spoken lists. (It was assumed by Cowan, 2001.) Nevertheless, in the study of Hitch et al., grouping was provided for the subject. The result does not necessarily imply that subjects are capable of imposing their own grouping on lists that are not grouped in presentation. The convergence of estimates from many procedures examined by Cowan (2001) resemble the findings of Figure 4.5 and suggest that subject-imposed grouping in the presence of articulatory suppression was not an important factor.

When items to be recalled are nonverbal items that cannot easily be rehearsed because they cannot be converted to simple labels (e.g., dot locations; Jones, Farrand, et al., 1995) or very long phrases that cannot be verbally rehearsed because of time limitations (e.g., proverbs; Glanzer & Razel, 1974), there may be no need to block rehearsal. For lists of 4, 7, or 10 dots in Jones, Farrand et al., respectively, Cowan (2001) estimated 3.5, 3.8, and 3.2 items in storage.

Glanzer and Razel (1974) estimated only two items in short-term memory, but their estimates for lists of shorter items was similarly low. The estimates were for free recall and, as Cowan (2001) pointed out, they may be underestimates because they assumed that long-term memory was equivalent in the medial and final serial positions, which is contradicted by the negative recency effect that is often found in long-term free recall (Craik, Gardiner, & Watkins, 1970). Also, it is possible that there is some effect of output interference for very short lists after all, if the duration of the output interference is very large as it is in the case of memory for proverbs.

Despite the exception mentioned, then, the overwhelming bulk of evidence of this type is convergent with the evidence from an information overload in suggesting a fundamental working memory capacity limit of three to five chunks of information.

Evidence Type 3: *Examination of performance discontinuities.* In the examples for the first two types of data from Cowan (2001), the dependent measure was recall (or recognition), and the critical issue was that, in critical situations in which rehearsal and grouping of stimuli into larger chunks presumably cannot take place, up to about four elements can be remembered. Here, however, the focus is on data sets in which smaller or larger numbers of items can be processed, but not in the same way; there is a discontinuity in the error rate or the reaction time after some small number of items.

An often-discussed example is the subitizing process discussed in Chapter 1 stemming from the early work of Jevons (1871); the ability to enumerate up to about four items rapidly and almost without error, without counting, in contrast to the slower and more error-prone enumeration that occurs for larger numbers of items (with the reaction time increasing more steeply, and approximately linearly, as a function of the number of items after four). An example of subitizing is shown in Figure 4.6, from the often-cited article of Mandler and Shebo (1982). The top panel shows that exposure duration only begins to matter for sets of four items or more, and stops mattering after about eight items, when most responses are erroneous; the middle panel similarly shows that reaction times go through a relatively flat phase for one to three or one to four items, then shift to a relatively steep phase, and then another flat phase after about eight items; and the bottom panel shows that the responses are not biased until after about eight items. These data can be explained if there is a subitizing region (about one to four items), a counting region (about four to eight items), and an estimation region (more than eight items or so), in which there is not enough time to count.

Some have been unimpressed by the discontinuity in the data for subitizing. After all, there could be psychometric scaling problems such as the compressed range of data for the extremely small numbers of items. There are two studies that help allay that worry using neuropsychological dissociations. Dehaene and Cohen (1994) examined patients who had simultanagnosia, which they defined as "a deficit of the visual perception of complex scenes, with preserved recognition of individual objects" (p. 960). These patients sometimes see only some of the elements of a scene. What is critical for the study is that the patients have difficulty counting. It was found that they were able to enumerate two and sometimes two objects without a problem, but that performance was much more subnormal for large numbers of objects. This provides additional justification for the distinction between counting and subitizing. As Dehaene and Cohen note, the disease could have lowered the subitizing limit compared with normal individuals.

Watson and Humphreys (1999) published research on a similar topic: "The Magic Number Four and Temporo-Parietal Damage: Neurological Impairments in Counting Targets Amongst Distractors." (I was unaware of this highly relevant article until after Cowan, 2001, was published.) They examined a patient with right temporoparietal damage who could both count and subitize when there was no distraction, but who was unable to count objects among distractors (e.g., red dots among blue distractors). Nevertheless, the patient was able to enumerate three and four objects accurately. That two different neurological deficits result in dissociations between counting and subitizing, under different stimulus conditions, strengthens the point that they reflect different processes.

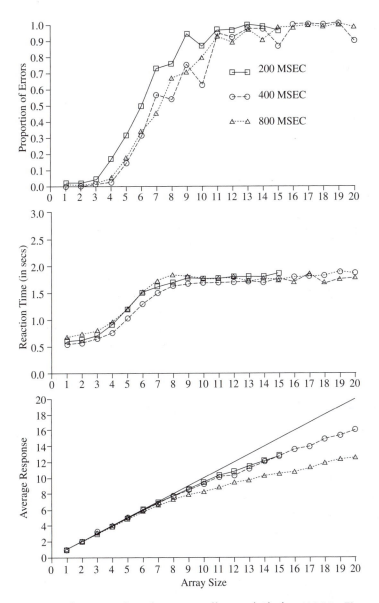

FIGURE 4.6 Subitizing data from Mandler and Shebo (1982, Figure 3). (Top) Proportions of errors as a function of set size for three different exposure durations (graph parameter). (Middle) Reaction times. (Bottom) Average responses. The first two panels show that the data can be classified into a subitizing region (roughly set sizes one through four), a counting region (roughly set sizes four through eight), and an estimation region when there are too many items to count quickly (roughly about set size eight).

Previously it was mentioned that some attribute subitizing to a pattern-matching process (e.g., Logan & Zbrodoff, 2003; Peterson & Simon, 2000). It is important, therefore, that there also are other types of procedures that show marked performance discontinuities between the within-capacity and beyond-capacity range. For example, in multiobject-tracking procedures, some of the objects on the screen flash and become targets. When they stop flashing, both targets and distractors move randomly around the screen at a fixed rate. After they stop, one object becomes the probe, and the subject must indicate whether the probed item was a target or a distractor. It is possible to do that task with three, and sometimes four, items (Pylyshyn & Storm, 1988; Yantis, 1992). This seems to reflect the number of objects that can be monitored by attention at the same time.

It seems likely that there are special task demands that should lead to somewhat different estimates for different procedures, such as the need for vigilance and speed in keeping up with changes in the multiobject tracking task. It is the similarity in the capacity estimates based on these various procedures, despite somewhat different task demands, that most impresses me.

Evidence Type 4: *Examination of indirect effects of the capacity limits*. In the evidence from Cowan (2001) reviewed so far, the dependent measures have been the number of items recalled accurately or the speed with which a certain number of items can be processed. The fourth and final category of evidence Cowan discussed comprised situations in which there was some other measure that led indirectly to an inference about working memory capacity. We already have discussed one type of evidence that could fit this description. The research on the timing of recall responses indicates that responses are made in bursts of a limited number of items (e.g., Broadbent, 1975; see Figure 4.1).

Another type of example comes from evidence in which there is no obvious indication that capacity is limited, but for which a theoretical account of performance includes a capacity limit. One type of task for which that is the case is the visual-search task. Shiffrin and Schneider (1977) distinguished between visual search tasks with *variable mapping* and tasks with *consistent mapping* and suggested that only the former type requires effortful, controlled processing, whereas the latter type uses automatic processing. However, we will see evidence of a capacity limit even in the case of consistent mapping.

Some explanation is needed first. In a task with variable mapping, there is no highly learned target set. For example, in one trial, the task may be to search for the letter *g* among several other letters, whereas, in the next trial, the task may be to search for the letter *w*, and *g* is eligible to appear as a distracting stimulus. In contrast, in a search task with consistent mapping, some stimuli belong consistently to the target set and others belong consistently to the distracting set. The letters *g* and *w* might always be targets to be found among other letters. Tasks with consistent mapping also can be set up without extensive training, by relying on previously learned distinctions. An example would be searching for the presence of a digit among distracting letter stimuli. The typical finding highlighted by Shiffrin and Schneider (1977) was that tasks with variable mapping result in performance levels that deteriorate steadily as the number of distracting stimuli increases, whereas tasks with consistent mapping produce flat performance functions that do not depend on the number of distracting stimuli (provided that the number is not large enough to make the stimuli difficult to perceive). The reason basically was thought to be that variable mapping requires a slow, possibly serial (one-item-at-a-time) search of the items in the array to find the target, whereas consistent mapping allows a parallel search of all letters at the same time.

Of interest here, however, are some findings suggesting that there are limits even to a search that occurs with consistent mapping. In the searches producing a flat slope, there may have been enough time for items to be searched, but the situation may be different when there is only a short time for a search to take place.

A relevant experiment was conducted by Sperling, Budiansky, Spivak, and Johnson (1971). They presented series of 6 to 12 arrays, each of which included up to nine characters in a 3 × 3 pattern. Each array had items in the same locations. All but one of the characters were letters, but the critical item, somewhere in the middle of the sequence, was a digit. The required response was to indicate where the digit appeared (e.g., bottom row, right side). Sometimes, the identity of the digit (a 2 or a 5) also had to be indicated, but other times the subject knew it in advance; that proved to be relatively unimportant. The time between arrays in the series varied from very short to several hundred milliseconds. Critically, the number of items in the entire display (counting up items across arrays) was 2, 3, 4, 9, 16, or 25. What was found was a large discrepancy in the pattern obtained with 2 to 4 characters on one hand, and 9 to 25 characters on the other hand. When the time between arrays was higher than about 60 ms, the efficiency of a process of apprehending or "scanning" characters was higher for the larger arrays. (This efficiency was expressed in terms of ms/letter scanned, and it could be estimated on the basis of the proportion correct in each condition along with a simple mathematical model of how many items had to be scanned to achieve that proportion correct.) In contrast, when the time between arrays was very short, about 30 ms or less, better efficiency was achieved for arrays that included a total of only two to four characters.

A type of model that can explain such a pattern of data, with reference to a basic capacity limit, was proposed by Fisher (1982, 1984) and is illustrated in Figure 4.7. The model posits a limited-capacity buffer. Each item that is apprehended must occupy a slot in the buffer for a period long enough to allow an evaluation of whether it is a target item (a digit among the letters) or not. In this particular example, the buffer allows the evaluation of up to four characters at once. When a character has been processed to the point that this buffer storage is no longer needed, a slot is freed up. The buffer shows that four characters from the first array are to be evaluated (*b, x, f, t*) and that the evaluation has been completed for only one of those characters (*b*) by the time the second array arrives. This means that only one slot is available for a character from the second array (*r*) to be evaluated and the rest will be lost. For the two arrays together, five items were evaluated or scanned. This type of model explains the data of Sperling et al. (1971), indicating that it is efficient to receive many items at the same time, but only if there is enough time for that many items to be processed. With very fast presentation times, it is more efficient to receive items three or four at a time than it is to receive them two at a time, the graphs show; but higher numbers of items presented at once cannot be as efficient when the presentation time per array is so short.

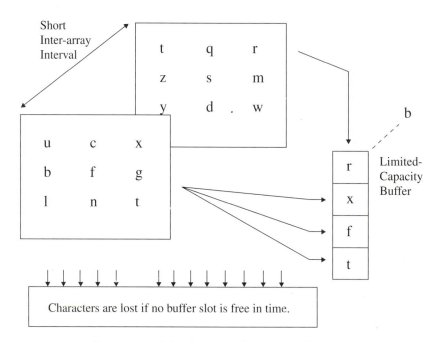

FIGURE 4.7 Illustration of the theoretical account of Fisher (1984).

Fisher (1982, 1984) went beyond that verbal description and tested a mathematical model of evidence of this sort. His description of the assumptions of the model was as follows (Fisher 1984):

(1) Encoded stimuli in the visual cortex are scanned once for placement on a comparison channel; (2) the time between arrivals of stimuli to the comparison channels is exponentially distributed with rate parameter l; (3) the time to compare a stimulus with a prespecified target is exponentially distributed with rate parameter m; (4) at most k comparison channels can execute in parallel; (5) stimuli in iconic memory are equally likely to be replaced by the characters or masks which appear next to the input streams; (6) masks are not placed on the comparison channels; and (7) the system is in a steady state. Note that it is assumed that the two dimensional coordinates of a stimulus are retained in the visual cortex. (p. 453)

Within a field termed queuing theory, this verbal description fits what is termed *Erlang's loss formula*. Fisher fit the data from multiple-array studies to the formula and reported the index of fit (Π^2) as a function of the estimate of the capacity of the buffer, k.

Fischer (1984) generally found that the best fits to the data were obtained with k values of 3 or 4. Figure 4.8 shows the values of fit for each value of k from 1 to 7, averaged across four subjects who were studied intensively.

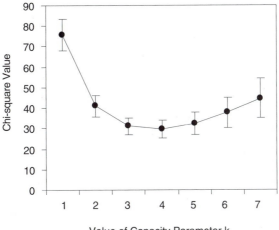

FIGURE 4.8   After Fisher (1984): chi-square value (with standard error) as a function of the value of the model parameter k.

(Other experiments show fit worsening steeply when even higher values of k are assumed.) When one looks at the raw data, no discontinuity is found. Yet, to arrive at a good model of the data, a capacity limit of a handful of items must be assumed. This is what is Cowan (2001) meant by indirect evidence of a capacity limit.

This account of the research reviewed by Cowan (2001) is incomplete. It is meant to give a flavor of the type of evidence discussed in the review. The strength of the review was in setting up principles for examining evidence and then finding that, when this was done, there was a striking confluence of results. When items were familiar, so that they could be assumed to reflect no more than one chunk of information per stimulus, and when the situation seemed to prevent rehearsal, grouping, or readout directly from sensory memory, normal adult humans could retain about three to four chunks of information at a time, on average, in many types of situations. It is hoped that others will try out this type of analysis on their favorite data, and eventually that it will be possible to judge the extent to which this analysis has merit. The work of Cowan, Chen, and Rouder (2004), discussed in Chapter 3, was a step toward confirming the analysis more experimentally, and it produced encouraging results.

☐ CONTINUING EVIDENCE

To see the field as I see it, one cannot think of Cowan (2001) as summarizing all of the available evidence regarding capacity limits, even with the commentaries included. Given the great diversity of situations in which evidence on capacity limits can arise, new evidence is apt to be trickling in all the time, both from new studies and from old studies that were overlooked. I will present a few of these to give a flavor of this trickling in with evidence for capacity limits in working memory.

In one kind of procedure, immediate recall is cued in a way that does not encourage phonological rehearsal or serial order information. Information from several categories is presented and one category is cued for recall. The expectation is that items from the relevant category must be transferred from an activated representation that is not capacity limited to a capacity-limited form of storage (such as the focus of attention in the model of Cowan, 1995, 1999). In the early example of this procedure, Reid, Lloyd, Brackett, and Hawkins (1961) presented a stream of exemplars from several semantic categories and occasional category names, as in the series, *Berlin, Willow, Moscow, Dartmouth, Elm, CITY, Golf, Ford, Soccer, TREE, College* …. Whenever a category name was presented, the required response was to recall the preceding words from the cued category.

In the example given, on hearing the word *CITY*, the correct response was to repeat the cities Berlin and Moscow. The mean *storage load* was defined as the number of items presented, but not yet recalled. When the word *CITY* was presented, the storage load was five (Berlin through Elm). After recall, the storage load was reduced to three (because Berlin and Moscow had been recalled) and then increased to six before the word *TREE* was presented. Within runs such as these, but longer, the load varied. The *average* storage load of a particular series was 2.5, 3.5, 4.5, or 5.5 items. The category to be recalled included one, two, or three exemplars of the category.

The processing requirement of this situation is an interesting one. The knowledge that testing would occur on the basis of semantic cues should help to focus attention on that level instead of on the phonological level that is ordinarily helpful for rehearsal (Baddeley, 1986). There was also the need to include only those categories for which untested exemplars have been presented. The variation in the number of items to be remembered at any one time within a series also would seem to prevent any fixed assignment of items to serial positions. Under these circumstances, the relevant factor for recall would be the number of items to be remembered.

Subjects practiced this task over a period of 4 days. The result of this experiment is shown in terms of a capacity estimate in Figure 4.9 (top panel). To construct this figure, the proportion correct for each load on each day had to be derived from the data. Then, the proportion correct

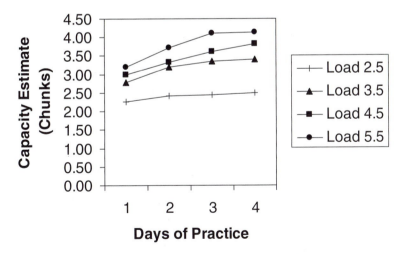

FIGURE 4.9 Data from Reid, Lloyd, Brackett, and Hawkins (1961). Capacity estimate as a function of days of practice for four different values of the imposed memory load.

was multiplied by the load to determine the average number of items estimated to be in working memory. For example, for an average load of 3.5 items, if 85% of the items that were supposed to be recalled were recalled correctly, the estimate of items held in working memory (the capacity) would be 3.5 × .8 = 2.8 items. The interesting finding is that performance increased with the increasing number of items to be retained in memory, i.e., the load, only up to a limit of about four items. Subsequent studies with related methods (Cohen & Sandberg, 1977; Haarmann, Davelaar, & Usher, 2003) have yielded similar results and will be discussed later in the discussion of individual differences in working memory.

Boutla, Supalla, Newport, and Bavelier (2004) examined the short-term-memory and working memory spans of individuals using English and American Sign Language (ASL). The result was a span of only about five items in ASL, versus the usual seven or so for English speakers. This difference was observed both for monolinguals and for bilingual speakers of English and ASL. This was the case even with controls for the duration of producing the list and other factors such as interitem phonological or sign similarity. Yet, performance levels on a more complex sentence span task did not differ in English versus ASL. One interpretation of this result is that the natural usefulness of a phonological rehearsal process accounts for the advantage ordinarily found for English sequences. Either using ASL or using a complex task with English materials interferes with that rehearsal process and leaves little beyond a core working memory capacity, within the range of 4 ±1 items.

Last, new evidence comes from Ericsson, Delaney, Weaver, and Mahadevan (2004), who used a variety of analytic methods to dissect the skills of a celebrated mnemonist, Rajan, who could remember long lists of digits. Whereas previous research (Thompson, Cowan, & Frieman, 1993) suggested that Rajan differed from ordinary individuals in a basic capacity, the study of Ericsson et al. suggested that the difference was in a knowledge structure that had been built up. For example, Ericsson et al. indicate that:

> Experiment 2 also revealed details about the internal structure of the 10-digit groups that were inconsistent with Thompson et al.'s ... hypothesis of an underlying basic "raw" capacity to store digits. They hypothesized that Rajan stored digits by associating each digit with its corresponding spatial location, resulting in 10–15 "slots" within each digit group ... our analysis of the digit sequences that had verbally reported associations suggested that Rajan would group immediately adjacent digits together into 2-digit, 3-digit and 4-digit groups (p. 209).

Other data will be presented in Chapter 6, as part of the discussion of why such limits exist.

In sum, there are abundant studies that appear to suggest a fundamental limit of three to five chunks of information in adults when supplementary storage mechanisms are disabled. Chapter 5 discusses dissenting views; Chapter 6 discusses reasons why the proposed capacity limit may exist.

☐ CHUNK LIMITS AND FEATURE-CONTENT LIMITS

In a rapidly moving area of science, 2 years can be a long time. There have been some important advances since I agreed to write this book in 2002. All along, I believed that the notion of a mechanism with a capacity limited to a fixed number of chunks in an individual was likely to be an oversimplification to be amended by future research in anomalous situations; these could include stimulus sets for which the chunks are not distinct from one another and stimulus sets for which the notion of an "object" or chunk does not fully summarize some complex or multidimensional information that has to be maintained for success in the task. If the chunk-capacity limit were to be modified by additional factors in a systematic way, I would not view that as a failure of theory, but as a success, analogous (in a small way) to Newton's theory of gravitation viewed from the perspective of Einstein's advances. Albert Einstein once explained:

> Creating a new theory is not like destroying an old barn and erecting a skyscraper in its place. It is rather like climbing a mountain, gaining new and wider views, discovering unexpected connections between our starting point and its rich environment. But the point from which we started out still exists and can be seen, although it appears smaller and forms a tiny part of our broad view gained by the mastery of the obstacles on our adventurous way up. (Asimov and Shulman, 1988, p. 326)

The advance underlying this philosophical detour involves the feature within each object or chunk. Luck and Vogel (1997), in their research with comparisons between arrays of objects, included conditions with multi-featured objects. They found that the capacity for such objects was as high as the capacity for single-featured objects. That finding was partly verified by Wheeler and Treisman (2002), who found, for example, that subjects could perform just about as well when made responsible for both the color and the shape of an object as when made responsible for only one of these stimulus features (at least, when the probe array was limited to just the tested object).

Wheeler and Treisman (2002) failed to replicate the finding of Luck and Vogel (1997) that subjects could keep track of an inside color surrounded by a different outside color in the same object, as easily as they could keep track of homogeneous color squares. The difference was tentatively attributed to higher luminance values in the Luck and Vogel study, which could have been bright enough to produce color blending. However, Xu (2004) showed that there was an advantage for retention of N two-colored objects as opposed to $2N$ single-colored objects, provided that one part of the object (in this study, round shapes) used one set of color features and another part of the object (in this study, tails) used a different set of color features.

Alvarez and Cavanagh (2004) took this idea further by using complex objects and showing how they affected capacity. They used the following stimuli, arranged here from simpler to more complex: colored squares, English block letters, line drawings of common elongated objects, Chinese characters, irregular polygons, and shaded cubes of various orientations. The complexity rating of objects of a particular type was empirically defined on the basis of a visual search task. A single object was to be found among an array of objects of the same class, and complexity was defined as the mean slope of the search reaction time function across array sizes. A two-array comparison procedure also was carried out for each object type and it was found that the working memory capacities of the different object types were linearly related to their complexity ratings. For the most complex objects (the shaded cubes, it turns out), the capacity was fewer than two objects, but for maximally simple objects (colored squares), the capacity approached an intercept of slightly more than four objects. (Convergent evidence that object complexity affects capacity was obtained with gratings [Lakha & Wright, 2004].)

To compare this finding of Alvarez and Cavanagh (2004) with previous research, one might appeal to the notion of integral and separable stimulus features (Garner, 1974). In the stimuli of Wheeler and Treisman (2002), the multifeatured objects presumably involved perceptually separable features. Each feature type could be encoded separately in the sensory memory system and then attention could be turned to the sensory representation (or feature map) that turned out to be relevant, or even to one feature map after another if necessary for the task. In the stimuli of Alvarez and Cavanagh, however, the features appear more integral. The vertical line of a letter has no meaning except as it relates to other lines in the letter, the shading and shape of one face of a cube is not indicative of the cube's orientation until the shading and shape of multiple faces are perceived together in an integral fashion, and so on.

Several different theoretical resolutions are possible here. The simplest resolution might appear to be one in which only the total amount of informational complexity, and not the number of objects or chunks, matters for working memory. The capacity limit of about four objects (or chunks) in working memory would be the result of using maximally simple stimuli, whereas, for more complex stimuli, the same working memory capacity has to be allocated to fewer objects.

That solution may be problematic, however. It does not explain why multiple, separable stimulus feature types do not place a larger load on working memory than do single-featured objects (Luck & Vogel, 1997; Wheeler & Treisman, 2002). One could hypothesize that the capacity limits reside in the feature maps themselves (as Wheeler & Treisman did), but that solution appears to contradict evidence that simple features in a field are encoded in parallel, with no strict capacity limit (Treisman, 1988).

Results of two recent neuroimaging studies (Jiang & Song, 2004; Xu, 2004) offer a new solution, and what appears to me to be a dramatic illustration that neuroimaging research may be of use in guiding models of cognition. Xu used functional magnetic resonance imaging to examine the neural correlates of performance in two-array comparison tasks. With the same objects, there was an easy task (remembering whether each object in an array included a hole) and a hard task (remembering the contour of each object). Two areas of the brain with different response properties were found. The lateral occipital complex (LOC) responded in a manner that mirrored behavioral performance. For the easy task, capacity increased to about four objects as the array size increased, and so did the signal strength in the LOC. For the hard task, capacity leveled out at about two objects, and so did the signal strength in the LOC. In contrast, the intraparietal sulcus (IPS) responded to the number of objects. From one to three objects, the signal strength increased. Then it leveled off with four or six objects. This happened in a similar manner no matter whether the easy- or the hard-working memory task was assigned. Thus the IPS had an object limit, whereas the LOC had a limit that depended on task difficulty.

Jiang and Song (2004) also found a dissociation between the number of objects and the task difficulty, but in a slightly different way. In each trial, a first array included irregular polygons in different colors and required memory for the colors, shapes, or both together. The probe stimulus was a single object that could have changed shape or changed color (depending on the task). Behaviorally, color memory increased to a capacity of about four items, whereas shape memory leveled off at about two to three items (consistent with Alvarez & Cavanagh, 2004), as does memory for the combination of shape and color at a slightly larger set size. Responses to the working memory load were observed in the right parietal cortex. It was found that the magnitude of the brain response depended on the task difficulty. The highest mean signal strength was obtained for the shape task and the lowest signal strength was obtained for the color task. However, for each task, the signal strength function across set sizes leveled off at four items, regardless of the overall level of the function. Thus the overall level of the function was consistent with behavior whereas the shape of the function was the same regardless of level.

Xu (2004) and Jiang and Song (2004) offered similar theories of capacity, combined here in Figure 4.10. A mechanism capable of registering objects (or opening object files, according to the terminology of Kahneman, Treisman, & Gibbs, 1992) is limited to a fixed number of objects: in the example, this is depicted by four slots. However, there is a fixed amount of "juice" that represents the information needed to distinguish between one object or another. The more complex the discrimination, the more juice is needed in each slot. In this example, there is enough of this juice to fill only two of the four slots sufficiently to allow a working memory representation adequate for array comparisons. More research is needed to define the necessary juice but the search-time measure of Alvarez and Cavanagh (2004) provide an estimate of it.

There is an alternative to the theory depicted in Figure 4.10. Sakai and Inui (2002) examined working memory for shapes with multiple convex limbs and found that working memory was limited to shapes with about four such parts. It is possible, then, that a simple slot theory can account

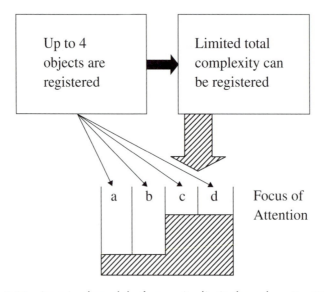

FIGURE 4.10 A revised model of capacity limits based on Xu (2004) and Jiang and Song (2004).

for capacity-limited working memory if we allow that complex objects need to occupy more than one slot. It may be that such "objects" have to be broken down into smaller units to be compared with other, similar objects. However, in some cases, it is difficult to see how the complexity of an object can be reduced by breaking it down into parts. Also, this alternative theory cannot easily explain the functional magnetic resonance imaging evidence that the IPS responds to the number of objects, regardless of their complexity (Xu, 2004). Perhaps a common strategy for examining a complex shape when it is presented alone is to break it down into subobjects, whereas that strategy may be impossible when multiple complex objects are presented at once. So, the model in Figure 4.10 may provide a more adequate overall analysis, with the proviso that objects may be broken into smaller parts when that is both helpful and feasible.

Having fleshed out my view of capacity, Chapter 5 situates it with respect to other views in the literature, Chapter 6 delves into possible reasons why capacity limits occur, and the epilogue offers some practical applications of the capacity concept.

Other Views of Capacity Limits

It is interesting to consider the process by which the review of Cowan (2001) was accepted for publication in *Behavioral and Brain Sciences*. That journal has a special mission in publishing theoretical reviews that are controversial and therefore are good topics for commentary. Many short commentaries are published after every "target article," along with the author's reply to the commentaries. When I first submitted my manuscript, many of the peer reviews came back with the comment that this was a good summary of results on capacity limits, but that it was not especially controversial. This sort of review could have resulted in an editorial action in which the article would be rejected, with advice to submit it to a more conventional journal that did not specialize in controversy. However, of the eight or so reviewers of the original manuscript (many more reviewers than most journals use), one or two did not at all trust my theoretical analyses. Most importantly, Herb Simon suspected that I rifled through the literature looking for the number 4. Because of the minority of commentaries of this nature, the article was controversial enough for the journal.

In my next draft of the article, which ended up as Cowan (2001), I made sure to explain why the article was controversial. Why was it necessary to do so? Interestingly, people tend not to notice when they accept contradictory beliefs. I suspect that some reviewers were willing to accept the capacity limit I proposed but, in another mood, would also feel comfortable with some contradictory theoretical beliefs. Stances both pro and con were familiar from previous literature and therefore might not seem objectionable.

Cowan (2001) advanced two main hypotheses: first, that there is a fixed-capacity mechanism with a typical limit of three to five chunks of information and, second, that the limited-capacity mechanism is the focus of attention. There are stark disagreements in the literature about both of those contentions. Cowan (2001, p. 88) listed seven contrasting views: (1) that there are capacity limits but that they are close to Miller's seven plus or minus two; (2) that short-term memory has time limits but not capacity limits per se; (3) that there is no special short-term memory mechanism; (4) that there may be no capacity limits, only the need for practice or behavioral scheduling conflicts; (5) that there are separate capacities for different materials; (6) that storage and processing have separate limits; and (7) that capacity limits are task-specific. Based on the commentaries and other recent literature, we can also add (8) that the limit is one thing at a time; (9) that there is a one-chunk limit and a separate four-chunk limit; (10) that there is a two-chunk limit; and (11) that there is a limit in the number of feature bindings, not objects. So many views for a noncontroversial topic! I will discuss the motivation for these different views, including some evidence postdating Cowan (2001), and respond briefly to each in turn (except that the time-limited view will be omitted, given its coverage in Chapters 1 and 3). It is worth noting in advance that some of the noncapacity concepts can be combined with capacity limits. For example, as we have already seen near the end of Chapter 3 (Chen & Cowan, in preparation), a theoretical model can include both capacity limits and forgetting over time, or interference that worsens as a function of time.

☐ THE SEVEN-ITEM VIEW

It is undeniable that, in many ordinary situations, people are able to recall about seven items. Therefore, it is not surprising that Miller's (1956) casual estimate of capacity limits was a hit. It has been used in quite recent work on capacity limits, such as Lisman and Idiart's (1995) neural model of short-term memory limits.

Some theorists resisted a reassessment of capacity limits by Cowan (2001). Notably, Pascual-Leone (2001) stuck to the original estimate of about seven items. His grounds for doing so had to do with the need to account for processing and storage. His general view was that processing and storage in working memory come from a common resource. In a task in which attention is prevented from carrying out grouping processes, the storage estimate comes to about four items, but the processes involved in carrying out the task, in his estimate, occupy the equivalent of the missing three or so items, for a total of about seven. For example, he suggested that the task of memory for unattended speech (Cowan, Nugent, Elliott, Ponomarev, & Saults, 1999) involved resources necessary to carry out the attended task of rhyming pictures.

The reason why I did not make this same assumption is that I assumed that the processes involved in carrying out the task are mostly automatic. Such processes are assumed not to take limited-capacity processing, unlike controlled processes. When processes become automatic, they are assumed to be carried out without an appreciable commitment of attentional resources (Shiffrin, 1988). If we do not make this assumption, it leads to some unsettling conclusions. Pascual-Leone continued:

> The situation is very different in the attended-digits task. In this task subjects' full attention is devoted to digits; and attention may not be needed to recall digit order because forward serial order (natural to language!) was considerably practiced during the span pretest task (Cowan et al. 1999) (p. 137).

However, if this explanation is accepted for ordinary recall, it is difficult to know how to interpret the task of running memory span, which does not involve a dual task and still results in only three or four items recalled.

A critic might still suggest that running span involves a continual updating process. The subject might continually add the most recent item to the list held in working memory and drop the least recent. However, recall that the research of Hockey (1973) argues against this type of method for rapidly presented lists. Subjects perform best when instructed to listen passively. The only retrieval process seems to be one in which, after the list ends, information is retrieved from a sensory or phonological store of the most recent items.

An alternative assumption might be that it is the passive store, not the storage mechanism used in active retrieval, that causes the limit of recall to three or four items in running memory span. For example, sensory and phonological memory for less recent items may have faded before the test. However, that account would not explain the very similar estimates of the number of items recalled obtained by Cowan et al. (1999) in a situation in which there were marked primacy effects as well as recency effects (in memory for unattended lists).

If one is not willing to accept the assumption that the estimates of 3 or 4 items recalled come from tasks in which the procedures are automatized, and believes instead that the procedures all require substantial resources, it seems that one ends up having to postulate a total resource demand of up to 10 items to account for the storage and processing involved in ordinary digit span. To me, this view does not seem tenable.

☐ THE ONE-MEMORY VIEW

A more cogent threat to the notion of a capacity-limited faculty is the notion that all of memory can be explained with a common set of rules regarding interference and item distinctiveness, a unitary-memory view (e.g., Brown, Preece, & Hulme, 2000; Crowder, 1993; McGeoch, 1932; Melton, 1963; Nairne, 2002; Neath & Surprenant, 2003). According to this sort of view, the limits in recall that Cowan (2001) pointed out result from a limit in distinctiveness of items in a series. A series of three is a natural set because it includes a beginning (benefiting from being the leading edge of the series), an unambiguous middle, and an end (benefiting from being the trailing edge of the series). That is, there are clear features of placement distinguishing between all of the stimuli in the small set. Items within a set of four are almost as distinguishable because the two middle items can be viewed as "next to" the beginning and ending items, respectively.

Nairne and Neath (2001) supported this hypothesis in a dramatic fashion. They presented subjects with lists of two through nine nouns and asked for pleasantness ratings of the nouns, without informing the subjects that they later would be asked to recall the nouns. Afterward, a filler task was presented for 5 min in which a task involving geometric figures was to be carried out. After the filler period, there was a surprise test in which subjects were given the words for each list and had to indicate the order in which the words had occurred. The proportion of items placed in the correct serial position depended on the number of words in the list. The estimated mean list length at which 50% of the items were correctly placed was 5.15 items, and the estimated mean list length at which all items could be correctly placed was 3.75 items. These figures are in the same range as those that Cowan (2001) offered. It was therefore argued that there is no special short-term holding mechanism, but that the same distinctiveness principles explain the recall limits for memory over short and long terms.

This data set would be a problem for a model in which the short-term and long-term stores are separate representations that can hold separate copies of an item in parallel (e.g., Shallice & Warrington, 1970, and possibly the working memory model of Baddeley, 1986). According to that sort of view, there is no known reason for the limit on long-term recall. According to an embedded-processes view (Cowan, 1999), though, it is understandable. The limit is said to be in the focus of attention, which is needed for all deliberate responses. In principle, it need not matter whether the focus of attention is aimed toward a sensory field coming from recent stimulation or toward a memory field coming from a prior episode. In either case, the limit is in how many chunks of information can be conceived or apprehended at once. In both cases, the limit refers to specific items, often identified by their relation to serial positions or to one another.

This conception of how short- and long-term stores may be related is uncommon, but not new. Broadbent (1971) made a similar point regarding evidence in favor of the unitary memory view, such as the finding of proactive interference in the Peterson and Peterson (1959) procedure by Keppel and Underwood (1962):

> There remain to be considered two points urged by interference theory: the existence of effects on short-term memory from previous long-term experiences, and the continuity which seems to exist between memory at long and short periods of time. The first of these must be admitted straight away, and is perfectly consistent with a view of short-term memory as due to recirculation into and out of a decaying buffer storage. ... In general one must beware of concluding that the appearance in short-term memory of an effect known from longer-term studies is evidence for identity of the two situations. ... Only the success or failure of attempts to show *differences* between the two situations is of interest in distinguishing the theories. (pp. 342–343)

Another recent article is similarly provocative (Logan & Zbrodoff, 2003). Although it does not state a unitary memory view, it would be compatible with one. It examines an alternative theory of the subitizing data, the pattern-matching theory. According to this theory, people can learn patterns of objects and use these learned patterns to identify the number of objects in the field. As the number of objects gets larger, the number of distinguishable patterns becomes greater and, therefore, the need to use counting increases (e.g., Peterson & Simon, 2000). Logan and Zbrodoff examined this theory by collecting similarity judgments between patterns with the same numerosity and different numerosities. The ratings clearly showed that displays in the subitizing range (1 to 3 items) were rated more similar to one another when the numerosity was the same, and more dissimilar to displays of different numerosities, than was the case for displays in the counting range (4 to 10 items).

Several points can be made in reply. First, it seems possible that the learning of patterns is not a *result* of their perceived similarity but a *cause* of their judged similarity. Displays of small numbers of items may be judged similar precisely because they have similar numbers of objects, and this information may be available to consciousness (without counting) only for items in the subitizing range.

Second, there appears to be something like subitizing in the auditory modality not involving patterns. Garner (1951) measured the accuracy of enumerating tones as a function of the number of tones and the time between tones. With fast presentation rates (10 or 12 tones/s), it appeared that performance was maintained at about 75% correct only with 4 or 5 tones. Of course, at relatively slow presentation rates, subjects may begin to use counting processes. ten Hoopen and Vos (1979) examined the counting of tones that sometimes were organized into groups and found that, if a similarly fast presentation rate was used, the accuracy of enumeration was superior for grouped tones but only with groups of two, three, or four tones, not with larger groups of tones.

Third, the entire phenomenon of subitizing actually may be in need of further research because there are extraneous cues available. In most or perhaps all studies of subitizing, the number of items is confounded with the amount of surface area (or, in the auditory studies, temporal duration) covered by all of the stimuli together. One might be able to estimate the numerosity by examining the total surface area. To do a subitizing study correctly, it seems necessary to vary the sizes of objects (or duration of tones) within a display to eliminate the spatial (or temporal) extent cues. Spatial extent has been shown to be important in infant studies (e.g., Feigenson, Carey, & Hauser, 2002; Feigenson, Carey, & Spelke, 2002) but, to my knowledge, has not been examined in adult studies of subitizing. When that is done, the present prediction is that rapid enumeration will still be possible for displays of two, three, or four objects at most. It is not theoretically clear to me whether the similarity analysis of Logan and Zbrodoff (2003) should hold up under such circumstances. This is an important area for future research.

There is no reason to abandon the notion of a capacity-limited mechanism based on evidence that has been taken to argue for a one-memory view.

☐ THE UNLIMITED-MEMORY VIEW

There are at least two different grounds on which researchers have suggested that there may be no limits to working memory. Ericsson and Kirk (2001) suggested that when skilled performers are used, the limits described by Cowan (2001) are far exceeded:

We question the effectiveness of procedures advocated by Cowan to eliminate storage in LTM [long-term memory] and restrict recall to independent chunks from pure STM [short-term memory]. Many of the "prototypical" pure STM studies Cowan cites in Table 2 involve recall of meaningful stimuli, such as unrelated words, presented while subjects are engaged in rehearsal suppression. To test how effectively these procedures control encoding, we examined how skilled and expert participants performed under such conditions. In contrast to the studies cited by Cowan, rehearsal suppression during encoding had little or no effect on skilled expert performers. (p. 120)

I do not disagree with the premise that expertise allows people to, in a practical sense, circumvent the capacity limits that I have described. A hallmark of intelligence is the ability to adapt to new situations and manage to carry out new tasks, and it is in such a situation that working memory capacity limits apply. It is in such a situation, also, that strategies such as rehearsal and grouping stimuli together can be used to try to overcome the capacity limits. Expertise involves previously constructed data structures in memory, which can allow excellent performance without the heavy use of special strategies (though only in the domain of expertise). However, I predict that a close look at what experts do will indicate that they are subject to the same capacity limits and that their expertise can be expressed in terms of the use of larger chunks (and more complex data structures) than novices are able to use. Thus, for example, a chess expert might be able to alternate between several games, but should not be able to make moves in two different games with the left and right hands concurrently. An expert can rotate from game to game quickly, making a move in each one and proceeding to the next game but, according to the present view, this occurs with the assistance of long-term memory (as described by Ericsson & Kintsch, 1995). It should not be possible actually to keep a large number of games in the focus of attention at one time.

Another objection to the use of the idea of capacity limits comes from a very different theoretical framework, in which attempts have been made to see how much processing can be explained without resorting to capacity limits. Meyer and Kieras (1997) developed a provocative theory of task conflicts. Unlike the usual theory of task conflicts, which depends on some notion of a resource conflict, or else on a response bottleneck (e.g., Pashler, 1994), Meyer and Kieras showed that the same data often can be accounted for without resource limitations. Instead, response conflicts were said to result from situations in which the subject had to make sure to emit the responses in the appropriate order, which involved withholding one response until another could be safely completed without interruption.

Although the merit of this approach is still under debate, it can at least be said that such an approach does not seem suitable as a replacement for limited resources of some sort in many of the procedures that I have discussed. When subjects have ample time to make their responses but there is an overload of information at the time of stimulus presentation, it is not easy to see how a scheduling conflict could account for limitations in performance. Perhaps there is some analogous model that could be made in such cases. If so, it would be useful to learn what such a model would look like.

□ THE MULTIPLE-CAPACITIES VIEW

Whereas the previous points had to do primarily with the limitation in working memory capacity, the present point has to do also with the theoretical account of that limit. The set of evidence examined by Cowan indicated a similar limit of three to five chunks of information on average, for verbal, nonverbal, visual, and auditory materials alike. For this reason, it seemed parsimonious to assume that all of these kinds of information are constrained by a single capacity limit from a central process that they all share. Another view, though, is that there is not one central capacity but, rather, separate capacity or resource limits for different types of information processing (e.g., Wickens, 1984).

First, let me clarify that the distinction is more than just the idea of multiple working memory faculties. My own embedded-processes view (Cowan, 1988, 1995, 1999) posits the existence of activated memory on one hand and the subset of that activated memory that is in the focus of attention on the other hand. However, only the focus of attention is assumed to be limited by capacity in chunks. The limit in activation is assumed to result from some combination of decay and interference.

It still would be possible for a multiple-capacity view to predict a similar limit in the capacity of recall for different types of materials. It could happen if all sorts of materials are subject to the same limitations having to do with principles of distinctiveness between items in a set. So, the multiple-capacities view could challenge the nature of capacity limits without challenging an empirical generalization stating that there is a limit of three to five items when familiar items *in a particular processing domain* are used and chunking and rehearsal are prevented.

This issue will be revisited in the next chapter, when the discussion focuses on the reasons for the capacity limits, because it depends on the presentation of new data.

☐ THE VIEW OF SEPARATE STORAGE AND PROCESSING LIMITS

As with the previous point, this one has more to do with the explanation of capacity limits than it does with the empirical generalization that such a limit exists. One common view of working memory is that it has a resource limit that is shared between storage and processing (e.g., Logan, 1979). Indeed, that was the rationale for using measures that tie up both storage and processing in order to assess individual differences in capacity (Daneman & Carpenter, 1980; Pascual-Leone, 2001). However, Daneman and Carpenter did note that storage did not seem to interfere with processing as much as would be expected on the basis of a common workspace (reflecting findings also of Baddeley, 1986; Baddeley & Hitch, 1974; Klapp, Marshburn, & Lester, 1983; Oberauer, Demmrich, Mayr, & Kliegl, 2001).

Previously I have suggested that, whenever there is an adequate opportunity for a rehearsal loop to be set up and used for the memory load, it need not interfere with a processing task that does not use that same rehearsal loop. Indeed, with development from childhood to adulthood, the attentional requirements of verbal rehearsal tend to disappear (Guttentag, 1984). Most researchers who have failed to show a common resource between storage and processing seem happy to believe that it is because storage depends on passive buffers with no strict capacity limit per se, though with limits resulting from decay or interference (e.g., Baddeley, 1986; Bayliss, Jarrold, Gunn, & Baddeley, 2003). That view is not strictly in conflict with my own views (Cowan, 1988, 1999, 2001).

There is at least one theoretical view, though, in which two different capacity limits are said to apply. Specifically, Halford, Phillips, and Wilson (2001) and Halford, Wilson, and Phillips (1998) maintained that there are separate types of capacity limit for storage and processing. Storage limits can be stated in terms of chunks, whereas Halford et al. (1998, 2001) found that they had to state processing limits in terms of dimensions, the number of ideas that had to be related to one another to describe the complexity of a concept.

The tone of my reaction previously was to minimize the difference between storage and processing demands by indicating that storage

demands, as with processing, could be restated as relations between enti-
ties. To understand this, first consider the following illustration of processing complexity (Halford et al., 1998): "... the premises 'Tom is smarter
than John, John is smarter than Stan' can be integrated into the ternary
relational instance monotonically smarter (Tom, John, Stan)" (p. 821).
My initial reaction was to minimize the formal difference between storage
and processing (Cowan, Saults, & Nugent, 2001): For example:

> "in-present-array (x, q, r, b)" could describe the quaternary relation
> leading to a whole report response in Sperling's (1960) procedure.
> "Monotonically later $(3–7, x, 2, 4–8)$" could describe a quaternary
> relation leading to partially correct serial recall of an attended list
> of digits for which 3–7 is a memorized initial chunk; x represents
> a place marker for a digit that cannot be recalled; 2 represents an
> unchunked digit; and 4–8 represents another memorized chunk. ...
> If this analysis is correct, there is no reason to expect a separation
> between processing and storage. The reason why a storage load
> does not much interfere with processing is that the storage load and
> the process do not have to be expanded in the focus of attention at
> the same time. (p. 113)

The latter statement was based on the concept that items could be held
as activated portions of long-term memory while some processing was
carried out.

In their response to my target article, Halford et al. (2001) pointed out
that there are implications of the relational representation that were not
specified in this illustration that I gave. For example, does "in-present-
array (x, q, r, b)" include information as to the relative locations of these
items in the array? Can one access any of the items using the others as
cues? If the items are not related to one another in a narrowly specified
manner, then a quaternary relation is not really involved.

Phillips and Niki (2002) carried out an experiment using behavioral
and functional magnetic resonance imaging results to distinguish between
the demands of storage and processing. The stimuli, in different experiments, were Japanese kanji, Japanese hiragana, numbers, and shapes.
In each case, the method involved paired recognition. Using letters to
represent stimuli, a condition in which pairs AB and CD were learned
involved four unique items but only unary relations between them. A condition in which pairs AB, CD, and EF were learned involved six unique
items but still only unary relations. In contrast, a condition in which AB,
AD, and CB were learned involved only four unique items, but binary
relations between them. One had to know that it was all right for A to
precede either B and D, whereas it was all right for B to follow either A

or C. Put into operation in this way, it was found that there was some effect on the number of items on errors, response times, and active areas of the brain, but that there was an even bigger and more pervasive effect of the binary relations. One can see from this example that the idea of processing complexity may have a lot to do with the idea of interference between concepts (e.g., between *AB* and *AD*), which has been noted by other investigators as a source of difficulty in working memory (e.g., Conway & Engle, 1994; Lustig, May, & Hasher, 2000; Rosen & Engle, 1997). Phillips and Niki (2003) sought additional stimulus control by extending the result to lists with different index lengths but the same number of items and item associates.

Although it is clear that storage and processing demands are different, it is not as clear to me that they do not draw on a common resource. For example, a relation between several items cannot be understood unless the items themselves are retained in memory. The ternary relation "monotonically smarter (Tom, John, Stan)" may be easier to understand and keep in mind if one knows the three people involved than if one does not, simply because it eases the working memory storage load. More work is needed on the effects of storage loads on the amount of relational complexity that can be understood.

The effect of this discussion is to uphold the four-chunk storage limit in simple situations but to cast doubt on whether the idea of holding a few separate chunks is really adequate to understand the range of processing situations. This simplification is probably not enough to understand all processing; we eventually will need to know such things as whether one must consider a continuum of association strengths, as opposed to just the binary distinction between very strong associations within a chunk versus very weak associations between chunks; whether one must consider the specific nature of bindings between ideas in working memory; how competing associations are to be held; how irrelevant information is to be inhibited; and so on. The four-chunk storage limit that I have documented is meant as a starting point under the simplest of circumstances, on the road to the eventual goal of quantifying working memory storage limits in more complex situations. It was not meant as an end point.

☐ THE TASK-SPECIFIC CAPACITY VIEW

This is what Cowan (2001) perceived to be the modal view in the field. It is the usually unstated view whereby one assumes that the observable capacity limits are task-specific and determined by many factors. This view is one of healthy skepticism; one should not be overly hasty in accepting a simple rule on the basis of insufficient data. The view may be partly the result of a sophisticated reading of Miller's (1956) article, in which the capacity limit was stated as a rhetorical device to allow a discussion of several research areas within the same talk, rather than being proposed as an honest-to-god law of nature.

The problem with this view, in my opinion, is that it has been coupled with an attitude in which the task of searching for a storage capacity limit has been made into a low priority. Skepticism toward a capacity limit should not detract from a search for it. One can liken it to the concept of gravity, which might have had to go through several stages of development before gaining scientific acceptance. It seems obvious that gravity exists as a general rule until one considers that some objects do not come down (e.g., planets, stars) or come down only very slowly (e.g., leaves, birds). The law of gravity could not be established until data were collected on systems in which the extraneous factor of wind resistance was controlled (in the study of planetary motion). As Cowan (2001) noted:

> The known history of the discovery of gravity seems consistent with this progression of thinking. Tycho Brahe established a wealth of observations on planetary movement, an arena in which there is little wind resistance unlike earthly applications of gravity. Johannes Kepler used Brahe's observations to establish regularities or laws of planetary motion, though without really understanding the general principles behind the laws; and later, Isaac Newton "stood on the shoulders" of Brahe and Kepler to establish more general laws of gravitational force. Albert Einstein later reformulated the law of gravitation in a more penetrating manner that tied it to other forces in the universe, representing it as curvatures in space; and surely the final word is yet to come. (p. 156)

For the concept of a capacity limit, Miller's (1956) observations led to a naive acceptance of a law that was followed by the skepticism of many researchers after more careful reflection. Broadbent's (1975) chapter on the basic capacity limit could then be compared with Kepler's attempt to establish regularities in the rule, with other factors (wind resistance; chunking and rehearsal) held constant. If we can understand more about the regularities pointed out by Broadbent (1975) and elaborated on by Cowan (2001), then the investigation of capacity limits should eventually reach the stages of Newton and Einstein, in which the regularities in the data are understood on a more principled basis.

In sum, a capacity-limited mechanism is only one component of how many items can be recalled; there are other factors to be taken into account, including the use of activated memory (or, according to multicomponent concepts of working memory, passive buffers), and the amount of interference or other items to be inhibited in order to recall the correct items. Such factors have to be minimized or taken into account (like wind resistance) for a limited capacity to be observed. In Chapter 6, I will contribute what I can to an understanding of theoretical reasons for capacity limits.

Certain data have been cited as evidence that it is wrong to conclude that there is any sort of underlying fixed capacity. One type of evidence that has been cited is the well-known memory-search task of Sternberg (1966). In this task, a probe item appears and one must indicate, as quickly as possible, whether the probe was a member of the memorized set or not. The reaction time to make a correct response increases as a linear function of the number of items in the memory set. This occurs across memory sets ranging from one to six items. What has been pointed out by several investigators (e.g., Jou, 2001) is that one might have expected a different reaction-time function on the basis of a fixed capacity limit. One might have expected that, with one through four items, a constant fast reaction time should be found, with increases in that reaction time as the size of the memory set increases beyond four items.

It is true that the memory-search data must constrain the theoretical view. It seems inconsistent with a theory in which about four items are held in a form in which they are immediately accessible equally, no matter whether there are one, two, three, or four items, and with additional items having to be accessed into the capacity-limited store before the search can be completed. However, another possible model is one in which the capacity-limited resource (attention?) must be divided between items. This division causes slowing of access to any one item in the capacity-limited store, accounting for the linear reaction-time function. This implies a capacity-limited, parallel-access model (e.g., Ratcliff, 1978; Van Zandt & Townsend, 1993).

A remaining point is that a four-chunk capacity limit would appear to predict that the reaction-time function would remain linear only up through four items (i.e., when recall can be based on a capacity-limited store). For higher numbers of items, the reaction times would follow a different course; they could be predicted to flatten out at higher levels of reaction times if retrieval were accomplished through a slower, but capacity-unlimited, manner after four items (e.g., retrieval from activated memory outside of the focus of attention). This is almost what happens; however, the flattening-out does not occur after four items, but after six items. For example, Burrows and Okada (1975) found a linear performance function with a slope of 37 or 57 ms per item (in different experiments) for memory sets of 2, 4, or 6 items, as opposed to a linear function with a slope of only 13 ms per item for sets of 8 to 20 items.

Why is the break point in the function typically at six items rather than four? One hypothesis consistent with Cowan (2001) is that the ability to rehearse the items typically allows six or seven items to circulate in and out of the capacity-limited store, but not more. If rehearsal could be blocked, the prediction is that only about four items would be included in the initial, faster part of the performance function with a steeper slope.

I have not found the appropriate data set to test such a prediction. However, an experiment by Okada and Burrows (1978; Experiment 2) is relevant. Their subjects learned lists of 2, 4, 6, 8, 12, or 16 spoken words and then responded to a set of trials with one list in mind at a time. On some trials, there was a memory load consisting of items from a newly presented set of two, four, or six items. In these trials, the subject was to respond "yes" if the probe came from either the learned set or the newly presented set, and "no" otherwise. The reaction-time data are shown in Figure 5.1. There was a large effect of the presence versus absence of a newly presented set of words, though only a small difference between a load of two, four, or six newly presented words. Therefore, rehearsal of the memory load may have served primarily as a source of articulatory suppression preventing rehearsal of the memorized target set. Interestingly, the presence of a load had the most effect on reaction times for a prelearned list of six words, not for shorter or longer prelearned lists. Perhaps it was lists of six words that were typically rehearsed, and therefore suffered from effects of a memory load that prevented that rehearsal. Words within lists of eight or longer may have been retrieved from long-term memory a few at a time, given that there would be too many to rehearse all at once.

In sum, the evidence from search tasks is compatible with a theoretical account in which a limited storage capacity can be divided among up to four items, or among up to about six (or seven?) items using a rehearsal process to supplement the capacity-limited faculty.

□ THE ONE-CHUNK VIEW

The one-chuck view arose from several commentaries in Cowan (2001) and should not have been a surprise to me. As far back as the work of Cherry (1953), it has been observed that people can only fully attend to one channel of information, or message, at a time. It would be a natural assumption that people can only attend to a single chunk of information at a time, as well.

The trouble with that extrapolation is that a message rapidly conveys multiple chunks of information. From those chunks, a coherent semantic

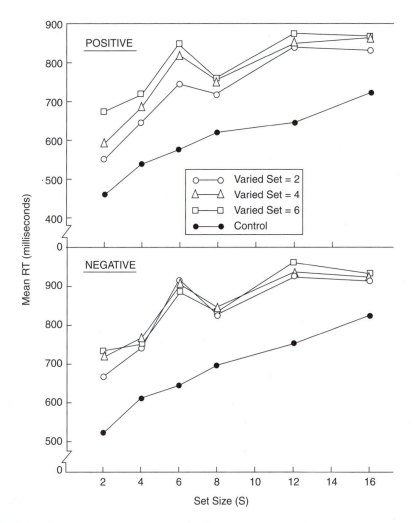

FIGURE 5.1   Reproduced from Okada and Burrows (1978, Figure 2). (Top) For target-present (positive) trials, mean reaction time (RT) as a function of memorized memory-set size (*x* axis) and concurrent working-memory memory load (graph parameter). (Bottom) Comparable data for target-absent (negative) trials. Notice the singularly large effect of a memory load, compared to no-load control trials, for set size six.

structure often can be built. The difficulty in sharing attention between two messages may be an attentional constraint that is completely separate from the working memory capacity limit, or it may just be an overload in the number of chunks coming in at the same time and the complexity of building two semantic structures at once.

The one-chunk view appeals to intuition. For example, Baars (2001) indicated that "The evidence comes from numerous studies of ambiguous figures and words, in which only one interpretation can be conscious at any instant" (p. 115). One has to be careful with such evidence, however. The inability to perceive only one interpretation of an ambiguous figure may come from the fact that the two interpretations are incompatible (i.e., from interference between the interpretations), not from a capacity limit. If several different ambiguous figures were presented at once, might they not all have interpretations at the same time? A competing intuition is that it may be necessary for two objects both to be in the focus of attention if those objects are to be compared with one another.

McElree (1998, 2001) appealed to more objective evidence of a capacity limited to a single chunk. It was based on the notion that items in the focus of attention should be retrieved more quickly than items outside of that focus. He sought to measure the rate of retrieval of various items in a list to determine how many were in the focus at the time of test. McElree (1998) presented lists of words followed by probes and examined reaction times using a response-signal speed-accuracy tradeoff procedure (Wickelgren, Corbett, & Dosher, 1980). One-syllable nouns were presented on the computer screen one at a time (for 400 ms/item), followed by a visual mask for 500 ms, and then a recognition probe. The probe stayed on the screen for anywhere from 43 ms to 3000 ms, followed by a tone cue. A rapid response was supposed to be made after the tone, indicating whether the probe item was in the list. The tone was meant to influence how much time was available for processing before a response was to be made, thereby altering the bias more toward speed or toward accuracy. In a speed-accuracy tradeoff function, accuracy is plotted as a function of processing time, a function capturing the "retrieval dynamics."

It was found that the last item in the list had a faster retrieval dynamic, or ascent to an asymptotic level, than did the other list items, which did not differ. McElree's (1998) favored interpretation of that finding was that the last item in the list is in the focus of attention, whereas other items in the list are not.

There are other possible accounts, however. It may be that the remaining attentional capacity is distributed among some of the other items, different ones on different trials so that no one item stands out on average.

In another experiment, McElree (1998) presented items grouped in sets of three in a row from the same semantic category. In that case, the more rapid retrieval came not only from the last item, but from the entire last semantic category. The interpretation was that the three items in the last category formed a chunk and that the chunk was in the focus of attention. Thus it was said that the focus of attention is capable of holding only a single chunk of information.

An alternative interpretation is that, although the semantic similarity between three items draws attention to all three, they do not form a single chunk in working memory. It is not clear that semantic similarity would be enough to form a chunk. Instead, if attention ordinarily were distributed among several items in the list, always including the final item but also several items from earlier on, then the semantic similarity might be enough to draw most or all of the attention to the final three items in the list, but as separate chunks.

McElree (2001) continued the theme with additional, clever experimentation. There were four different tasks, some of which were rather difficult. In a one-back task, the subject must determine whether the present item matches the previous item in an ongoing list of letters. In a two-back task, the subject must determine if the item matches the next-to-last item. For example, for the sequence *B, B, F, J, K, J, J...*, the answers (starting with the *F*) are no, no, no, yes (because the first and second *J*s match), and no. In a three-back task, the answers for this same sequence (starting with the first *J*) are no (the first *B* ... the first *J*), no (the second *B* ... *K*), no (*F* ... the second *J*), and yes (the first *J* = the third *J*). So far, this is a commonly used manipulation to cause increasing levels of difficulty.

What was unique about McElree's (2001) study is that he also used a *three-back inclusion* task. In this task, the subject must respond "yes" if there is a one-back, two-back, *or* three-back match. The notion was that three items, rather than just one, would be needed and that the retrieval time would be slower if all three could not be held in the focus of attention at the same time. The most critical result was that the retrieval dynamic was faster for three-back matches in the three-back exclusion condition than it was in the three-back inclusion condition. The idea was that attention could not be divided well in the three-back inclusion condition, so that information more often had to be retrieved from the episodic record. In the author's words:

> Two important findings were reported. First, the speed (SAT [speed-accuracy tradeoff] rate) of retrieval decreased as *n* increased in both variants of the *n*-back task. The slowing of retrieval indicates that the *n*-back target could not be maintained consistently in focal attention. ... Second, retrieval speed was significantly faster in the 3-back exclusion task than in the 3-back inclusion task. The dynamics advantage for the exclusion task implicates the role of limited-capacity control processes that circumvented the need for a search process by maintaining a target item within the focus of attention. It also suggests that three sequentially presented items cannot be reliably maintained in focal attention. (p. 828)

The first of these findings is not surprising. Clearly, no matter whether the focus of attention can include only one item, or as many as three or four items, less recent items are more difficult to maintain within the attended set. The second finding is key but it has alternative possible interpretations. McElree (2001) appears to assume that, in the three-back exclusion task, items that are one or two back are not kept in the focus of attention, even though they will be needed as targets a moment later. An alternative assumption is that attention is divided among all three, but with the present status of only the third-back item marked "present target." In the three-back inclusion task, all three items would be marked "present target." The reaction time dynamic difference between three-back exclusion and three-back inclusion could come because the search process involves one item in the case of exclusion and three items in the case of inclusion. Thus, in this alternative interpretation, one must assume that it is possible to search just a subset of the items in the focus of attention in the exclusion task (items with present-target status). McElree (2001) rejected this possibility on the grounds that McElree (1998) found no difference in the retrieval rates between three items in a row from the most recent semantic category (just in asymptotic levels). He also noted that the speed for the triad was no slower than is found for the last item in experiments in which items are not semantically grouped. The critical comparisons have not been carried out within a single experiment.

Another possible difference between the exclusion and inclusion tasks is in how simple or complicated the required updating process is. In the exclusion task, the turnover in target status is complete. When an item n arrives, item $n - 3$ is the only target and, when $n + 1$ arrives, $n - 3$ becomes a nontarget lure and $n - 2$ becomes the target instead. In contrast, in the case of the inclusion task, items $n - 3$, $n - 2$, and $n - 1$ all are targets together. Then, when item $n + 1$ arrives, the former group of targets must be split up. Item $n - 3$ is no longer a target, but items $n - 2$ and $n - 1$ still are, along with item n, the most recent probe, which is now a target. So, it easily could be argued that the complexity of the updating process itself, rather than the inclusion of multiple targets, is the reason that subjects may have trouble maintaining three items in focal attention in the three-back inclusion task. (Theoretically many investigators have suspected the same about running memory tasks but, as I have explained previously, with a fast presentation rate at least, subjects can only receive items passively in that task, rather than constantly updating; see Hockey, 1973.)

Cowan (2001) rejected n-back tasks as a measure of the contents of the focus of attention and suggested a simpler, slightly different test:

> Finally, it is necessary to exclude procedures in which the capacity limit must be shared between chunk storage and the storage of

intermediate results of processing. One example of this is the "*n*-back task" in which each item in a continuous series must be compared with the item that occurred n items ago (e.g., Cohen et al. 1997; Poulton, 1954) or a related task in which the subject must listen to a series of digits and detect three odd digits in a row (Jacoby, Woloshyn, & Kelly, 1989). In these tasks, in order to identify a fixed set of the most recent *n* items in memory, the subject must continually update the target set in memory. This task requirement may impose a heavy additional storage demand. These demands can explain why such tasks remain difficult even with *n* = 3. ... It may be instructive to consider a hypothetical version of the *n*-back task that would be taken to indicate the existence of a special capacity limit. Suppose that the subject's task were to indicate, as rapidly as possible, if a particular item had been included in the stimulus set previously. Some items would be repeated in the set but other, novel items also would be introduced. On positive trials, the mean reaction time should be much faster when the item had been presented within the most recent three or four items than when it was presented only earlier in the sequence. (p. 89)

McKone (2001) noted that she had carried out just such an experiment previously (McKone, 1995; Experiment 4). The most recent item was to be judged either *new* (never presented) or *old* (presented before). If the previous presentation was one, two, or three items ago, *old* judgments were faster than if the previous presentation was earlier, with no further increases in the response time.

As McKone (2001) noted, the functions were not equivalent for matches one, two, or three items ago. These data, reproduced in Figure 5.2, are inconsistent with the idea that all items are equally represented in working memory. Nevertheless, the data of McElree (1998, 2001) and McKone (1995) seem compatible with a capacity-limited faculty that encompasses several items at once.

Garavan (1998) also suggested that the focus of attention is limited to a single chunk of information. He presented two types of figures, a rectangle and a triangle, and the task for the subject was to keep track of how many of each was presented. If the count for the same shape was incremented twice, the reaction time was faster than when there was a switch. In another experiment, a stimulus-priming account was ruled out. Garavan suggested that this switching cost occurred because only one count could be held in the focus of attention in order to be updated. The other count was presumably held in the activated portion of long-term memory.

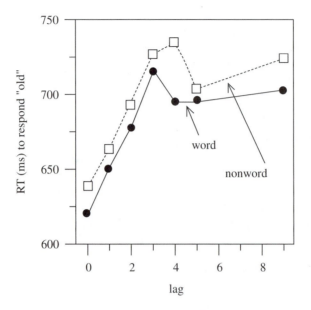

FIGURE 5.2 Reproduced from McKone (2001). Reaction time (RT) to respond "old" to a repeated word or nonword (graph parameter) as a function of the lag (number of intervening stimuli).

My objection to this conclusion is that it could be differences in stimulus status, rather than a capacity limit of one item, that causes the switch cost. Imagine an experiment in which there were two different counts that both had to be updated when one signal was given (e.g., update the counts of a red triangle and square when you see a red screen), whereas two other counts had to be updated when another signal was given (e.g., update the counts of a blue triangle and square when you see a blue screen). These could be made nonredundant by mixing in other trials in which only one of the four items was to be updated. I would predict a reaction-time advantage for *both* of the no-switch items over both of the switch items, which in this case presumably would implicate two items in the focus of attention at once. The limit of a single item could be a limit built into the experiment, as opposed to built into the mind.

In any case, the single-chunk focus of attention has been reassessed by Verhaeghen, Cerella, and Basak (2004). They found a one-chunk focus of attention using a reaction-time measure modeled after the work of McElree (1998, 2001). However, with practice, they found that the focus of attention expanded to about four items. Perhaps there is a shift in subjects' typical strategy from a focus on a singe item or chunk at a time at the beginning of the experiment to a focus on a larger amount when the task itself became more automatic. (This is different from the notion of chunking, in that the four items held in the focus differed from one trial to the next and therefore could not have resulted from learning of multi-item chunks.)

Usher, Haarmann, Cohen, and Horn (2001) proposed a model that could serve as a compromise between the one-chunk view and the four-chunk view. They proposed that attention could zoom in to focus on as little as one chunk of information intensively or zoom out to apprehend up to four or so chunks at a time. That is another plausible explanation of the results. It is compatible with a suggestion that McElree and Dosher (2001) made that the focus of attention includes one item for sequential presentations versus up to four items for simultaneous presentations. However, as will be explained in Chapter 6, another measure of capacity in sequential presentations, based on susceptibility to proactive interference, indicates a capacity limit of about four items (Cowan, Johnson, & Saults, 2005).

In sum, we do not really understand the reasons why some types of evidence point toward a four-chunk limit and other types of evidence may point toward a one-chunk limit. However, there are reasons to question whether the one-chunk limit is real, or only apparent.

☐ THE ONE-CHUNK CENTER, FOUR-CHUNK SURROUND VIEW

Oberauer (2002) suggested a view that incorporates both the one-chunk limit of Garavan (1998) and McElree (2001) and something like the four-chunk limit of Cowan (2001) into a single model of processing. In the words of Oberauer:

1. The activated part of long-term memory can serve, among other things, to memorize information over brief periods for later recall.
2. The region of direct access holds a limited number of chunks available to be used in ongoing cognitive processes.
3. The focus of attention holds at any time the one chunk that is actually selected as the object of the next cognitive operation. The limits of working memory capacity, as measured by various tasks … presumably reflect the limited number of independent elements that can be held in the region of direct access at the same time. This region, therefore, corresponds most closely to what Cowan (1995, 1999) named the *focus of attention*. The capacity limit of working memory probably arises from two factors, partial overwriting of representations in

> working memory and crosstalk between the elements in the region of direct access when one of them must be selected for processing. ... (p. 412)

This model is like that of the embedded-processes model of Cowan (1999) with two differences. The capacity-limited region that Cowan identified as the focus of attention is here called the region of direct access. Within it, a one-chunk focus of attention is established (i.e., one level of embedding beyond what Cowan posited).

The evidence for this view was a modification of a task first used by Salthouse, Babcock, and Shaw (1991). In Oberauer's version of it, there were two rows of numbers, only one of which was selected as the active set. Within that active set, one number was selected to be updated on a particular trial. It was observed that reaction times were unaffected by the number of items in the passive set (one or three), but did depend on the number of items in the active set (one or three). This was presumably because only the active set was held in the capacity-limited "region of direct access," whereas the passive set was presumably held in the capacity-unlimited "activated portion of long-term memory." Additionally, reaction times were faster when the same location within the active set was selected as in the previous trial compared with when there was a switch from one location to another within the active set. This was presumably because of the limit in the focus of attention to one location.

My thoughts on this data set are similar to my thoughts on Garavan (1998). The apparent capacity limits are built into the experiment but not necessarily built into the human information processing system. It could be that another level of privileged access could be built into the experiment. For example, within the active set, suppose that the target to update was twice as likely to occur at the central location than at the left or right locations. Perhaps the subjects are told of this distribution of trials. It might well be found that there are then at least three levels of reaction time: the fastest time for items in the central location on nonswitch trials; the next-fastest times for items either in the central location on switch trials, or at the peripheral locations on non-switch trials; and the slowest reaction times for items in the peripheral locations on switch trials. Add to this the difference between the active and passive sets, and it would appear as if one would need yet one more level of embedding in the model, beyond what Oberauer (2002) posited.

Another possible interpretation, though, is that the model of Cowan (1999) is basically right: that the levels of embedding include only the activated portion of long-term memory and, within it, the capacity-limited focus of attention (subsuming the entire region of direct access of the model of Oberauer, 2002). What Oberauer's data would add to this model is the need to assume that not all items are of equal status within the capacity-limited focus of attention. Instead, the most recently accessed item would have a special designation or tag within that focus that other items in the active set would not have. We have already seen from other evidence (e.g., Sternberg, 1966; also McKone, 1995, shown in Figure 5.2) that the items within the limited-capacity set cannot all be of equal status.

☐ THE TWO-CHUNK VIEW

As Gobet and Clarkson (2004) note, "An important task of any mature science, but all too often neglected in psychology (Grant, 1962; Meehl, 1967; Simon, 1974) is to carry out experiments narrowing down the quantitative estimates of the parameters of its theories." They carried out experiments on copying and remembering chess boards using a refined methodology in which the chess boards were computerized to examine the number of chunks of information copied and the number recalled. This computerized methodology eliminates the problem that was encountered with real chess boards, that the subject's hand is limited in how many chess pieces can be picked up at once, which in turn limits the way in which the chess arrangement is reconstructed. (The study also included real chess boards but the conclusions were similar and I will focus on the computerized setup.) The authors suggest, on the basis of their evidence, that the capacity estimate offered by Cowan (2001) may be an overestimate and that the true capacity limit is closer to two chunks than to four. The chunks involved are complicated structures. The subjects included chess novices, Class B players, and masters, and the boards that they were to copy or recall were either real games or random placements. The indication of a chunk boundary was whether the time period between recalls (not counting the mouse-transition time) was more than 2 s. This was reasonable inasmuch as, in the copying task, recalls without glancing back at the model almost always occurred with intervals of less than 2 s between piece placements, whereas longer intervals occurred between glances. The size of chunks was, of course, larger for real games than for random boards and larger for more experienced players. At one extreme, for random pieces with novices, the mean of individuals' median chunk size was less than three pieces, whereas, at the other extreme, for real games and experts, the chunk size was about seven pieces.

The critical evidence from this study was that the number of chunks copied, when the setup remained available, far exceeded the number of chunks recalled. For novices, this difference was most clearly notable. They copied about eight chunks but recalled fewer than two. Class B players copied five to six chunks in real chess games (larger chunks), but recalled fewer than three. Experts encoded only about three huge chunks in real games and recalled about three; but for randomly placed boards, they encoded five to six chunks and recalled only about two of them. In general, then, the number of chunks recalled was closer to two than to four.

It is possible that this type of design illustrates a boundary of the concept of chunks. Cowan, Chen, and Rouder (2004) found that there were some apparent chunks in immediate recall that could not be recalled in a cued-recall test that required long-term recall. Similarly, some of the elaborate chunks set up in the copying task might have been temporary chunks that could not be retained well enough so that one chunk could be put on the board while the other chunks were retained in memory.

Another possible explanation, though, is that the encoding time was too brief in the recall task. The board to be recalled was presented for 5 s and then removed. In contrast, in the copying task, repeated glances at the board were possible. It seems quite possible that encoding all of the chunks on a board often takes more than 5 s but that, in the copying task, this encoding time was divided between multiple glances. Thus it would be possible to transfer one chunk to the response board without having encoded all of the chunks on the board. In the one case in which encoding was likely to be rapid (for masters encoding real chess boards), all three encoded chunks generally were recalled.

Another potential indication that the estimate of two chunks is too low is an anomaly of this study. A second method was used to determine chunks, and that was a method in which subjects were to indicate meaningful partitions of the chess board by drawing circles around partitions. In past experiments, this manipulation typically has produced results similar to the 2-s delay rule but, in this study, the partitioning method produced substantially smaller chunks. Perhaps the chunks used in copying and recall actually were superchunks (as in the recall of long digit lists by trained experts described by Ericsson, Chase, & Faloon, 1980), and the focus of attention shifted back and forth between the superordinate level and the chunk level during recall, which would allow a simple chunk span to be exceeded.

To suggest that I could provide a definitive explanation of all of the many, seemingly conflicting results in the literature would be pretentious. The most important message of this chapter is probably that a determination of the capacity limit of working memory is, indeed, more controversial than many people have realized and is a fertile area for research in the near future. Metaphorically, it is not only that each blind man touches a different part of the elephant, but also that most of the blind men have assumed that all of their colleagues are experiencing the same thing. Yet, to me, even with awareness of this pitfall, the extant data still seem consistent with a basic capacity limit of three to five chunks, usually closer to three than to five.

☐ THE BINDING-LIMIT VIEW

Davis, Welch, Holmes, and Shepherd (2001) took the alternative view that capacity is limited in a manner that is not object-based. They suggested that there are two ways in which binding must be accomplished for a scene to be fully perceived. Features within objects must be bound together to form the objects in the perceptual representation, and objects must be bound together to form the scene. Although it was proposed that within- and between-object types of binding are based on different streams of neurons, it was also proposed that the limit in capacity is related to the total number of bindings that must be carried out.

Cowan (2001) replied to a version of this view. The stimuli that Davis et al. used to reach their conclusions seemed fraught with possible confounding factors, such as the uncontrolled use of symmetry as a perceptual cue. Nevertheless, it is a theory that cannot be ruled out, at least not until it is specified more completely. There is a lot of evidence that perception is object-based, but it is not absolutely clear that working memory limits are object-based. For example, the specific binding between objects may place a demand on working memory that cannot be expressed in terms of objects alone (Wheeler & Treisman, 2002), although it is also possible that when the objects are saved, the bindings between these objects are saved along with them. It is theoretically possible that the capacity limit in chunks is an indirect effect of a more fundamental capacity limit expressed in terms of the number of binding operations, although I certainly would not be able to fill in the details of a conversion equation between binding operations and chunks.

Why the Capacity Limit?

People tend to talk about what they have to say, not what there is to be said. So it is that we have spent six chapters focusing on *what* the capacity limits are and *how* capacity is limited, with not much thought about *why* capacity is limited. That is, for me at least, a much more difficult question, though one with potentially a much larger theoretical yield. Now we will turn to this difficult and important question.

There are many ways to answer. First, though, the question must be clarified. One could ask, positively, why it is possible to apprehend as many as four chunks simultaneously. Alternatively, one could ask, negatively, why it is not possible to apprehend many more chunks. One could also ask why the capacity changes with age and differs among individuals. All of these questions come up, though none of them can be answered definitively at present.

There are many ways in which one can answer any particular "why" question. In considering them, I will borrow a structure from Aristotle that was explained and applied to psychological questions by Killeen (2001). He noted four kinds of explanation, seeking different kinds of causes of a phenomenon. *Efficient* causes are determiners or necessary precursors. For capacity limits, the efficient causes could be factors that influence whether an item can be retained in a working memory task. The concurrent memory load and the type of load would be two such factors. *Formal* causes are models. A model of working memory would be a description of what its parts are and how each one operates. *Material* causes are substrates or mechanisms. In the case of working memory capacity, what is most relevant is the brain mechanisms that permit it. *Final* causes are functions; they are teleological. For final causes, one could discuss reasons why it was important in evolution for the capacity to be as large as it is, and perhaps benefits of the capacity not being even larger (or, at least, costs that outweigh the benefits). I will try to organize the discussion according to these types of causes, although they seem to overlap.

Before proceeding, it is important to emphasize that I am not talking here about the causes of performance on working memory tasks, broadly conceived. I am focusing on the limited amount that can be recalled without the help of grouping stimuli into new chunks, rehearsing them, or committing them to memory. Working memory broadly conceived is of great interest, but it is clearly too complex to be explained whole cloth at present. Moreover, the capacity-limited aspect of working memory is of fundamental philosophical interest if it is the part directly related to conscious experience (e.g., Baars & Franklin, 2003). Performance on working memory tasks could include many factors: the ability to control attention (see studies by R. Engle, M. Kane, and colleagues), the ability to switch, and not only to control attention (Cowan, Hitch et al., 2003; Hitch et al., 2001; Miyake et al., 2000), the knowledge base in the area (Ericsson & Kintsch, 1995; Hambrick & Engle, 2001), phonological abilities (Baddeley, Gathercole, & Papagno, 1998; Gathercole, Willis, Baddeley, & Emslie, 1994), visuospatial abilities (Logie, Della Sala, Wynn, & Baddeley, 2000), mathematical or numerical abilities (Geary & Widaman, 1992; Logie & Baddeley, 1987), and the ability to withstand a delay without rehearsal (Cowan, Nugent, Elliott, & Saults, 2000; Towse, Hitch, & Hutton, 1998). What I am questioning here is, more narrowly, the reason for the core capacity limit in chunks (a limit of three to five chunks on average in many tasks) that is seen when grouping and rehearsal strategies are either prevented (Cowan, 2001) or taken into account (Cowan, Chen, & Rouder, 2004). Under these carefully controlled circumstances, capacity limits are observed, and I would like to know why.

☐ EFFICIENT CAUSES (DETERMINERS) OF CAPACITY LIMITS

The question of what determines capacity limits can be divided into more specific questions. (1) Is there a central limit or are there domain-specific limits? (2) If the limit is central, how does the capacity-limited mechanism differ from other aspects of working memory? (3) Is the capacity limit the same for everyone or, if not, does it vary in ways that have important implications for the performance of complex tasks? (4) Is there a certain type of information that resides in the limited-capacity region, such as information binding together different features of the objects or chunks that are included?

Is there a Central Limit or Only Domain-Specific Limits of Working Memory?

Following Cowan (2001), there are similar limits in the number of chunks that can be retained in either vision or audition, for either verbal or non-verbal materials. However, one must be careful in drawing inferences from those findings regarding the nature of the capacity limits. The data could reflect either a central limit that pertains to all domains or separate limits in different domains, each perhaps sharing an organizing principle that produces similar capacity limits in the different domains.

Analogies with other psychological processes may help foster this necessary caution. Dissociations between findings are not sufficient to argue for separate domains. For example, the presentation of words pertaining to clothing tends to interfere with memory for other words about clothing presented in the same session, and words pertaining to fruit tend to interfere with memory for other presented words about fruit (Wickens, Born, & Allen, 1963). We would not conclude from this that there must be separate systems to process clothing and fruit. Rather, there is a principle of semantic similarity involved, and it may be retrieval from a single memory store that is susceptible to that principle. Conversely, similarities between findings are not sufficient to argue for a common domain, either. For example, there are rather similar psychophysical functions for the perception of brightness and loudness (Stevens, 1975), but one still would not want to argue that vision and audition reflect a common sensory system.

Wheeler and Treisman (2002) examined variations of the visual-array procedure of Luck and Vogel (1997) to determine what individuals knew about the binding between features. They concluded that there was a limit for how many bindings between features could be maintained concurrently, a conclusion to which we will return shortly. Additionally, however, they found that multiple types of features could be retained concurrently up to a certain limit. In one experiment, subjects who did not know if they would be tested on color or shape information did just as well as they did when they knew they would be tested on shape alone. To explain this, Wheeler and Treisman suggested that "feature values from different dimensions are each stored in parallel in their own dimension-specific cache, within which feature values compete for limited capacity representation but between which there is little or no competition" (p. 61). Although this is one possibility, it is also possible that the individual modalities include no such limit. The limit in recall (shown by decreasing performance with increasing set sizes) might occur at the point at which a central focus of attention must be aimed at a particular feature map in working memory, after the recall cue is presented. In that case, the actual limit would be central, not domain specific. The limit would be in the capacity of the focus of attention, no matter from which feature map information would be drawn.

One can find results that appear to support either a central limit or domain-specific limits. A finding that strongly suggests a central resource limit is one in which event-related potentials were collected and the P300 component was examined in a dual-task situation (Sirevaag, Kramer, Coles, & Donchin, 1989). The P300 is a component of the event-related potential response, an electrical response of the brain measured at the scalp, that is taken to reflect a strategic process such as the updating of working memory (for a discussion of possible interpretations, see Verleger, 1988). Sirevaag et al. had subjects control a cursor using a joystick, tracking a target moving in one or two dimensions in discrete jumps. The cursor was controlled by either the velocity or the acceleration of the joystick, so there were four levels of difficulty of the tracking task. In the other task, a series of high and low tones was heard, and the subject was to count the occurrences of one of the tones. Clearly, these two tasks share little in the way of motor movements or processing modalities. Yet, when the tasks were performed together, the P300 components elicited by the two tasks showed reciprocity: the larger the P300 was to the targets in the tracking task, the smaller it was to the tones, and the sum of P300 amplitudes in the two tasks was nearly constant across conditions. If the P300 reflects a resource that is used to perform the tasks, it apparently is of limited capacity that can be divided between the two tasks. Just et al. (2001) similarly found a constraint of one task on the effect of another task on neural activation in a functional magnetic resonance imaging (fMRI) task.

Still, given that the response showing the constancy is an electrical component of debatable psychological interpretation (Verleger, 1989), it would help to examine performance on two tasks, at least one of which is taken to indicate a capacity limit free of rehearsal and grouping effects. In Chapter 2, we examined the studies of Morey and Cowan (2004), Morey and Cowan (in press), Stevanovski and Jolicoeur (2003), and Jefferies, Lambon Ralph, & Baddeley (2004), suggesting that there is, at least sometimes, a central component of attention involved in the working memory maintenance of items to be recalled.

How is the Central, Limited-Capacity Portion of Working Memory Unique?

The previous section provides a sketch of how people may carry out memory tasks in which materials are presented in two domains at once. This still leaves open the question of what happens when only one task is presented at a time. Is there still an advantage for the subject to using a central capacity to encode and maintain the stimuli? What is the advantage to the subject as opposed to a more passive, automatic form of storage (such as the phonological loop or visuospatial sketch pad of Baddeley, 1986)?

One advantage of the capacity-limited form of storage appears to be that it assists in avoiding proactive interference from previously encountered information. Evidence in this regard was obtained by Halford, Maybery, and Bain (1988). They used a procedure modeled after the ever-popular task of Sternberg (1966), in which a list of items is followed by a probe item and the subject's task is to determine whether the probe item was present in the list as quickly as possible. In their experiments, the list items often shared similarities with items in the previous list. They were semantic similarities in one procedure and phonological similarities in another procedure. In either case, the theoretical rationale was that proactive interference should occur during the retrieval process but that items held in an active portion of working memory, such as the focus of attention, need not be retrieved and therefore should not suffer from proactive interference. The finding was that there was proactive interference (slower reaction times to the probe) when the list contained 10 items, but not when it contained only 4 items. In children, there was proactive interference when the list contained four items, but not when it contained only two items. Thus the mechanism immune to proactive interference had a larger capacity in adults than in children.

One limitation of this study by Halford et al. (1988) is that the list items all were presented simultaneously. Theoretically, it may be that the focus of attention in adults accommodates about four items simultaneously when they are presented simultaneously, but accommodates fewer when they are presented in sequence, one at a time, as in most studies of list recall. Cowan, Johnson, and Saults(2005) extended this type of task to situations in which items were presented either simultaneously or sequentially. To increase the amount of proactive interference, four previous trials contained most of the same words to be used in the high-interference trial. In contrast, low-interference trials comprised words drawn from a semantic category that was used nowhere else in the experiment.

The results were similar for simultaneous and sequential list procedures. Whereas Cowan et al. (2005) plotted their results averaged across these procedures, the results are presented separately for the two procedures in Figure 6.1. Post hoc Newman-Keuls tests indicated that, for simultaneous presentation, the effect of proactive interference was significant only for eight-item lists, whereas, for sequential presentation, the effect was significant for both six- and eight-item lists. Simultaneous presentation may promote grouping, which could increase the amount that can be held in the capacity-limited portion of working memory. In any case, there was no proactive interference at all for three-item lists, which is fitting given that most adults have a capacity limit of more than three items, according to Cowan (2001). There was no significant proactive

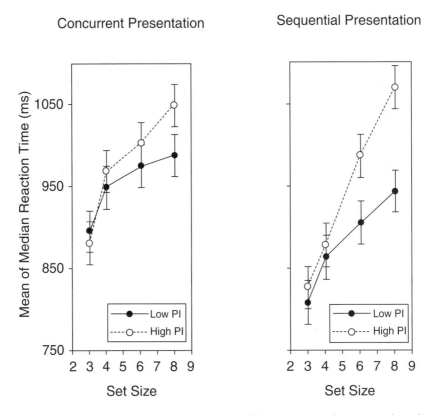

FIGURE 6.1 Based on the data set reported by Cowan, Johnson, and Saults (2005). (Left) For word lists with concurrent presentation of words, mean of median reaction times to a probe item as a function of the memory set size (x axis), for conditions of high proactive interference (PI; dashed lines) and low PI (solid lines). (Right) Comparable data for lists with sequential presentation of words in the list. PI was observed only for the larger set sizes.

interference for four-item lists, either, though one can detect in the figure a slight trend in that direction. These results generally support the notion that the capacity-limited portion of working memory, presumably the focus of attention, can maintain storage of about four elements in a manner that is relatively invulnerable to proactive interference.

Are there Individual Variations in Limited-Capacity Storage?

We have discussed two aspects of attention that theoretically are related to working memory: the control of attention and its ability to hold onto the goal of a task despite interfering information (e.g., Kane & Engle, 2003) and the focus of attention with its capacity limit (e.g., Cowan, 2001). In the case of the control of attention, it is clear that it varies among individuals and is related to working memory performance. Working memory capacity is highly correlated with the g or general factor in intelligence, and with other intellectual tasks (Conway et al., 2002; Daneman & Merikle, 1996; Engle, Tuholski, Laughlin, & Conway, 1999; Kail & Hall, 2001). It is a good bet that the control of attention similarly correlates with various intellectual tasks, although that may not have been demonstrated directly. In adult aging, there is evidence on the importance of the ability to inhibit prepotent incorrect responses (e.g., Hasher, Stolzfus, Zacks, & Rypma, 1991), suggesting that some loss of the control of attention may be important to account for the cognitive effects of aging. There are similar reports regarding children's difficulty in inhibiting prepotent responses (e.g., Bjorklund & Harnishfeger, 1990), suggesting that the control of attention is an important aspect of life-span development and individual differences.

What about the *capacity* of attention as opposed to its control? Does it, too, vary among individuals in a way that is important for complex cognitive tasks, and is it related to higher level cognition? One would expect that it is if, in fact, attention is a commodity that is capable of zooming in to hold on to a goal in the face of interference or zoom out to apprehend a handful of items within a field (cf. Cowan, 2004, 2005; Usher, Haarmann, Cohen, & Horn, 2001).

Tuholski, Engle, and Baylis (2001) tested this notion using an enumeration task. They found that, although high- and low-span individuals differed in their counting speeds, they did not differ in how many items they could subitize, which could be estimated by the first appearance of a curvilinear trend in the reaction times as a function of the number of items to enumerate. The subitizing cutoff point was calculated as

3.25 items ($SD = .81$) for low-span individuals and 3.35 items ($SD = .67$) for high-span individuals. Thus the effect size was only about 0.14 SD units (not significant). Note, however, that young and elderly adults differ in their subitizing range according to another study (see Basak & Verhaeghen, 2003).

Other measures that Cowan (2001) advocated as indices of the capacity of the focus of attention do correlate with working memory and with various cognitive-performance measures.

One straightforward example is a meta-analysis by Mukunda and Hall (1992). They looked at all available studies in children and in adults in which particular types of working memory measures were correlated with various aptitude tests on a within-age basis. Among the usual working memory measures, the correlation was relatively high for reading span (11 tests, $R = .43$) but lower for operation span (6 tests, $R = .23$) and counting span (3 tests, $R = .28$). It was also low for simple digit span (53 tests, $R = .22$). However, one measure that Cowan (2001) advocated as an index of the capacity-limited store with little ability to rehearse or group information, running memory span, had a correlation more comparable to reading span (11 tests, $R = .40$).

Another capacity-related measure was developed by Cohen and Sandberg (1977) in an experiment with Swedish children 12 and 13 years of age. A series of nine spoken digits was presented on each trial, usually at the rapid rate of four digits per second. Following the list, a cue indicated whether recall was supposed to be of the first, second, or third set of three digits. The fast presentation rate was designed to minimize the use or effectiveness of rehearsal. Previous studies indicated that the end of the list is the part least likely to benefit from rehearsal and most likely to be recalled directly from a short-term store. This, for example, accounts for the negative recency effect in final free recall (Craik, Gardiner, & Watkins, 1970). This procedure was administered to seven different groups of children. Four of those groups received nine lists at the rapid rate for complete serial recall before going on to the partial-recall procedure described previously. In those subjects, it was found that the most recent portion of the list was the portion most likely to be related to intelligence. The correlation was quite high, ranging from .45 to .68. All but one of the correlations for the earlier two parts of the list were insignificant. Three other groups of children began immediately with the partial recall procedure. In those children, the correlations were quite a bit lower, ranging from .10 to .42. In all seven groups, the correlation of the first part of the list with intelligence was insignificant.

A case can be made that the presence of full-list recall entrained subjects to restrict rehearsal to the early parts of the list, which forced recall of the end of the list to rely on maintenance mechanisms not relying upon rehearsal. In contrast, subjects who received the partial-recall trials first often may have developed a strategy in which rehearsal was distributed across all portions of the list. So it appears not to be rehearsal that correlates with intelligence but, rather, a storage mechanism related to the recall of recent items.

Bunting (2003) further investigated the procedure of Cohen and Sandberg (1977) and replicated the finding of a correlation with intelligence (in this case, using Ravens Progressive Matrices) only for the more recent portion of the list. He also showed that this correlation depended on the relatively large amount of proactive interference that had built up at the end of the list. The interpretation offered by Bunting was that attentional control is used to overcome proactive interference. A slightly different interpretation would be that holding items in the focus of attention makes them immune to proactive interference, which is in keeping with what Halford et al. (1988) and Cowan et al. (2005) found.

In a second experiment, Cohen and Sandberg (1977) replicated their effect and also found strong correlations between running memory span (with rapidly presented digits) and intelligence. The digits were presented 6/s or 9/s and correlated with intelligence at $r = .59$ and $r = .56$, respectively. These correlations are higher than what is usually obtained for working memory tasks. A third experiment showed that these correlations could not be accounted for simply by the buildup of proactive interference within a trial. Running memory span with 6, 9, 12, and 15 digits rapidly presented before a test on the last three digits correlated with intelligence at $r = .70, .55, .58,$ and $.69$, respectively. Proactive interference may only have to reach a moderate level for retrieval from memory to become ineffective, thus making performance depend on what information is still in the capacity-limited portion of working memory.

Haarmann, Davelaar, and Usher (2003) developed a task similar to one used earlier by Reid Lloyd, Brackett, and Hawkins (1961), described in Chapter 4. In the Haarmann et al. task, nine words were presented and a semantic cue indicated that three words were to be recalled (e.g., "*lamp, pear, tiger, apple, grape, elephant, horse, fax, phone*, FRUIT? Correct answer: *apple, pear, grape*"). This item recall with semantic organization would not appear to be ideal for phonological rehearsal and may occur through a memory search in which one category is uploaded from the activated portion of long-term memory into the focus of attention. The task resulted in relatively high correlations with measures of text comprehension ($r = .37$, compared with .35 for reading span) and spoken sentence comprehension ($r = .35$, compared with .30 for reading span).

Cowan et al. (in press-a) examined three tasks that Cowan (2001) would take as indications of the capacity-limited faculty: running memory span, memory for ignored speech (after Cowan, Nugent, Elliott, Ponomarev,

& Saults, 1999), and memory for visual arrays (after Luck & Vogel, 1997). We have examined them along with digit span and two measures of working memory span: listening span and counting span. We also have examined four measures of intelligence: Ravens Progressive Matrices, the Peabody Picture Vocabulary Test, and the pattern analysis and vocabulary subtests of the Stanford-Binet intelligence test. We have collected these measures in a developmental sample including elementary school children and adults, but have then conducted some of the analyses with age-group partialed out. Our results clearly show the measures of capacity to predict intelligence more successfully than does digit span. They are not as successful as the working memory-span measures, but we believe that we have been able to localize the differences to domain-specific skills rather than the control of attention. For example, in accounting for the nonverbal intelligence tests with age-group and the verbal intelligence test scores both partialed out, part of the remaining variance is held in common between the capacity tests and the working memory tests; another part is unique to the counting-span test (but not the listening-span test) and therefore seems to reflect a specific nonverbal skill. In this analysis, the digit-span test accounted for no variance.

This test and other results suggest that the control of attention as measured in working memory tests and the capacity of attention may closely covary. They may come from the same or closely related mechanisms in the brain.

An account of why simple span tasks do not have comparably high correlations with aptitude tests in adults (e.g., Daneman & Merikle, 1996) is that individual differences in the capacity-limited portion of memory do not have such an impact on simple span tasks because other processes play a large role. These other processes include the ability to group and rehearse the list. If this is the case then, in young children who do not rehearse or group items efficiently, simple span tasks should rival working memory (storage plus processing) span tasks in the extent to which they correlate with complex tasks. That has been found in several studies. In a study of children 8 and 11 years old, Hutton and Towse (2001) found correlations between digit span and spatial, mathematical, and reading tests of $r = .36, .45,$ and $.45,$ respectively, and comparable correlations between operation span and those same tests of $r = .35, .48,$ $.48,$ respectively. In another study with children in that age range, Cowan, Towse et al. (2003) carried out partial correlations controlled for age and found that the correlations with the verbal, quantitative, and nonverbal sections of the Cognitive Abilities Test were about as high for digit span ($r = .45, .37,$ and $.38,$ respectively) as for listening span ($r = .49,$ $.39,$ and $.29,$ respectively). Those for counting span were not significant in this experiment.

Kail and Hall (2001) did find a distinction between simple span and storage plus process types of working memory span in children. The simple spans included memory for digits, letters, and words. The complex span included listening and reading span, and a task in which the child had to identify the lowest number in a list and then remember the lowest numbers of several lists for later recall. The storage plus processing tasks provided a better prediction of the criterion task. However, that criterion task was reading recognition, not a general intelligence measure. Moreover, the children spanned between 7 and 13 years of age, so it is likely that the older children were distinguished from the younger ones on the basis of grouping and rehearsal processes. Much of the advantage of the storage plus processing measures was in the age effects. Table 1 of Kail and Hall can be used to calculate the partial correlations between various span measures and the reading recognition test, with age partialed out. In Study 1, the partial correlations were, for letter and word spans, .17 and .27; for reading and listening spans, .30 and .25, respectively. In Study 2, the correlations were, for digit and word spans, .34 and .20; for reading, listening, and least-number spans, .32, .29, and .31, respectively. Notice that, in Study 1, simple word span outperformed listening span and that, in Study 2, simple digit span outperformed all three storage plus processing spans. Viewing the literature as a whole, there is a clear, consistent advantage for storage plus processing tasks over simple span tasks only in adults (and probably in older children), it appears.

Hale, Bronik, and Fry (1997) found that working memory task performance (recall of series of digits or spatial locations) was affected by domain-specific interference in both children and adults, but was affected by interference from a domain different from the primary memory task in 8-year-old children, but not in 10-year-old children or adults. This finding illustrates that simple working memory tasks involve central executive processes and attention more in young children than in adults, which can explain why these tasks tap broad cognitive abilities in children.

Oberauer, Lange, and Engle (2004) presented research leading them to a conclusion consistent with Cowan et al. (in press-a). They found that dual-task costs were not general across verbal and spatial domains. There was little evidence for a general ability to resist interference or coordinate dual tasks as a core of working memory. Instead, the authors concluded:

> Adding a secondary task that uses representations of the same domain would largely disable the slave systems, such that dual-task performance reflects mainly the capacity of more central mechanisms such as the episodic buffer (Baddeley, 2000). Individual differences in dual-task costs would then reflect quantitative or qualitative differences between people in their ability (or willingness)

to use efficient specialized strategies for serial recall (in Cowan's framework), or differences in the efficiency of the slave systems utilized for serial recall in the single task condition (in Baddeley's framework). Under such a view, it would not be surprising that the single-task benefits added by specialized subsystems, or by task-specific strategies, are not correlated across domains, and are not particularly strongly related to independent measures of working memory. Hence, we might regard "simple" span tasks as the more complex measures, in that they reflect more of a mixture of different sources of variance. Whereas the starting point of our work was the equation "complex span = simple span + controlled attention" (Engle et al., 1999), it might be more fruitful to turn things around: simple span = complex span + specialized mechanisms or strategies. (p. 94)

Does the Central Capacity Limit Specifically Pertain to Binding?

Although this question may appear arbitrary, it actually is critical for the notion of capacity limits. The difference between activated elements from the memory system, which presumably occur without a capacity limit (Cowan, 1999), and a limited-capacity storage mechanism is that only the latter implies context-specific knowledge, which in turn implies some sort of binding between items and the context in which these items were encountered. Illustrating this difference, suppose one were presented with the word *cat* subliminally. It could prime recognition of the related word *dog* without an explicit recollection of having seen *cat* in the experiment, but an explicit recollection is needed to answer questions about having seen the word *cat* (e.g., Balota, 1983). Explicit recollection is more dependent on attention than is implicit memory or familiarity (Cowan, 1995).

Two types of binding include (1) associations between the features of an object (e.g., knowledge that the most recent display contained a red square and a blue triangle, as opposed to a blue square and a red triangle) and (2) association between objects and the context in which they occurred (e.g., knowledge that the digits 4, 7, and 6 occurred in the first through third serial positions of the most recently presented list or, at least, knowledge that they were part of that list). A straightforward interpretation of the theoretical framework of Cowan (1988, 1995, 1999), discussed in Chapter 2, makes it clear that the portion of working memory that involves the focus of attention must have a lot to do with how ideas are associated or bound to one another. There was said to be an unlimited amount of activation of features corresponding to recently encountered stimuli. However, only a limited subset of activated features can be in the focus of attention at any one time. The focus of attention is said to be instrumental in binding features that make up individual objects and events and in binding objects to the context. However, there is some apparently contradictory evidence and it is necessary to look carefully at the role of attention in binding at encoding, maintenance, and retrieval, both within and between objects.

Binding and Attention

The role of attention in creating and maintaining binding was earlier proposed by Treisman and colleagues (e.g., Treisman, 1988; Treisman & Gelade, 1980). It was proposed fundamentally on the basis of findings indicating that subjects could search through a visual array looking for a unique feature (e.g., a red item among blue ones, or a square among circles) at a speed that was almost independent of the number of items in the array, whereas, in contrast, the search for a conjunction of features (e.g., a blue square among blue circles and red squares) was highly dependent on how many items were in the array. The more items in the array, the longer the reaction times. So, it seemed that there was a capacity limit in the ability to perceive conjunctions between features.

Mandler (1985) further suggested that all items in the focus of attention and in awareness are bound together (i.e., integrated):

> The organized (and limited) nature of consciousness is illustrated by the fact that one is never conscious of some half dozen totally unrelated things. In the local park I may be conscious of four children playing hopscotch, or of children and parents interacting, or of some people playing chess; but a conscious content of a child, a chess player, a father, and a carriage is unlikely (unless of course they form their own meaningful scenario). (p. 68)

However, Luck (2004) recently summarized evidence that retaining binding information in working memory is no more attention-demanding than retaining the two features that comprise the binding. When objects are perceived, apparently so is the binding information within the object, provided that it is simple binding between two features.

Binding and Working Memory Capacity

Cowan (2001) suggested that a capacity limit applied not to items per se, but rather to bindings between items, or between items and context. For example, in a digit-span experiment, it does not make sense to suggest that the digits are the objects for which capacity is limited. All 9 (or 10) digits are probably in a high state of memory activation throughout most of the experiment. Instead, what counts is knowledge that certain digits were members of the most recent list and, beyond that, knowledge of the correspondences between items and serial positions and between multiple items forming a chunk. Similarly, in a visual-array comparison experiment, what is important is the knowledge that certain colors were present in the most recent array and, beyond that, knowledge of the spatial locations of particular colors (in experiments in which knowledge of spatial position is required). It is memory for such bindings—the episodic information— that was said to be limited in capacity.

Luck and Vogel (1997) made a distinction between bindings within an object and bindings between an object and a spatial location. They found that subjects could retain multiple features of an object, bound together, for multiple objects at once. For example, when an object could change in either color or orientation, the ability to compare two arrays was no worse than when it could change only in one of those features. In contrast, subjects could retain only a limited number of location-specific objects in an array (about four).

Wheeler and Treisman (2002) replicated the findings of Luck and Vogel (1997), except that they found that colors within a multicolored object had to be retained separately and taxed working memory capacity separately. (That finding was obtained with objects comprising an inner, small square of one color and a surrounding area of a different color.) Wheeler and Treisman also examined the situation in which it was a conjunction of features that had to be recalled. In different experiments, they did this with the features of color and location and with the features of color and shape. They tested for the binding by swapping features so that, for example, a square that was previously blue became red in the second array, and a square that was previously red became blue. With this type of change between arrays, no new features were introduced.

Two kinds of tests were used in different experiments. In one kind of test, two arrays were presented as described previously. In a second kind of test, the probe was not a complete array but only the critical item that may have changed from the array. In the experiment involving location and color, for example, presentation of a colored square at the center of the array meant that one was to indicate whether that color had appeared in the first array, whereas presentation of a black square somewhere in the visual field meant one was to indicate whether an item had been presented at that location. This method worked because the array to be retained contained no objects at the center of the visual field and no black objects, so that center location and black could serve as neutral probes. Finally, in the binding condition, presentation of a colored square somewhere in the array other than the center meant that one was to indicate whether that specific color had appeared in that location or not, given that the designated color had appeared somewhere in the array, and that some color had appeared at the designated location.

Figure 6.2 summarizes the results of four experiments in Wheeler and Treisman (2002). The results make it clear that it is almost as easy to retain two features and then to be tested on one of them (bars marked *Both*) as it is to retain just one feature. Also, it appears that the results for binding information depend on how testing is done. When the probe is

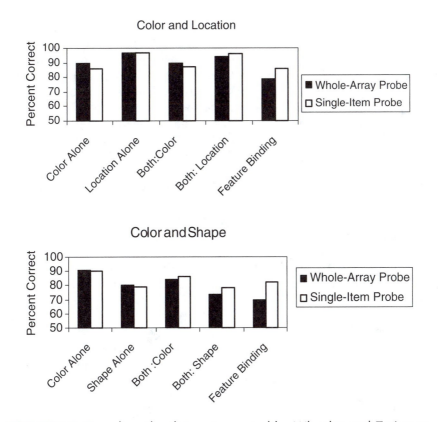

FIGURE 6.2 Based on the data set reported by Wheeler and Treisman (2002). (Top) Trials with color and location as the relevant features in visual-array-comparison tasks. For whole-array probes (black bars) and single-item probes (white bars), the percentages of correct responses are shown as a function of the feature or feature combination for which the subject is held responsible (*x* axis). (Bottom) Comparable data for trials with color and shape as the relevant features.

an entire array (black bars), there is a deficit for binding information. However, when the probe is a single item (white bars), retaining the binding information is no more difficult than retaining the more challenging of the two features. This last finding, and other similar evidence that Wheeler and Treisman reviewed, suggests that features are automatically retained as bound objects after they are encoded.

Why, then, is there a disadvantage for binding information when the probe is an entire second array? Although Wheeler and Treisman (2002) did not fully explain this result, one possible explanation is that binding information is saved automatically but that *access* to that binding information is capacity limited. Objects are saved as bindings between elements and the number of objects that can be saved in such a manner depend on working memory capacity at the time of encoding. However, when one is trying to compare a probe with the array, each object has to be *unpacked* for the features to be compared. If k objects can be saved in working memory, this does not mean that k objects with two features per object can be compared to an additional k objects with two features per object, all at once. Perhaps the binding information is too fragile for that.

The situation of comparing multiple objects with multiple features per object seems analogous to several children opening similar Christmas presents in the same room. The chances of each child going home with all of the cards, plastic markers, and other parts belonging to him or her, and not any of the parts from another child's presents, are slim. The advantage of unpacking one object at a time for comparison may be similar to the advantage, which many others have discussed, of unpacking one chunk at a time (e.g., Tulving & Patkau, 1962).

Wheeler and Treisman (2002) offered a different type of account of capacity limits, in which it was supposed that different feature maps (for color, shape, and so on) had separate, albeit comparable, capacity limits. It seems more parsimonious to assume that the feature maps are capacity-unlimited, but that the limitation comes into play when the focus of attention must help to store information or retrieve it from these feature maps. Then, the same capacity limits are obtained no matter whether it is features or integrated objects that are to be retrieved.

Cohen and Ivry (1989) carried out a study that strengthens this logic and suggests that (1) items are, in fact, stored with their location information, and (2) the location information from multiple objects in different places is usually confused only if the objects are attended at the same time. Each array included a digit in the center of the array, at the fixation point and two peripherally located letters: O, and either F or X. The O was presented in one color and either F or X was presented in another color. The task was to report (by key presses) first the digit, then the color of the target letter, and then its identity (F or X). A binding or conjunction error would consist of reporting the target letter in the color that the non-target letter, *O*, actually was presented. It was found that, unless the *O* and target letter were within 1 degree of visual angle of each other, conjunction errors were not made. In a subsequent experiment, the initial task was to report two digits that sometimes flanked the letter stimuli, in which case the letters would be *inside* of the initial focus of attention. When that was the case, conjunction errors were made between the color of the *O* and the target letter, even when these two letters were far apart in the array. In sum, items automatically carried location information and the errors in the binding of features (in this study, letter identity and color) occurred primarily between the features of simultaneously attended objects.

Binding and Individual Differences

There is a question of whether the formation and maintenance of the bindings between features comprising an object require attention beyond what is devoted to encoding and retaining the features themselves. Given that some authors have suggested attention-related concepts to explain individual differences and age differences in working memory (e.g., Engle et al., 1999; Hasher, 1991), it generally has been assumed that attention differences would lead to age and individual differences in binding. However, this assumption needs to be reexamined in light of the finding of Cohen and Ivry (1989) that features may be automatically bound to locations.

It is clear that there are some age differences in binding. For example, Chalfonte and Johnson (1996) quizzed younger and elderly adults on memory for arrays of colored line drawings of common objects they had studied and found several types of deficiencies in the elderly. First, they were deficient when quizzed on the locations of objects in the array. There was no comparable deficiency for the identities or colors of objects. Second, they were deficient in the binding between features. Thus they were less likely than young adults to recall which items were presented in which colors, or which items were presented at which locations. However, it cannot be determined from this study what the role of attention is in this age-related deficiency.

It is clear from other research that at least some age differences in binding and association cannot be explained by differences in focused attention. Naveh-Benjamin, Hussain, Guez, and Bar-On (2003) had young and elderly adults study pairs of words and then tested them on recognition of either the words or the word pairs. In the latter type of test, the words were always drawn from those that had been studied but these words sometimes were paired incorrectly. The young adults also were tested on words studied during a secondary, tone-identification task to divide attention. The results are reproduced in Figure 6.3, for the item tests (top panel) and the association tests (bottom panel). There was a striking deficit for associative information in the elderly. Moreover, this associative deficit was not reproduced with divided attention in the young adults. This suggests that forming associations, even between words, does not require highly focused attention *beyond what is needed to encode the objects or features* that are to be bound. In a related study of young adults, Naveh-Benjamin, Guez, and Marom (2003) showed that associative information is not differentially affected by divided attention; it is affected by dividing attention only to the same extent as item information is affected.

I suspect that forming an association between two words and carrying out the tone task still does not stress working memory capacity to its limit. This findings of Naveh-Benjamin, Hussain, et al. (2003) do suggest, though, that associations or bindings between at least two elements can take place in parallel with other attentive processing. Unpublished research in our laboratory, some of which has been carried out jointly with Naveh-Benjamin, further suggests that dividing attention does not selectively impair information about the binding between colors and locations in the array-comparison task of Luck and Vogel (1997); it impairs memory for colors at least as much as it impairs memory for the locations at which specific colors appeared. Other studies similarly suggest that auditory and visual grouping can occur without focused attention (Driver, Davis, Russell, Turatto, & Freeman, 2001; Macken, Tremblay, Houghton, Nicholls, & Jones, 2003; Scholl, 2001). The general conclusion may be, therefore, that a level of attention to objects sufficient to allow them to be encoded also results in an encoding of the binding information; divided attention does not selectively impair the encoding of binding.

A Special Role of Retrieval

There are conflicts in the literature regarding the role of attention in binding that might be resolved with reference to the concept of *unpacking* objects or events at the time of retrieval. For example, consider the finding of Macken et al. (2003) that multiple auditory streams can be formed in an ignored channel; that is, that auditory events are automatically bound into groups extending over time on the basis of their similarities and differences. In contrast, the finding of Carlyon, Cusack, Foxton, and Robertson (2001) suggested that streaming does not take place without attention.

The difference between these two studies is that the methods of Carlyon et al. (2001) require that subjects judge the auditory streams, whereas Macken et al. (2003) simply found that the streams alter the interference

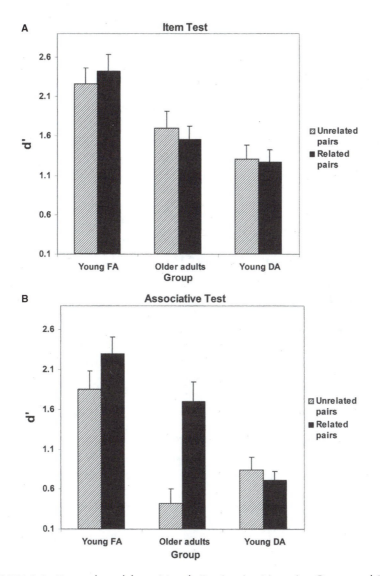

FIGURE 6.3 Reproduced from Naveh-Benjamin, Hussain, Guez, and Bar-On (2003, Figure 2). (A) Sensitivity (d′) of memory in a test for words presented in unrelated pairs (gray bars) or related pairs (black bars). The three clusters of bars indicate young adults with full attention (FA), elderly adults, and young adults with divided attention (DA). (B) Comparable data for a test of the presented paired associations. Dividing attention in the young lowers performance overall but does not reproduce the extreme, differential deficit obtained in the elderly for new associations between unrelated words in a pair.

effects of auditory stimuli on a visually presented memory task (i.e., an explicit versus implicit memory distinction). The resolution of these apparently contradictory findings may be that streaming requires attention only if the task requires that the stimuli be unpacked to be reported, as in the study of Carlyon et al. but not Macken et al. The more general hypothesis is that binding information may be easy to encode and maintain, but that many cases produce information overload at the time of retrieval if too many feature bindings must be attended at once. This statement has obvious relevance, for example, to the findings of Wheeler and Treisman (2002) illustrated in Figure 6.2. It also explains why word association did not depend on attention more than object encoding, in a task in which only one pair of words had to be associated at a time (Naveh-Benjamin, Hussain et al., 2003).

Model of Feature Bindings and Their Use in Processing

Figure 6.4 presents an illustration of a model of performance that is my best attempt to explain the pattern of evidence regarding binding, given the available evidence. It is shown with respect to the array-comparison task of Wheeler and Treisman (2002), but the processes are meant to apply to all situations of binding.

According to this model, some attention is needed for the encoding of items into working memory; however, divided attention is possible. Encoding is limited to about four items, assuming that they cannot be combined into larger chunks in the time available. That is shown in the top row of the figure.

Once encoded, the maintenance of items can be attention-free *for a short period filled with no interfering stimuli*, as shown in the second row of the figure. However, that maintenance is susceptible to interference from various sources, presumably including internal noise and external stimulation. If the retention period is long (e.g., longer than 1 s) or contains other stimuli, attention becomes increasingly necessary to defend the representations from interference. The passive buffer stores within the model of Baddeley (1986) or Baddeley and Logie (1999) serve the same purpose as activated memory here, and similarly would be vulnerable to interference or decay.

When a probe is presented, as in the third row of the figure, the task is to compare that probe with the representation in working memory. The spotlight of attention now must be divided between the representation in memory and the probe, as shown by the dashed lines tied to the bottom row of the figure. However, if the probe is a repetition of the entire first array, with a change possible in any item, as in Option A in the figure's bottom row, this increases the working memory load and consequently

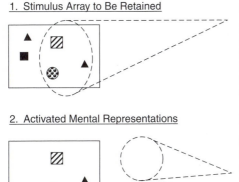

1. Stimulus Array to Be Retained

Attentive Encoding

Up to ~4 objects encoded in working memory with multiple features per object (e.g., location, color, shape, size). Rapid presentation: binding errors are possible.

2. Activated Mental Representations

Maintenance: Attention is Optional

Brief maintenance of k objects automatically; features are bound to one another as encoded above (BUT attention is needed to ward off effects of decay and interference.)

3. Probe-Stimulus Array

Attentive Comparisons of Arrays

Possibility of contamination from features of now-irrelevant objects within the memory representation in A. The total working-memory load affects performance.

A   OR   B

FIGURE 6.4 Proposed roles of attention at three stages of an array-comparison task. (Top) Attention is needed to store the correct bindings when multiple items are encoded at once. (Middle) Attention is needed to preserve the correct bindings in the face of interference and long delays. (Bottom) Attention is needed for correct bindings when multiple items in the second array are to be compared to multiple items in the first array.

increases the possibility of mistaken recombinations of features from different objects in the memory representation (i.e., illusory conjunctions) as objects are unpacked for comparison with the multiple items in the probe array. If the probe is a single item that may have changed, as in Option B, then it is possible to focus attention on a smaller set of feature bindings, one in the memory representation and one in the probe, which removes the added burden of attending to multiple feature bindings. If the item in question is part of the memory representation, as depicted in the figure, then performance will be correct.

This model is tentative, but it provides one explanation for the pattern of binding results discussed previously, and especially the finding of Wheeler and Treisman (2002) that the recovery of binding information was far less successful when the entire array to be recalled was repeated in the probe stimulus, as opposed to a single-item probe (see Figure 6.2).

In situations in which only one binding is to be created or retrieved at a time, working memory capacity is not likely to be exceeded and a dual task may not affect binding beyond its effect on feature or item storage (e.g., Naveh-Benjamin, Hussain et al., 2003). Indeed, although Naveh-Benjamin, Hussain et al. obtained an aging deficit in binding or association between words, it was attributed largely to degradation in hippocampal systems, not to degradation in attention-related systems in the brain.

The model may eventually be tested in a wide variety of applications. For example, in serial recall, the items must be bound to serial positions. Cohen and Sandberg (1980) examined various types of serial recall measures in 12- and 13-year-old children and concluded from their data that individual differences in intelligence were best predicted by the "encoding of items-in-order into an already-loaded store" (p. 319). What may be at issue here is the attempt to retrieve too many item-to-serial-position bindings at once, given the limited capacity of the attention-related portion of working memory.

☐ FORMAL CAUSES (MODELS) OF CAPACITY LIMITS

Formal causes are sets of assumptions that, taken together, make clear predictions about data, much as Newton's gravitational law and Einstein's general theory of relativity make predictions about the movement of objects. A set of formal causes, or formal model, of working memory could simply lead to a description of the data without increasing our understanding of it. However, there would be more explanatory power in a model that did not include a capacity limit as one of the assumptions of the model, but derived a capacity limit from other principles for which there is independent justification.

Usher et al. (2001) briefly described one such model. In it, the capacity limit emerged from a consideration of the overlap between concepts:

> An alternative neurobiological account ... explains the capacity limitation in terms of inherent properties of competitive networks. ... The main idea for consideration is that while LTM (Long Term Memory) is mediated by structural changes in connectivity, STM (Short Term Memory) (which is associated with awareness) is mediated by neuroelectric reverberations ... subject to competitive interactions, whose need has often been discussed in experimental and computational neuroscience ... the system shows a sharp

capacity limitation where only a small number of items can be simultaneously maintained. This capacity depends on the excitation and inhibition parameters and is within the range of 3–5 items. ... Functional considerations demonstrate the system cannot increase its capacity beyond this range by diminishing the inhibition β parameter even further. Due to the recurrent excitation and to small overlaps in the input (or in the representations themselves) a minimal amount of lateral inhibition is required to prevent the activation [from spreading] to all the memory representations. (pp. 151–152)

This brief description is enough to illustrate how formal models might well help answer the question of why capacity limits exist and how they are implemented. Formal models in this field have attempted to incorporate the neurobiological level, and some of these models will be discussed in the next section.

☐ MATERIAL CAUSES (MECHANISMS) OF CAPACITY LIMITS

It is first helpful to discuss the neural basis of the working memory system. After that, it is possible to discuss the neural basis of a capacity limit.

Are there Frontal and Parietal Attentional Systems?

Most of the recent literature on the relation between the brain and working memory focuses on the role of the frontal lobes in the control of attention (e.g., Kane & Engle, 2002). Although this important link to brain function has been established beyond a doubt, there are other important brain areas to consider. In my previous book (Cowan, 1995), I made broad suggestions about what areas of the brain might be involved in working memory. These suggestions were based primarily on evidence from neuropsychological syndromes and animal lesion studies. The suggestions included: (1) a high involvement of frontal areas of the brain in the control of attention; (2) a high involvement of parietal areas in the focus of attention; and (3) a high involvement of the perceptual processing areas in the retention of modality-specific, short-term memories. At the time, the field was most interested in the frontal areas and there was some tendency to place the attention-related portion of working memory squarely in those areas (e.g., Goldman-Rakic, 1992). Nevertheless, there were other researchers who emphasized that the frontal and parietal systems act as separate, but interconnected, regions with slightly different functions (e.g., Posner & Peterson, 1990; Posner & Rothbart, 1991; Schacter, 1989). Damage to the frontal lobes more often results in a loss of control and planning, whereas damage to the parietal lobes more often results in impairments in attention and consciousness, such as unilateral neglect (typically, lack of awareness of stimuli in the right side of space) and anosognosia (lack of awareness of a physical disability or problem). Cowan suggested that, in a typical working memory task, the frontal lobes contain pointers to the appropriate information in the parietal lobes and other posterior parts of the brain, and therefore keep the appropriate neural systems active to maintain the representation of the stimuli. The inferior parietal areas (and adjoining temporal areas) appear to receive input from multiple sensory systems and therefore may be a site of the representation of integrated or abstract information (Postle & D'Esposito, 1999). This view is different from the view that others have made popular (e.g., Goldman-Rakic, 1992), in which the frontal systems themselves hold the information in working memory. Evidence of specialized areas of the frontal lobe to hold different types of visual information (Wilson, O'Scalaidhe, & Goldman-Rakic, 1993) may be misleading because different animals were used to observe different features.

Ruchkin, Grafman, Cameron, and Berndt (2003) recently assembled a large amount of psychophysiological evidence in support of the basic view of Cowan (1995). Their abstract states that studies of event-related potentials show coactivation of frontal and posterior systems during working memory storage, including the same posterior areas involved in the encoding of the stimuli and long-term memory representations related to these stimuli. They show that the posterior activation is prolonged in working memory retention by the activity of the prefrontal cortex. On the basis of this evidence, they argue against the need to posit separate, specialized short-term storage buffers (e.g., Baddeley & Logie, 1999) and favor the general notion of activated portions of long-term memory, with the addition of new links between long-term concepts within the working memory representation.

The view that there are distinct short-term buffers was attributed to Baddeley (2001b), who was said to appeal to the existence of syndromes in which individuals lose short-term memory abilities while maintaining intact long-term memory abilities, or vice versa. Ruchkin et al. (2003) argued that a loss of short-term memory can occur because some aspects of phonological processing are lost, whereas semantic and lexical processes are preserved. For example, individuals with short-term memory loss also lose the ability to learn new words (Baddeley, Papagno, & Vallar, 1988). Individuals with a semantic short-term memory deficit (Romani & Martin, 1999) have difficulty forming semantic long-term memories, Ruchkin et al. noted. In the case of long-term memory loss with preserved short-term memory, they suggested, the inability to preserve new associations (through damage to the hippocampal system or to the frontal areas involved in carrying out mnemonic processing) does not imply that the long-term storage areas differ from short-term storage areas. They suggested that long-term memory deficits "can be due to impaired binding processes involving hippocampal-neocortex connections responsible for eliciting simultaneous activations across long-term stores that lead to an episode being stored (Rickard & Grafman 1998)."

The discussion of a study by Prabhakaran, Narayanan, Zhao, and Gabrieli (2000) exemplifies the difference in interpretation. They found that information requiring integration or binding of elements results in more activation of the right prefrontal cortex than when no such integration is required. Baddeley (2001b) took this as an indication of a neural area subserving an episodic buffer, but Ruchkin et al. (2003) restated the results in a way that does not imply a specialized store. They suggested that "a more precise interpretation of the fMRI data is that the right prefrontal cortex participates in the process of maintaining binding information in an active state" (p. 711). That is very different from the assumption that the bound information is located in the frontal area. Similarly, areas of the brain implicated for Baddeley's specialized phonological and visuospatial stores would be interpreted by Ruchkin et al. as areas involved not only in buffer storage, but also in processing and long-term storage of the code-specific information. They are parts of the activated portion of long-term memory of Cowan (1995, 1999).

Awh and Jonides (2001) similarly suggested that the mechanisms of attention and spatial working memory overlap; that spatial working memory is attention applied to the same areas involved in spatial perception to prolong the activation of memory in those areas.

Chein, Ravizza, and Fiez (2003) went further in accumulating neuroimaging evidence in favor of an embedded-process type of model. They concluded:

> Cowan's model offers the opportunity to reconceptualize the mappings between working memory processes and their neural substrates in three important respects. First, Cowan proposes an attentional scanning procedure that relies upon internal shifts of attention. We have shown that patterns of activation within the inferior parietal cortex are consistent with such a function. Second, Cowan posits that attentional scanning is only one potential

strategy for maintaining information in working memory, while speech-based rehearsal is a second strategy. We argue that patterns of activation within the inferior parietal cortex can serve to detect the employment of attentional scanning over speech-based rehearsal strategies. ... Third, Cowan places the representations that support the maintenance of information within the long-term memory system in distributed cortical regions. We argue that this offers a way to reconcile otherwise contradictory findings. (pp. 332–333)

Chein (2003) further supported the embedded-processes model with fMRI research by showing that, in a list-recall task, articulatory suppression affected phonologically related areas, whereas irrelevant sounds affected attention-related areas, in line with task analyses offered by Cowan (1995).

What is the Locus of the Storage Capacity Limit?

Within the general theoretical framework shared by Ruchkin et al. (2003) and Cowan (1995, 1999), it is possible to distinguish between two different neural accounts of attention-related capacity limits. Ruchkin et al. agree with me in suggesting that the frontal lobes carry pointers to the activated information in the posterior part of the brain. They suggested that the capacity limit is a limit in how many pointers can be carried at once. In contrast, Cowan (1995, 1999) saw portions of the parietal lobe as the seat of the focus of attention, the place where various sensory and interpretive processes converge and are integrated. According to that view, the limitation in capacity may not be a limitation in how many pointers can be held but, rather, in how many independent chunks of information can be pointed to.

Several theorists have ventured to discuss neural reasons why capacity may be limited. These theories have to do with the need to avoid interference between items held simultaneously in working memory; a capacity limit is the necessary price of avoiding too much interference. One such theory was described in the section on formal causes of capacity limits (Usher et al., 2001). According to that, activation of the memory system would go out of control if capacity were not limited to about four items at once. The other type of theory that has been discussed widely appeals to the manner in which features of an item are bound together, yet without a confusion between items. This type of theory was suggested long ago by Milner (1974) in an essay on visual shape recognition: "cells fired by the same figure fire together but not in synchrony with cells fired by other figures. … Thus, features from a number of figures could be detected and transmitted through the network with little mutual interference, by a sort of time-sharing arrangement" (p. 532). That is to say, binding of the features of an item relies on synchrony of firing of the feature detectors of that item, and separation of different items (as opposed to illusory conjunctions) relies on nonsynchrony. Assuming that the brain must cycle back to a particular item within a certain interval to maintain its activation in working memory, it follows that only a limited number of items could be maintained at once. This has been the basis of several recent explanations of capacity limits (e.g., Lisman & Idiart, 1995; Luck & Vogel, 1998).

There is a physiological basis to support this conjecture of timing and time-sharing as a basis of object identification and capacity limits. Gray, König, Engel, and Singer (1989) examined two cortical columns of neurons in cats representing different portions of the visual field and found that the two columns correlated when they were stimulated by different parts of the same object, but not if they were stimulated by different objects. Synchronization of features (at a frequency of about 40 Hz, what is termed the *gamma band*) did seem to define the neural representation of objects, a hypothesis that has been explored many times since then. Recent studies have extended this finding to humans and have tied it to attention (e.g., Herrmann, Munk, & Engel, 2004). Tiitinen et al. (1993) found that a 40-Hz oscillatory cycle was enhanced by attention. Rodriguez et al. (1999) reported electrical synchronizations between widely separated scalp locations 180 to 360 ms after presentation of a silhouetted human profile, but not after a random field. Miltner, Braun, Arnold, Witte, and Taub (1999) found synchronized activity after a conditioned stimulus, a lighting change followed by shock, but not after a lighting change that was not followed by shock. Recent work in humans also links this oscillatory activity to working memory. Tallon-Baudry, Bertrand, Peronnet, and Pernier (1998) and Tallon-Baudry, Kreiter, and Bertrand (1999) found enhancements of activity in the range of 40 Hz (and a slower range) during a delayed match-to-sample task in humans, and Sarnthein, Petsche, Rappelsberger, Shaw, and von Stein (1998) found that the synchronization between frontal and posterior regions of the cortex (including, but not limited to, the 40-Hz frequency region) was increased from baseline during a visuospatial working memory task. For reviews suggesting that working memory may be fundamentally an activated subset of long-term memory, that the activation involves coordination between frontal and posterior regions, and that it involves gamma-band oscillations, see Engel and Singer (2001), Ruchkin et al. (2003), and Ward (2003).

Several more recent studies tend to support the view that the capacity limit is more strongly related to parietal regions presumably representing the focus of attention, as opposed to frontal regions presumably containing pointers to that attentional focus and controlling attention. These studies used visual-array comparison tasks modeled after Luck and Vogel (1997). We have already discussed the recent studies of Xu (2004) and Jiang and Song (2004) that found capacity-limited parietal regions.

Vogel and Machizawa (2004) cued subjects to attend to colored squares on one side of the visual field on each trial while ignoring squares on the other side, so that the extra electrical negativity in event-related potentials on the side of the scalp contralateral to the attended field could be used as an index of working memory maintenance of the attended squares. This extra activity persisted to the presentation of the second array and its magnitude demonstrated a capacity limit comparable to the behavioral limit. In particular, the amount of negativity increased as a function of the number of attended color squares up to three or four, after which there was no further increase in the level of electrical activity. Similar to what Cowan (2001) reported behaviorally, there were individual differences in both behavior and event-related electrical activity. The individual differences in electrical activity were measured as the difference in activity between two and four attended objects. This measure was highly correlated with the behavioral measure of capacity, $r = .78$.

Vogel, McCollough, and Machizawa (2004) used this measure to determine the relation between individual differences in the scope of attention and individual differences in the control of attention. They did that by including objects in a color that was task-relevant and other objects in a color that was task-irrelevant. The magnitude of the capacity-related activation of the brain included the irrelevant objects for low-span individuals, but not for high-span individuals. Therefore, consistent with what Cowan et al. (in press-a) proposed, individual differences in the scope of attention were highly related to individual differences in the control of attention.

Todd and Marois (2004) examined fMRI responses during an array-comparison task and found specific posterior regions that responded in a manner similar to the behavioral response, the intraoccipital and intraparietal sulci. The activity levels in these areas increased as the number of objects to be retained increased to four, after which it leveled off like the behavioral results. (The behavioral and brain functions were strikingly similar.) The activity in these areas was greater for three objects than for one object during encoding and maintenance, but not during retrieval. The activity in these brain regions was found to be independent of the presentation duration between 150 and 450 ms (similar to behavioral responses), not to be due to saturation of the dependent measure, and to respond similarly to a task in which the variable feature was object orientation rather than color. It also responded similarly even in a task in which location-specific information was not needed (because the color of the probe was either old or new and was presented in the center of the display). This study truly seems to establish a specific neural basis of visual working memory capacity limits. The anterior cingulate region responded with an approximately linear increase in activity as a function of the set size (which went from one to eight items), but did not show a capacity limit. It therefore supports the notion of an involvement of the frontal region in encoding or maintaining working memory, but with the capacity limit localized in the posterior activity associated with the representation itself, not with attentional control.

It is clear that additional research with these procedures of Vogel and Machizawa (2004) and Todd and Marois (2004) should tell us a lot about the nature of capacity limits. For example, imagine a situation in which auditory and visual information must be maintained, either on separate trials or at the same time. One important question is how much overlap there would be between the regions of representation for the auditory and visual information. (Perhaps the intraoccipital sulci would be specific to visual stimuli, whereas the intraparietal sulci would be active for both modalities). Another important question is whether, for a dual-modality presentation, activity in any common areas would depend on the total number of stimuli to be maintained, and whether the amount of activity in any modality-specific areas would occur automatically or only as a function of continued attention devoted to that modality. The model presented in Figure 6.4 suggests that if the maintenance period is unfilled, it should not be necessary to keep attention focused on the task during the retention interval (at least over a few seconds) to maintain the capacity-limited representation.

What are the Brain Links between Capacity Limits, Attention, and Intelligence?

We have discussed the neural basis of working memory storage, but one thing that remains to be discussed is how brain mechanisms of capacity-limited storage and attention are involved in complex cognitive tasks, such as intellectual aptitude tasks.

A recent study using positron emission tomography showed a relation between activity in the lateral prefrontal cortex and performance on a difficult task that was correlated with fluid intelligence (Duncan et al., 2000). Gray, Chabris, and Braver (2003) found that this area and a broader network that also included other frontal, parietal, and temporal regions correlated with fluid intelligence as measured by Ravens Progressive

Matrices. More specifically, though, the information distinguished between individuals with higher versus lower intelligence scores was performance in a three-back task on trials in which the test stimulus was a lure matching an item presented recently in some position other than three-back. It was this ability to reject difficult lures for which the brain areas responded differently in subjects with high and low intelligence. The left lateral prefrontal cortex and parietal cortex bilaterally, taken together, explained more than 99% of the relation between fluid intelligence and accuracy on these lure trials. The relations were much weaker for nonlure trials.

The involvement of frontal areas and the importance of lure trials reinforce the notion that the control of attention, and specifically the use of attention to overcome interference, is key in distinguishing between individuals displaying higher versus lower fluid intelligence (Engle et al., 1999; Hasher et al., 1991; Kane, Bleckley, Conway, & Engle, 2001; Kane & Engle, 2003; Lustig, May, & Hasher, 2001). However, the importance of parietal areas is interesting inasmuch as those areas are not as often implicated in attentional control processes.

One reason for the parietal areas taking part in these effects may be that the attentional control region's purpose in the three-back task was to reload working memory, represented in the parietal regions, every time a new stimulus was presented. In that case, both the areas involved in causing the updating and the areas involved in holding the updated representations would be expected to respond.

In neural terms, such processes might have implications for the basis of individual differences in working memory capacity. It could be that the basic capacity, determined by factors such as the number of sets of synchronously firing neural features that can occur in oscillations within a fixed period (e.g., Lisman & Idiart, 1995), does *not* vary among individuals. Instead, it may be that the patterns of oscillations are set up in much the same way in all individuals but that, in more intelligent individuals and those with higher working memory spans, patterns are set up more appropriately and are maintained better in the face of interference because of the continuing contributions of attentional control.

Alternatively, it may be that more intelligent individuals can maintain more items in a capacity-limited store, even without the involvement of attentional control during the maintenance period. There could be many neural differences between individuals with more versus less intelligence, and it may be that attentional control and working memory capacity are just two areas in which the effects of neural differences are most easily observed. More research is needed in this interesting area, and it is not too difficult to see some avenues in which to proceed. The research should indicate whether the relationships between limited-capacity storage (presumably by the focus of attention) and intellectual aptitudes are direct or whether they are mediated by the involvement of attentional control in the efficient use of the limited-capacity storage.

Other Processes and Dissenting Voices

Although I have not come down firmly in support of an exact model of working memory, I have gravitated toward the view in which the control of attention and the focus of attention both are important in working memory, intelligence, and conscious experience. I would hasten to add that I do not mean to overlook the importance of other processes as well. There are legitimate and important roles of processing speeds (e.g., Salthouse, 1996), knowledge and practice (e.g., Ericsson & Kintsch, 1995), verbal memory abilities (e.g., Gathercole & Baddeley, 1993), visuospatial memory abilities (e.g., Hitch, Halliday, Schaafstal, & Schraagen, 1988; Logie et al., 2000), dual-task coordination (Logie, Cocchini, Della Sala, & Baddeley, 2004), and partially separable executive processes (Miyake, Friedman, Emerson, Witzki, & Howerter, 2000).

There is likely to be enough confusion among people with differing views that it is not entirely clear who agrees with whom. I emphasized this point in my commentary on Ruchkin et al. (2003); see Cowan (2003). Ruchkin et al. perceived their views as *proceduralist* in that the areas of the brain involved in the initial processing and long-term storage of particular information are also the areas activated in working memory of these types of information. The frontal attentional areas activate particular posterior regions of the brain involved in particular types of processing, including temporal areas for verbal information, occipital areas for visual information, and so on. They distinguished this view from one in which there are specialized *structures* for different types of working memory, a view attributed to Alan Baddeley (e.g., Baddeley, 1986). Nevertheless, regardless of whether one believes that there are specialized working memory structures or not, Ruchkin et al., Baddeley, and I all fall into the same general camp that maintains that there are at least specialized *processes* for working memory, and distinguishable processes for different types of working memory. We all appear to disagree with the view that a common set of processes predominates in all memory tasks, with no distinction between working memory and long-term memory processes (e.g., Nairne, 2002). My objection to such a view is that there are subtle but important differences between short- and long-term memory phenomena, some of which were detailed by Cowan (1995, pp. 118–134).

☐ FINAL CAUSES (FUNCTIONS) OF CAPACITY LIMITS

Some Initial Observations

Discussions of the functions of working memory capacity and its limits can only be asked within a general philosophical context. A starting point that is conventional within the scientific discourse is Darwin's (1859) theory of evolution. For example, consider the context of a religious, monotheistic view including a literal interpretation of the Bible, a view to which I do not personally subscribe. There may be no definitive answer to the capacity question from that view but one could speculate that God, being omnipotent and omniscient, must have no working memory limit. Although man was supposedly made in God's image, certain limitations might have been imposed to keep man in his place. It could be for that reason that people have limitations, in working memory capacity or otherwise. It is a shame, though, that the number of primary commandments (10) exceeds the magical number seven (Miller, 1956), and far exceeds the magical four (Cowan, 2001) unless some expert chunking processes have been carried out.

A starting point that is, naturally, more conventional within scientific discourse is Darwin's (1859) theory of evolution involving survival of the fittest. According to this view, one presumably would take into account that species mutate and that mutations that confer sufficient advantages to the species survive, along with the changed species. From this point of view, one would presume that there are reasons why it was helpful for humans and other intelligent species to have the ability to process some information in more detail at the expense of forgoing other information processing; that is, to have selective attention. If working memory were not limited, it might be more difficult to process any information in sufficient depth. It is easy to see this and to see also that it could be advantageous to be able to allocate attention flexibly, zooming in to focus on a small amount of information intensively or zooming out to apprehend a larger stimulus field (or to ruminate on a "soup" of interrelated thoughts, perhaps). The additional question that would require more thought here is why there would be any kind of advantage to limiting the number of objects that could be attended or apprehended at once to a mere handful, as opposed to spreading attention widely across many objects concurrently.

One simple answer might be that any organism has to operate in a short period and with limited metabolic resources. Perhaps the resources that it would have taken to have a larger working memory capacity were better spent on some other capabilities, such as physical prowess.

Another possible answer is that there is no good reason. In fact, it is entirely possible that a larger working memory capacity would have been preferable, was doable, but still did not happen. If this is the case, one might expect working memory capacity to expand in the future, assuming that it offers a sufficient survival advantage. The basis for this kind of reasoning is that evolution is a trial-and-error process and may not have reached perfection yet. (Or it may be that, as our technology develops, the need for working memory capacity increases.) One does not need to make the case that every aspect of the contemporary human is ideal for survival and necessary; the human appendix may not be necessary, for example, and inclinations toward suicide in some individuals probably are not ideal for the species' survival. Our current working memory capacity could just reflect our place in the middle of an ongoing evolutionary process, not an end point.

Efficiency of Search

An idea that seems more intriguing is that our working memory capacity is in some sense close to ideal. Several authors have made that argument on mathematical grounds. Two of them argued that a working memory capacity of about four items may allow the most efficient working memory search operations.

Dirlam (1972) carried out such an analysis on the basis of the assumption that memory is structured hierarchically. We organize our thoughts and perceptions according to certain categories, and then according to categories within categories, and so on, and ultimately according to items within those categories. The process that was modeled was one in which there is a search through memory to gain access to a particular item. The question asked was whether, with certain additional simplifying assumptions, one can identify the organization that would make memory most efficient, in terms of how many items should be grouped together to form a single chunk.

The specific example that was given was one in which there are 1024 items in memory, to be inspected one at a time until a particular one is located. If items were retrieved one by one in random order, on average it would take 512.5 inspections (halfway through the set) to reach the desired item; this is what is known as a *self-terminating search* because the search process ends when the desired item is found. The next assumption was that a categorical organization provides a benefit. For example, suppose the items were divided into four categories, with 256 items in each category. Suppose also that, for each category, one learned a category heading that, when inspected, indicated whether or not the desired item was included in the category, without that category having to be searched. Then one would have to inspect only 2.5 category headings on average (halfway between the second and third category of four) and then inspect 128.5 items within that category on average (halfway through the items in the category), for a total of 131 inspections.

It was then mathematically shown that, no matter how many levels of organization the memory system has, the average number of inspections is minimized if the average number of items on each level is 3.59. That is, the ideal is to have an average of 3.59 items per level 1 category, an average of 3.59 level 1 category headings within each level 2 category heading, and so on. (With a larger number of items or headings per category, additional inspections must occur within the selected category whereas, with a smaller number of items or headings per category, additional categories much be inspected.) The solution was found by expressing the number of inspections in terms of the number of categories per level and the number of items overall, and finding a minimum of the equation using differentiation (a basic technique of calculus).

Dirlam (1972) also carried out a second analysis in which it was not the mean number of inspections that was minimized, but the maximum number of inspections. If one allows the mean number of inspections to be a little larger, one can arrange things so that it rules out very long searches. In this case, the ideal comes out to the natural logarithm e, which is approximately 2.7.

MacGregor (1987) had a similar idea, apparently unaware of Dirlam's work; he did not cite Dirlam. He imposed many of the same assumptions, but imposed an additional simplifying constraint. He examined the case in which items are unorganized and the case in which there is one level of organization. His question was how many items there must be before the search process is facilitated by organization. I will present his reasoning in a bit more mathematical detail; the gist of the method can be understood even with somewhat less effort.

Let s = the expected number of elements examined to complete a search, where elements refer to either items or category headings. Let c_1 = the average number of items per category and let c_2 = the number of categories. The number of items in memory is n. The minimal value of n for grouping to be helpful was derived separately for a serial exhaustive search (i.e., search through all items before rendering the result) and for a serial self-terminating search (i.e., search ending when the target item is found).

For exhaustive search it was stated that $s = c_1 + c_2$ because all elements must be searched. We also know that $n = c_1 \times c_2$ (i.e., the number of categories times items per category equals the total number of items). Combining equations, we get $s = c_1 + (n/c_1)$. When this equation is differentiated to find the minimum value of s, the minimum occurs for c_1^2 = n, which, when combined with the equation $n = c_1 \times c_2$, further yields c_1 = c_2. For a self-terminating search, the derivation (which wasn't shown) differs, but it was said that the outcome, to this point, is the same.

The final steps of the derivation yield different results for the exhaustive and self-terminating searches. First, consider exhaustive searches. If there is no categorical organization, then $s = n$. If there is, $s = c_1 + c_2$. Given that $c_1 = c_2$ (see previous), $s = 2 \times c_1$. The one-level and two-level organizations result in the same number of elements inspected, therefore, when $n = 2 \times c_1$. Given the result that $c_1^2 = n$, it is easy to obtain a solution to these two equations jointly: $n = 4$. That is, when there are four items, it does not matter whether grouping is used or not but, when $n > 4$, grouping helps.

The logic for the self-terminating search was similar but the values for how many elements had to be searched was different. The result came to an n of approximately 5.83.

Dirlam (1972) and MacGregor (1987) both considered only serial searches. More recent studies favor a model in which memory-search processes occur for all elements within a category in parallel, in such a way that the search time is slower when there are more elements in the category, and terminates when the target element is found. That is, they favor a parallel, capacity-limited, self-terminating search (Ashby, Tein, & Balakrishnan, 1993; Ratcliff, 1978; Van Zandt & Townsend, 1993). It appears to me that MacGregor's analysis can be modified to consider this sort of search and leads to the same result as the serial, exhaustive search: $n = 4$. To see this, consider a constant unit of time t, such that the time S to search in parallel through n items until the target is found averages $n \times t$. (This function produces the linear search slope that is typically obtained.) If there is grouping, then the total search time will be $S = c_1 \times t + c_2 \times t$. Given that $n = c_1 \times c_2$, we can remove c_2 from the equation: $S = c_1 \times t + (n/c_1) \times t$ so that $S/t = c_1 + (n/c_1)$. The differentiation process is the same as one MacGregor used but with S/t in place of s, the number of searches. It indicates that S/t reaches a minimum when $c_1^2 = n$. Given that t is a constant, this minimum occurs at the same point at which S, the search time, reaches a minimum. Given that $n = c_1 \times c_2$, this further yields $c_1 = c_2$ as previously, so the search time with grouping in place, $S = c_1 \times t + c_2 \times t$, can be rewritten as $= 2 \times c_1 \times t$. The one-level and two-level organizations result in the same number of elements inspected, therefore, when $n \times t = 2 \times c_1 \times t$. Given that $c_1^2 = n$ at the point of minimization, it follows that $n = 4$ in order for grouped and ungrouped search times to be the same. That is, grouping helps when $n > 4$.

There are limits to how much stock can be placed in these calculations. They depend on several important assumptions about searching through category headings when items are grouped. First, they depend on the assumption that a search through the category headings somehow indicates which items are within each category, thus avoiding the need to search through the items within any category except the correct one. It is not unfathomable that this is the case, but it is unclear what the mechanism would be. Second, the calculations depend on the assumption that searching through a certain number of categories is equal in difficulty to searching through a certain number of items. I know of no particular reason to assume that that is true. So the fortuitous outcomes of these simulations cannot be given much weight at present. In the future, perhaps it will be possible to shore up the assumptions on which they depend. It is with that possibility in mind that the present summary may prove to be of use.

The Starting-Small Argument

Newport (1990) brought up an argument that is rather counterintuitive, but intriguing nonetheless. In search of why it appears that young children learn languages more readily than older individuals, she suggested that the lower working memory capacity of young children may actually be an advantage rather than a disadvantage. According to this line of thought, learners of language must understand relatively small units, such as words, before they can understand larger units, such as phrases and sentences.

In subsequent computer modeling of a connectionist program that learns syntax, Elman (1993) confirmed that learning went faster if, at first, the language was input in smaller units or the working memory limits of the learning device started small. However, Rhode and Plaut (1999) found no such advantage when semantic clues also were included. In their words:

> ... the network's ability to represent and maintain information about an important word, such as the head noun, is reinforced by the advantage this information provides in predicting information within embedded phrases. As a result, the noun can more effectively aid in the prediction of the corresponding verb following the intervening material ... One source of such correlations in natural language are distributional biases, due to semantic factors, on which nouns typically co-occur with which verbs. For example, suppose dogs often chase cats. Over the course of training, the network has encountered chased more often after processing sentences beginning *The dog who* ... than after sentences beginning with other noun phrases. The network can, therefore, reduce prediction error within the embedded clause by retaining specific

information about the dog (beyond it being a singular noun). As a result, information on dog becomes available to support further predictions in the sentence as it continues (e.g. *The dog who chased the cat barked*) …. These considerations led us to believe that languages similar to Elman's but involving weak semantic constraints might result in less of an advantage for starting small in child language acquisition. (p. 72)

Subsequent research with adult humans to some extent supported the advantage of starting small, however. Cochran, McDonald, and Parault (1999) tested it by presenting sign language, sometimes with adults who were under a working memory load (tone counting). They found that learning was in some ways better, though in other ways worse, when learning occurred under load. Kersten and Earles (2001) used a spoken artificial language with animations illustrating the concepts (involving two types of motion of two objects and two possible directions of motion). They started some subjects with single words and started others with all three words of a sentence. Starting with one word first resulted in overall better language learning.

Although the status of the "starting-small" hypothesis is unresolved, it seems worth noting that the hypothesis only makes sense if there is a limit in how well strategies can be used to deploy attention optimally. If working memory capacity is a matter of attention and an individual is able to influence his or her own learning experience by zooming in on fewer objects in the field more intensively, then a larger working memory capacity should never be a disadvantage. In the study that found clear advantages of starting small (Kersten & Earles, 2001), it was the stimulus set size that was manipulated. My prediction is that the results would not be replicated if it were instead the working memory load that was manipulated because subjects who are not under load can flexibly allocate attention until they feel that they are learning optimally.

Another possible advantage of starting small was offered by Kareev (2000). Detecting the structure of the world can be conceived as detecting imperfect correlations between features. Detected correlations can lead to hypotheses to be tested out with further evidence. For example, in English there is probably a correlation between whether a noun ends in the phoneme *s* and whether it is plural or not. Most plural nouns end in *s* (e.g., bugs, hats), but some do not (e.g., deer), and some singular nouns end in the phoneme *s* (e.g., goose). Kareev pointed out that if a population correlation is moderate in size, then the expected *sample* correlation depends on the sample size; smaller samples lead to larger modal correlations. For example, suppose that there is a population of objects coming in two colors and two shapes and that there is a .6 correlation between color and shape (e.g., the majority of squares are red and the majority of circles are blue). If one randomly selects six or eight items and calculates the sample correlation, its modal value is somewhat higher than .6. Kareev suggested that this provides support for the magical number seven plus or minus two (Miller, 1956). It should be noted, though, that if the sample comprised only four objects, the modal correlation approached 1.0. A revised argument, then, is that an individual considering at most four objects at a time would be more likely to notice a correlation than an individual considering eight items at a time. The cost of noticing more correlations would be that some spurious correlations would be noticed, also, but that would not be a serious error if the detected correlations simply become hypotheses to be tested out further (e.g., "plural nouns end in *s*" or "squares are red and circles are blue"). Kareev, Lieberman, and Lev (1997) found support for their hypothesis, showing that adults with lower memory spans were more likely to detect correlations in the range of .2 to .6 than were higher span individuals, at the cost of detecting more spurious correlations.

There is one more question that might be vexing to the less-is-more proponents. How much less is children's working memory? According to some investigators, the ability to be aware of the numerosity of one, two, or three objects is well-developed even in infancy (e.g., Feigenson, Carey, & Hauser, 2002a; Feigenson, Carey, & Spelke, 2002b) and in animals (Dehaene, 1997; Gallistel & Gelman, 2000), whereas it is impossible for these subjects to keep track of more objects. Yet, Cowan et al. (1999) found that, with a memory-for-ignored-speech procedure, children did remember fewer items than adults. Results of Rose, Feldman, and Jankowski (2001) within infants are in line with that. Infants 5 to 12 months of age were shown sets of one to four objects and then had to discriminate between each old object and a new one. There was development within this age range but, for each of the ages of infant studied, the modal infant could recognize two but not three objects from a set.

It is possible only to speculate why these studies appear to disagree. An important difference between the studies is that the method of Feigenson et al. (2002a, 2002b) required only that infants keep track of how many objects were presented, whereas the methods of Cowan et al. (1999), Rose et al. (2001), and Ross-Sheehy, Oakes, and Luck, (2003) required that the participants know the identities of objects. A fascinating and unanswered question is how these two capabilities relate to one another.

However, one newer study suggests that this may not be the critical distinction between studies. Ross-Sheehy et al. (2003) asked whether infants could detect changes within series of colored arrays and found that the changes were detected in 6.5-month-old infants with one object but not two, whereas 10-month-old infants could detect a change with an array size of four but not six objects. This study requires knowledge of the identity of the objects and yet reveals a capability more in line with what Feigenson et al. (2002a, 2002b) suggested.

Another possible difference between studies is that the ones showing capacities of three or four items in infants (Feigenson et al., 2002a, 2002b; Ross-Sheehy et al., 2003) used a simultaneous presentation of items to be held in working memory at the same time, whereas studies showing lower capacities in infants or children (Cowan et al., 1999; Rose et al., 2001) used a sequential presentation. However, Cowan et al. (in press-a) showed development in the visual array task.

Perhaps the basic attentional capacity does not undergo development but, rather, what develops is the ability to fill that capacity efficiently from a sensory-memory field (such as the stream of spoken digits in Cowan et al., 1999). Then, "starting small" would not be a cause of good learning but, rather, an effect. According to such a view, children (and other people beginning the process of learning a language) start small because their attentional capacity is filled with smaller chunks than adults or more experienced individuals.

It should be clear that the question of whether children start small, and in what way, as well as the question of why starting small is advantageous, and in what way, comprise fertile grounds for additional research.

☐ RECONCILIATION BETWEEN TYPES OF CAUSATION

We have now considered the reasons for capacity limits on four different levels of causation: essentially, the levels of determiners, formal models, mechanisms and substrates, and teleological functions. How are all of them to be evaluated? That is a difficult question, but it seems worth noting that all types of causation eventually must be considered together. It seems possible to do this in an evolutionary framework. To consider the literature on evolutionary trends is beyond the scope of this book and beyond my abilities, but I nevertheless think it may be useful to invent a story illustrating how the different levels of causation might work together. (For one evolutionary approach incorporating a general working memory factor, see Geary, 2004).

One can distinguish two fundamental types of behavior based on past learning. These might be termed *probabilistic* and *logical* modes of behavior. In the probabilistic mode, the strengths of different learned responses compete based on a simple summation and based on generalization gradients.

For example, an animal might see a larger animal and might recognize danger from previous encounters with other large animals (which were in some ways similar). There may be a tendency to want to run away and, the larger the animal might be, the greater that tendency might be. There may also be tendencies to freeze, hide, or attack the large intruder, and these tendencies will be weighed in the brain and the stronger one will win. In the logical mode, in contrast, behavior is based on a reasoning process that can yield predictions about the likely outcome of alternative possible behaviors. According to this principle, there may be a tendency to want to run but, if it is judged that an attempt to run is likely to fail (e.g., because the animal is cornered, the large intruder seems fast, or running is likely to draw attention), the animal can suppress that urge and instead freeze or try to hide without much movement. So both modes of behavior sometimes could lead to the same outcome but, it is assumed, the logical mode is more often correct.

It is likely that the logical model of behavior places a greater demand on attention and working memory. The use of attention is to select the inputs that seem most important and the behaviors that seem most helpful, while suppressing the relative weight of other inputs and activated behaviors (e.g., prepotent responses).

The simplest mode of attention would allow attention to one stimulus or behavior at a time, suppressing all others. However, that mode would not seem to allow a consideration of interactions between features. For example, in deciding whether to run or freeze, one must consider both the danger from the intruder and the likelihood of outrunning the intruder from one's present position. One can suppose that the attention function involves pulsating neural inputs that enhance the functioning of features belonging to an attended stimulus and makes their neural activity more synchronous. Perhaps it took additional brain evolution for attention to activate features of several objects or thoughts concurrently without losing their distinctiveness from one another (the function of oscillations discussed by Lisman & Idiart, 1995). Even then, the risk of too much overlap between object representations would limit the number of concurrently held items in working memory (Usher et al., 2001), avoiding inefficiency (Dirlam, 1972; MacGregor, 1987). Thus we have briefly considered a determiner of working memory (attentional processes), a mechanism (pulsating features representing objects), aspects of formal modeling (accounts of why overlap between object representations constrains working memory), and teleological reasons why working memory and its limits might evolve (the need to enhance processing of some stimuli or behaviors relative to others; efficiency of search).

It is possible that one may need to decide between hypotheses on different levels. For example, the concept of too much overlap between representations, in the area of formal modeling (Usher et al., 2001), and the concept of an optimal chunk size for efficient search (Dirlam, 1972; MacGregor, 1987) might both happen to be important, or it could be that only one of them is important. It is also possible that the ideas of causation at the different levels work together. Cowan (2001) illustrated this as follows:

> The process of scanning through the items in STM [short-term memory] has been employed theoretically by both the teleological and the physiological theorists. For example, the teleological argument that MacGregor (1987) built using an exhaustive scan resulted in the conclusion that the scan would be most efficient if the number of items per group were four. This conclusion was based on the assumption that the amount of time it takes to access a group to determine whether a particular item is present within it is equal to the amount of time it then takes to access each item within the appropriate group once that group is selected, so as finally to identify the probed item. This concept can be mapped directly onto the concept of the set of items (or chunks) in capacity-limited STM being represented by a single cycle of a low-frequency oscillation (5 to 12 Hz) with each item mapped onto a different cycle of a 40-Hz oscillation, riding on top of the 5 to 12 Hz oscillation. These figures are in line with the teleological data and memory capacity data reviewed above if the rate for the slow oscillation is close to about 10 Hz, so that four items would fit in each of the slower cycles. As suggested by Shastri and Ajjanagadde (1993) and others, the cyclic search process could be employed recursively. For example, at one point in a probed recognition process there could be up to four chunks in the capacity-limited store. Once the correct chunk is identified, the contents of STM would be replaced by the items contained within that chunk, now "unpacked," so that the contents of the chunk can be scanned in detail. In present theoretical terms, the focus of attention need not focus on multiple levels of representation at the same time. (p. 110)

I hope that I have shown that there is something to be gained in the exploration of working memory capacity limits by thinking about causation on multiple levels together.

Epilogue: Working Memory Capacity, Life, Death, and Cars

On Wednesday, August 13, 2003, a conversation with a reporter from the *Los Angeles Times*, Benedict Carey, startled me out of my scholastic thoughts. He was calling because, as he explained in a newspaper article published 5 days later, "a UC Irvine professor had driven to work and forgotten to take his 10-month-old son out of the car. The boy later died of heat exposure, as have at least three other young children left unattended in cars in the West this summer." He was seeking advice from memory researchers regarding whether it is possible that a responsible, loving parent could make this mistake, or whether it had to be a jaded excuse.

It was quite possible for a child to be forgotten in the car, I assured him. Schacter (2001) has recorded anecdotes about how people have forgotten other very important things. The perceived importance of an event is not enough to keep it in one's awareness or to return it from long-term memory back to awareness at the appropriate moment. I later received other telephone calls from other reporters concerning separate, unrelated incidents. In October, a mother in Cottage Grove, Wisconsin, had a sleepless night as her severely disabled 2-year-old son spent his first night in an institution; she left her 6-month-old daughter in the car the next day, forgetting to bring her to day care, and the baby died. There were other cases in New Jersey and in Montreal. Articles discussing these cases appeared in Canadian newspapers in mid- and late August. An aggrieved parent who had started a Web site on the problem (www.4rkidssake.org) said that between 2000 and mid-2003, 138 hyperthermia deaths had been tracked to children left in cars. However, according to other sources, many car deaths occur not only because of heat, but also because of asphyxiation, unfortunately because newer cars are made airtight to eliminate noise.

Taking the baby out of the car is a good example of what is termed *prospective memory*. It might be reasonable to suppose that the reporters contacted the wrong person, inasmuch as I have studied working memory and not prospective memory. However, prospective memory describes the task and not the mechanisms that are used to carry out that task. Those processes have to involve working memory heavily. This is likely to be true in two ways. One can succeed in a prospective memory task either by memorizing a set of relevant cues (e.g., "When I see the grocery store on my right, I will plan to turn right at the next intersection") or by maintaining the relevant plan in working memory without interruption (e.g., "turn right at Gilford Street ... turn right at Gilford Street"). The latter method clearly makes use of working memory. It is likely that the former method, involving memorization of a cue to be used later, also makes use of some of the same working memory processes (such as central executive processes) in a different way, to encode the cue effectively. Moreover, after the memorized cue is observed, the retrieved information about the prospective task still may have to be held for a short time in working memory. The cue may tell you to turn right at the first intersection after the grocery store, but an intervening event, such as traffic or conversation, might make you forget the information again before the prospective task can be carried out.

Recent research suggests that prospective memory can be lost quickly in some people. Einstein, McDaniel, Manzi, Cochran, and Baker (2000) assigned a task in which encountering the word "system" or "technique" within a reading passage was supposed to lead to the response of pressing a computer key. The key press was to be immediate or, in another condition, delayed by 30 to 40 s until the current task ended. This prospective memory task also was sometimes combined with a secondary task in which a handheld counter was to be pressed if two odd numbers in a row were heard within a number series. The participants were younger and elderly adults. The elderly had a disadvantage at the prospective memory task, as they often do, especially when the response was to be postponed and most especially under dual-task conditions. Einstein, McDaniel, Williford, Pagan, and Dismukes (2003) showed that forgetting of intentions over short periods (as short as 10 s) during distraction was difficult to overcome through strategies such as rehearsal.

In any area of life involving danger, it seems likely that there are multiple ways in which working memory is critically involved. In driving, for example, recent research has shown that performance is dangerously affected by telephone conversations (Strayer & Johnston, 2001). The interference does not come primarily from holding the telephone, as is assumed by driving restrictions put into law in many states within the United States, but rather from the conversational requirement—the planning and execution of language production and language comprehension.

Part of the problem is a phenomenon know as *inattentional blindness* (Rensink, 2002; Rensink, O'Regan, & Clark, 1997; Simons, 2000; Simons & Levin, 1998). Although people are very good at attending to a handful of elements or limited aspects of the current environment (Cowan, 2001), they are surprisingly poor at noticing much about the remainder of the environment. What they get from the environment appears to be, primarily, a schematic view of how all of the pieces fit together, with several salient chunks of information held in the focus of attention, but not much detail about those pieces. Of course, you usually notice abrupt environmental changes in situations such as one in which, say, you are driving and staring straight ahead when a light turns from green to yellow in the center of your visual field. An isolated physical change tends to be noticed (Broadbent, 1958; Cherry, 1953; Cowan, 1988, 1995, 1999; Sokolov, 1963). Imagine, though, that you have turned away from the light when it was green, perhaps to face the passenger while holding a conversation, and now have turned back to the road. The abrupt change in the light was missed and the different color (yellow instead of green) occurs along with a massive change in the entire visual field (from shifting one's gaze from the passenger to the straight-ahead view). Under such circumstances, you might notice the color change only if you preserve part of your working memory for the task goal of driving safely, along with a subgoal of being aware of changes in traffic conditions and signals. Usually, that will be the case. Holding a conversation could make you lose the drive-safely goal momentarily, at just the wrong moment.

In the test situations that have been used to examine inattentional blindness (e.g., Rensink, 2002; Simons, 2000), even having the appropriate task goal does not suffice. That is because the task goal is to examine a complex visual scene or array, examine another one that is separated temporally from the first (so that a simple abrupt change cannot be observed), and determine if anything has changed. A scene of people sitting at a restaurant might be replaced by another scene in which there are incidental changes such as a bottle being replaced by a glass or the color of a person's sweater changing. Many subjects do not notice such changes. These situations are formally similar to those in which a feature (e.g., color, orientation) of an element in an array changes from one array to another (e.g., Luck & Vogel, 1997). It is clear from that kind of procedure, as discussed throughout this book, that only about three to five elements from the first array typically can be preserved in working memory to allow a correct response.

The inattentional blindness phenomenon might easily translate into driving behavior. Imagine that you are driving along a country road with little traffic. The road winds among pine trees and some drifts of snow. As you drive along, you look away from the road for a moment and then look back. Even though you are staring straight ahead, there are many objects in the attentional field such as boulders, trees, and a picnic table along the side of the road, as well as several road signs. Given the complexity of all of this, inattentional blindness prevents you from realizing immediately that one of the objects at the side of the road is a deer. By the time you realize, the deer has stepped into the road and there is no way for you to stop without hitting it. Inattentional blindness has cost you the time and expense of a car repair, or possibly much worse. We sometimes pay for the limits in our working memory capacity. Becoming aware of these limitations in human information processing may allow us to minimize how much we pay.

Human social justice also pays a price for the limitation in working memory, and for our general unawareness of this limitation. This is demonstrated, for example, in a report by Goldinger, Kleider, Azuma, and Beike (2003), who showed that irrelevant aspects of a legal case (presented in a story or vignette) could influence decisions in a way that depended on working memory. The apparent reason was that the questions differed in cognitive complexity. For example, they explained (Goldinger et al., p. 82), that "… one story kernel involved Mark, a basketball season-ticket holder. In the control version, Mark attends a game, sitting in his usual seat. A light fixture falls from the ceiling, breaking his foot. In the counterfactual version, Mark takes advantage of an open seat closer to the floor, and the light falls on his foot." The question was how much money he should be awarded by the stadium owner. Logically, he was not at all responsible for his own injury, no matter whether he stuck to his usual seat or moved to another one. However, in the second version there is the temptation to speculate that, if Mark had not moved to a new seat, he would have been luckier and would not have been under the falling light fixture. It takes free working memory capacity to read about the second scenario while also realizing that the question of whether he would have been safe had he not moved is irrelevant to the case. It was found that lower span individuals awarded less money to the victim in the latter case, in which he had moved to a new seat, but only in a condition that required holding a memory load of six bisyllabic nonwords in addition to the story judgment. (There was a much smaller effect in high-span individuals.) I am reminded of a scene within the musical *Chicago* in which the slick lawyer explains how he liked to "razzle dazzle" the jurors.

The effect of a memory load during the judgment phase of the trial was almost as much as if the load were presented during both reading of the story and judgment. The razzle-dazzle process does not have to occur throughout the encoding process, but only at a point at which it is critical to access all of the relevant information and concepts at once.

Perhaps, though, it is time to emphasize the advantages of working memory rather than the drawbacks of its limitations. We have seen that working memory is a key aspect of human intelligence. It is most necessary to use working memory when the situation is one for which the person does not have a planned script to follow; it is useful for new situations in which it is difficult to keep in mind the rules of what is going on. This, too, is where human beings excel. They are not superior to other animals in any particular environmental niche, but they are better able to adapt to a new niche. They do so by using working memory to keep track of new, unfamiliar aspects of the environment.

Garlick (2003) has made the case that what differentiates individuals who are more intelligent from those who are less intelligent is the superior ability of the brains of more intelligent people to adapt to the environment. This type of view reconciles the high heritability of intelligence with the finding that neural connections are highly responsive to the environment. In fact, when the environment is poor and impoverished, the heritability of intelligence as measured in comparisons of twins is considerably lower than is found in more ordinary environments (Turkheimer, Haley, Waldron, D'Onofrio, & Gottesman, 2003).

If, as the present perspective suggests, new learning takes place when items residing in the focus of attention concurrently are linked together to form new episodic memories, then surely the manner in which attention is used to form these new links is a major area of individual difference also. We have seen that there are close correlations between the deployment and scope of attention, on one hand, and performance on complex cognitive tasks, on the other hand.

The study of working memory is telling us some very human things about ourselves, and about some of the underlying causes of our strengths and weaknesses as humans. There is much left to find out.

References

Allen, P. A., & Coyne, A. C. (1989). Are there age differences in chunking? *Journal of Gerontology, Psychological Sciences, 44*, 181–183.

Allen, P. A., & Crozier, L. C. (1992). Age and ideal chunk size. *Journal of Gerontology, Psychological Sciences, 47*, 47–51.

Alvarez, G. A., & Cavanagh, P. (2004). The capacity of visual short-term memory is set both by visual information load and by number of objects. *Psychological Science, 15*, 106–111.

Anderson, J. R., & Lebière, C. (1998). *Atomic components of thought*. Hillsdale, NJ: Erlbaum.

Anderson, M. C., & Green, C. (2001). Suppressing unwanted memories by executive control. *Nature, 410*, 366–369.

Anderson, J. R., & Matessa, M. (1997). A production system theory of serial memory. *Psychological Review, 104*, 728–748.

Andrews, G., & Halford, G. S. (2002). A cognitive complexity metric applied to cognitive development. *Cognitive Psychology, 45*, 153–219.

Andrews, G., Halford, G. S., Bunch, K. M., Bowden, D., & Jones, T. (2003). Theory of mind and relational complexity. *Child Development, 74*, 1476–1499.

Ashby, F. G., Tein, Y.-J., & Balakrishnan, J. D. (1993). Response time distributions in memory scanning. *Journal of Mathematical Psychology, 37*, 526–555.

Ashcraft, M. H., & Kirk, E. P. (2001). The relationships among working memory, math anxiety, and performance. *Journal of Experimental Psychology: General, 130*, 224–237.

Asimov, I., & Shulman, J. A. (1988). *Isaac Asimov's book of science and nature quotations*. New York: Weidenfeld & Nicolson.

Atkinson, R. C., & Shiffrin, R. M. (1968). Human memory: A proposed system and its control processes. In K. W. Spence & J. T. Spence (Eds.), *The psychology of learning and motivation: Advances in research and theory* (Vol. 2, pp. 89–195). New York: Academic Press.

Awh, E., & Jonides, J. (2001). Overlapping mechanisms of attention and spatial working memory. *Trends in Cognitive Sciences, 5*, 119–126.

Baars, B. J. (1988). *A cognitive theory of consciousness*. London: Cambridge University Press.

Baars, B. J. (2001). A biocognitive approach to the conscious core of immediate memory. *Behavioral and Brain Sciences, 24*, 115–116.

Baars, B. J., & Franklin, S. (2003). How conscious experience and working memory interact. *Trends in Cognitive Sciences, 7*, 166–172.

213

Baddeley, A. (2000). The episodic buffer: a new component of working memory? *Trends in cognitive sciences, 4,* 417–423.

Baddeley, A. (2001a). The magic number and the episodic buffer. *Behavioral and Brain Sciences, 24,* 117–118.

Baddeley, A. (2003). Working memory and language: an overview. *Journal of Communication Disorders, 36,* 189–208.

Baddeley, A. D. (1986). *Working memory.* Oxford, England: Clarendon Press.

Baddeley, A. D. (2001b). Is working memory still working? *American Psychologist, 56,* 851–864.

Baddeley, A. D., & Levy, B. A. (1971). Semantic coding and short-term memory. *Journal of Experimental Psychology, 89,* 132–136.

Baddeley, A., Gathercole, S., & Papagno, C. (1998). The phonological loop as a language learning device. *Psychological Review, 105,* 158–173.

Baddeley, A., & Hitch, G. J. (1974). Working memory. In G. Bower (Ed.), *Recent advances in learning and motivation* (Vol. VIII). New York: Academic Press.

Baddeley, A., Lewis, V., & Vallar, G. (1984). Exploring the articulatory loop. *The Quarterly Journal of Experimental Psychology, 36A,* 233–252.

Baddeley, A., & Logie, R. H. (1999). Working memory: The multiple-component model. In A. Miyake & P. Shah (Eds.), *Models of working memory: Mechanisms of active maintenance and executive control* (pp. 28–61). Cambridge, UK: Cambridge University Press.

Baddeley, A., Papagno, C., & Vallar, G. (1988). When long-term learning depends on short-term storage. *Journal of Memory and Language, 27,* 586–595.

Baddeley, A. D., Thomson, N., & Buchanan, M. (1975). Word length and the structure of short-term memory. *Journal of Verbal Learning and Verbal Behavior, 14,* 575–589.

Baddeley, A., & Wilson, B. A. (2002). Prose recall and amnesia: Implications for the structure of working memory. *Neuropsychologia, 40,* 1737–1743.

Balota, D. A. (1983). Automatic semantic activation and episodic memory encoding. *Journal of Verbal Learning and Verbal Behavior, 22,* 88–104.

Balota, D. A., & Duchek, J. M. (1986). Voice-specific information and the 20-second delayed suffix effect. *Journal of Experimental Psychology: Learning, Memory, and Cognition, 12,* 509–516.

Barrouillet, P., Bernardin, S., & Camos, V. (2004). Time constraints and resource sharing in adults' working memory spans. *Journal of Experimental Psychology: General, 133,* 83–100.

Barrouillet, P., & Camos, V. (2001). Developmental increase in working memory span: Resource sharing or temporal decay? *Journal of Memory and Language, 45,* 1–20.

Barrouillet, P., & Fayol, M. (1998). From algorithmic computing to direct retrieval: Evidence from number and alphabetic arithmetic in children and adults. *Memory and Cognition, 26,* 355–368.

Basak, C., & Verhaeghen, P. (2003). Subitizing speed, subitizing range, counting speed, the Stroop effect, and aging: Capacity differences and speed equivalence. *Psychology & Aging, 18,* 240–249.

Bayliss, D. M., Jarrold, C., Gunn, D. M., & Baddeley, A. D. (2003). The complexities of complex span: Explaining individual differences in working memory in children and adults. *Journal of Experimental Psychology: General, 132,* 71–92.

Becker, M. W., Pashler, H., & Anstis, S. M. (2000). The role of iconic memory in change-detection tasks. *Perception, 29,* 273–286.

Bjork, R. A., & Whitten, W. B. (1974). Recency-sensitive retrieval processes in long-term free recall. *Cognitive Psychology, 6,* 173–189.

Bjorklund, D. F., & Harnishfeger, K. K. (1990). The resources construct in cognitive development: Diverse sources of evidence and a theory of inefficient inhibition. *Developmental Review, 10,* 48–71.

Bousfield, W. A., Sedgewick, C. H., & Cohen, B. H. (1954). Certain temporal characteristics of the recall of verbal associates. *American Journal of Psychology, 67,* 111–118.

Boutla, M., Supalla, T., Newport, E. L., & Bavelier, D. (2004). Short-term memory span: insights from sign language. *Nature Neuroscience, 7,* 997–1002.

Bowles, A. R., & Healy, A. F. (2003). The effects of grouping on the learning and long-term retention of spatial and temporal information. *Journal of Memory and Language, 48,* 92–102.

Broadbent, D. E. (1958). *Perception and communication.* New York: Pergamon Press.

Broadbent, D. E. (1971). *Decision and stress.* London: Academic Press.

Broadbent, D. E., & Broadbent, M. H. P. (1973). Grouping strategies in short-term memory for alpha-numeric lists. *Bulletin of the British Psychological Society, 26,* 135.

Brooks, L. R. (1968). Spatial and verbal components of the act of recall. *Canadian Journal of Psychology, 22,* 349–368.

Brown, G. D. A., Preece, T., & Hulme, C. (2000). Oscillator-based memory for serial order. *Psychological Review, 107,* 127–181.

Brown, J. (1958). Some tests of the decay theory of immediate memory. *Quarterly Journal of Experimental Psychology, 10,* 12–21.

Brown, J. (1959). Information, redundancy and decay of the memory trace. In *Mechanisation of Thought Processes: Proceedings of a Symposium held at the National Physical Laboratory on 24, 25, 26, and 27 November, 1958* (pp. 729–752). National Physical Laboratory Symposium Number 10. London: Her Majesty's Stationery Office.

Bundesen, C. (1990). A theory of visual attention. *Psychological Review, 97,* 523–547.

Bunting, M. F. (2003). *Why working memory measures "work:" Proactive interference in tests of immediate memory.* Unpublished doctoral dissertation, University of Illinois, Chicago.

Bunting, M. F., & Cowan, N. (2004, November). *Working-memory retrieval takes attention: Effects of distraction under time pressure.* Poster presented at the annual meeting of the Psychonomic Society, Minneapolis.

Burrows, D. & Okada, R. (1975). Memory retrieval from long and short lists. *Science, 188,* 1031–1033.

Cantor, J., & Engle, R. W. (1989). The influence of concurrent load on mouthed and vocalized modality effects. *Memory & Cognition, 17,* 701–711.

Caplan, D., Rochon, E., & Waters, G. S. (1992). Articulatory and phonological determinants of word length effects in span tasks. *Quarterly Journal of Experimental Psychology, 45A,* 177–192.

Carlyon, R. P., Cusack, R., Foxton, J. M., & Robertson, I. H. (2001). Effects of attention and unilateral neglect on auditory stream segregation. *Journal of Experimental Psychology: Human Perception and Performance, 27,* 115–127.

Carr, H. A. (1933). The quest for constants. *Psychological Review, 40,* 514–532.

Carretti, B., Cornoldi, C., De Beni, R., & Palladino, P. (2004). What happens to information to be suppressed in working-memory tasks? Short and long term effects. *Quarterly Journal of Experimental Psychology, 57A,* 1059–1084.

Case, R. (1972). Validation of a neo-Piagetian mental capacity construct. *Journal of Experimental Child Psychology, 14,* 287–302.

Case, R. (1995). Capacity-based explanations of working memory growth: A brief history and reevaluation. In F. E. Weinert & W. Schneider (Eds.), *Memory performance and competencies: Issues in growth and development* (pp. 23–44). Mahwah, NJ: Erlbaum.

Case, R., Kurland, D. M., & Daneman, M. (1979). *Operational efficiency and the growth of M-space.* Paper presented at the annual convention of the Society for Research in Child Development, San Francisco.

Case, R., Kurland, D. M., & Goldberg, J. (1982). Operational efficiency and the growth of short-term memory span. *Journal of Experimental Child Psychology, 33,* 386–404.

Cattell, J. M. (1885). Über die Trägheit der Netzhaut und des Sehcentrums. *Philosophische Studien., 3,* 94–127.

Chalfonte, B. L., & Johnson, M. K. (1996). Feature memory and binding in young and older adults. *Memory & Cognition, 24,* 403–416.

Charness, N. (1976). Memory for chess positions: Resistance to interference. *Journal of Experimental Psychology: Human Learning and Memory, 2,* 641–653.

Chase, W., & Simon, H. A. (1973). The mind's eye in chess. In W. G. Chase (Ed.), *Visual information processing* (pp. 215–281). New York: Academic Press.

Chein, J. M. (2003). *Evaluating models of working memory: fMRI and behavioral evidence on the effects of concurrent irrelevant information.* Unpublished doctoral dissertation, University of Pittsburgh.

Chein, J. M., & Ravizza, S. M., & Fiez, J. A. (2003). Using neuroimaging to evaluate models of working memory and their implications for language processing. *Journal of Neurolinguistics, 16,* 315–339.

Chen, Z., & Cowan, N. (in press). Capacity limits and length limits in immediate recall: A reconciliation. *Journal of Experimental Psychology: Learning, Memory, and Cognition.*

Cherry, E. C. (1953). Some experiments on the recognition of speech, with one and with two ears. *The Journal of the Acoustical Society of America, 25,* 975–979.

Cleeremans, A., & McClelland, J. L. (1991). Learning the structure of event sequences. *Journal of Experimental Psychology: General, 120,* 235–253.

Cocchini, G., Logie, R. H., Della Sala, S., MacPherson, S. E., & Baddeley, A. D. (2002). Concurrent performance of two memory tasks: Evidence for domain-specific working memory systems. *Memory & Cognition, 30,* 1086–1095.

Cochran, B. P., McDonald, J. L., & Parault, S. J. (1999). Too smart for their own good: The disadvantage of a superior processing capacity for adult language learners. *Journal of Memory and Language, 41,* 30–58.

Cohen, A., & Ivry, R. (1989). Illusory conjunctions inside and outside the focus of attention. *Journal of Experimental Psychology: Human Perception and Performance, 15,* 650–663.

Cohen, J. D., Perlstein, W. M., Braver, T. S., Nystrom, L. E., Noll, D. C., Jonides, J., et al. (1997). Temporal dynamics of brain activation during a working memory task. *Nature, 386,* 604–608.

Cohen, R. L., & Heath, M. (1990). The development of serial short-term memory and the articulatory loop hypothesis. *Intelligence, 14,* 151–171.

Cohen, R. L., & Sandberg, T. (1977). Relation between intelligence and short-term memory. *Cognitive Psychology, 9,* 534–554.

Colom, R., Rebollo, I., Abad, F. J., & Shih, P. C. (in press). Complex span tasks, simple span tasks, and cognitive abilities: A re-analysis of key studies. *Memory & Cognition.*

Conrad, R. (1964). Acoustic confusion in immediate memory. *British Journal of Psychology, 55,* 75–84.

Conway, A. R. A., Cowan, N., & Bunting, M. F. (2001). The cocktail party phenomenon revisited: The importance of working memory capacity. *Psychonomic Bulletin & Review, 8,* 331–335.

Conway, A. R. A., Cowan, N., Bunting, M. F., Therriault, D. J., & Minkoff, S. R. B. (2002). A latent variable analysis of working memory capacity, short-term memory capacity, processing speed, and general fluid intelligence. *Intelligence, 30,* 163–183.

Conway, A. R. A., & Engle, R. W. (1994). Working memory and retrieval: A resource-dependent inhibition model. *Journal of Experimental Psychology: General, 123,* 354–373.

Conway, A. R. A., & Engle, R. W. (1996). Individual differences in working memory capacity: More evidence for a general capacity theory. *Memory, 4,* 577–590.

Conway, A. R. A., Kane, M. J., & Engle, R. W. (2003). Working memory capacity and its relation to general intelligence. *Trends in Cognitive Sciences, 7,* 547–552.

Cooke, N. J., Atlas, R. S., Lane, D. M., & Berger, R. C. (1993). Role of high-level knowledge in memory for chess positions. *American Journal of Psychology, 106,* 321–351.

Cowan, N. (1988). Evolving conceptions of memory storage, selective attention, and their mutual constraints within the human information processing system. *Psychological Bulletin, 104,* 163–191.

Cowan, N. (1995). *Attention and memory: An integrated framework.* Oxford Psychology Series #26. New York: Oxford University Press.

Cowan, N. (1999). An embedded-processes model of working memory. In A. Miyake & P. Shah (Eds.), *Models of working memory: Mechanisms of active maintenance and executive control* (pp. 62–101). Cambridge, UK: Cambridge University Press.

Cowan, N. (2001). The magical number 4 in short-term memory: A reconsideration of mental storage capacity. *Behavioral and Brain Sciences, 24,* 87–185.

Cowan, N. (2003). Varieties of procedural accounts of working memory retention systems. *Behavioral and Brain Sciences, 26,* 731–732. (Commentary on target article by Ruchkin et al.)

Cowan, N. (2004). Working-memory capacity limits in a theoretical context. In C. Izawa & N. Ohta (Eds.), *Human learning and memory: Advances in theory and applications. The 4th Tsukuba international conference on memory* (pp. 155–175). Mahwah, NJ: Erlbaum.

Cowan, N. (2005). Understanding intelligence: A summary and an adjustable-attention hypothesis. In O. Wilhelm & R. W. Engle (Eds.), *Handbook of understanding and measuring intelligence* (pp. 469–488). London: Sage.

Cowan, N., Baddeley, A. D., Elliott, E. M., & Norris, J. (2003). List composition and the word length effect in immediate recall: A comparison of localist and globalist assumptions. *Psychonomic Bulletin & Review, 10,* 74–79.

Cowan, N., Beschin, N., & Della Sala, S. (2004). Verbal recall in amnesiacs under conditions of diminished retroactive interference. *Brain, 127,* 825–834.

Cowan, N., Chen, Z., & Rouder, J. N. (2004). Constant capacity in an immediate serial-recall task: A logical sequel to Miller (1956). *Psychological Science, 15,* 634–640.

Cowan, N., Day, L., Saults, J. S., Keller, T. A., Johnson, T., & Flores, L. (1992). The role of verbal output time in the effects of word length on immediate memory. *Journal of Memory and Language, 31,* 1–17.

Cowan, N., Elliott, E. M., & Saults, J. S. (2002). The search for what is fundamental in the development of working memory. In R. Kail & H. Reese (Eds.), *Advances in Child Development and Behavior, 29,* 1–49.

Cowan, N., Elliott, E. M., Saults, J. S., Morey, C. C., Mattox, S., Hismjatullina, A., et al. (in press-a). On the capacity of attention: Its estimation and its role in working memory and cognitive aptitudes. *Cognitive Psychology.*

Cowan, N., Elliott, E. M., Saults, J. S., Nugent, L. D., Bomb, P., & Hismjatullina, A. (in press-b). Rethinking speed theories of cognitive development: Increasing the rate of recall without affecting accuracy. *Psychological Science.*

Cowan, N., Johnson, T. D., & Saults, J. S. (2005). Capacity limits in list item recognition: Evidence from proactive interference. *Memory, 13,* 293–299.

Cowan, N., Lichty, W., & Grove, T. R. (1990). Properties of memory for unattended spoken syllables. *Journal of Experimental Psychology: Learning, Memory, & Cognition, 16,* 258–269.

Cowan, N., Nugent, L. D., Elliott, E. M., and Geer, T. (2000). Is there a temporal basis of the word length effect? A response to Service (1998). *Quarterly Journal of Experimental Psychology, 53A,* 647–660.

Cowan, N., Nugent, L. D., Elliott, E. M., Ponomarev, I., & Saults, J. S. (1999). The role of attention in the development of short-term memory: Age differences in the verbal span of apprehension. *Child Development, 70,* 1082–1097.

Cowan, N., Nugent, L. D., Elliott, E. M., & Saults, J. S. (2000). Persistence of memory for ignored lists of digits: Areas of developmental constancy and change. *Journal of Experimental Child Psychology, 76,* 151–172.

Cowan, N., Saults, J. S., & Brown, G. D. A. (2004). On the auditory modality superiority effect in serial recall: Separating input and output factors. *Journal of Experimental Psychology: Learning, Memory, and Cognition, 30,* 639–644.

Cowan, N., Saults, J. S., Elliott, E. M., & Moreno, M. (2002). Deconfounding serial recall. *Journal of Memory and Language, 46,* 153–177.

Cowan, N., Saults, J. S., & Nugent, L. D. (1997). The role of absolute and relative amounts of time in forgetting within immediate memory: The case of tone pitch comparisons. *Psychonomic Bulletin & Review, 4,* 393–397.

Cowan, N., Saults, J. S., & Nugent, L. (2001). The ravages of absolute and relative amounts of time on memory. In H. L. Roediger III, J. S. Nairne, I. Neath, & A. Surprenant (Eds.), *The nature of remembering: Essays in honor of Robert G. Crowder* (pp. 315–330). Washington, DC: American Psychological Association.

Cowan, N., Towse, J. N., Hamilton, Z., Saults, J. S., Elliott, E. M., Lacey, J. F., et al. (2003). Children's working-memory processes: A response-timing analysis. *Journal of Experimental Psychology: General, 132,* 113–132.

Cowan, N., & Wood, N. L. (1997). Constraints on awareness, attention, and memory: Some recent investigations with ignored speech. *Consciousness and Cognition, 6,* 182–203.

Cowan, N., Wood, N. L., & Borne, D. N. (1994). Reconfirmation of the short-term storage concept. *Psychological Science, 5,* 103–106.

Cowan, N., Wood, N. L., Nugent, L. D., & Treisman, M. (1997). There are two word length effects in verbal short-term memory: Opposed effects of duration and complexity. *Psychological Science, 8,* 290–295.

Cowan, N., Wood, N. L., Wood, P. K., Keller, T. A. Nugent, L. D., & Keller, C. V. (1998). Two separate verbal processing rates contributing to short-term memory span. *Journal of Experimental Psychology: General, 127,* 141–160.

Craik, F., Gardiner, J. M., & Watkins, M. J. (1970). Further evidence for a negative recency effect in free recall. *Journal of Verbal Learning and Verbal Behavior, 9*, 554–560.

Craik, F. I. M., & Birtwistle, J. (1971). Proactive inhibition in free recall. *Journal of Experimental Psychology, 91*, 120–123.

Craik, F. I. M., & Lockhart, R. S. (1972). Levels of processing: A framework for memory research. *Journal of Verbal Learning and Verbal Behavior, 11*, 671–684.

Crowder, R. G. (1993). Short-term memory: Where do we stand? *Memory & Cognition, 21*, 142–145.

Crowder, R. G., & Morton, J. (1969). Precategorical acoustic storage. *Perception & Psychophysics, 5*, 365–373.

Daneman, M., & Carpenter, P. A. (1980). Individual differences in working memory and reading. *Journal of Verbal Learning & Verbal Behavior, 19*, 450–466.

Daneman, M., & Merikle, P. M. (1996). Working memory and language comprehension: A Meta-Analysis. *Psychonomic Bulletin & Review, 3*, 422–433.

Darwin, C. (1859). *On the origin of species by means of natural selection, or the preservation of favoured races in the struggle for life.* London: John Murray.

Darwin, C. J., Turvey, M. T., & Crowder, R. G. (1972). An auditory analogue of the Sperling partial report procedure: Evidence for brief auditory storage. *Cognitive Psychology, 3*, 255–267.

Davelaar, E. J., Goshen-Gottstein, Y., Ashkenazi, A., Haarman, H. J., & Usher, M. (2005). The demise of short-term memory revisited: Empirical and computational investigations of recency effects. *Psychological Review, 112*, 3–42.

Davis, G., Welch, V. L., Holmes, A., & Shepherd, A. (2001). Can attention select only a fixed number of objects at a time? *Perception, 30*, 1227–1248.

de Groot, A. D. (1965). *Thought and choice in chess.* The Hague: Mouton.

Dehaene, S. (1997). *The number sense: How the mind creates mathematics.* New York: Oxford University Press.

Dehaene, S., & Cohen, L. (1994). Dissociable mechanisms of subitizing and counting: Neuropsychological evidence from simultanagnosic patients. *Journal of Experimental Psychology: Human Perception and Performance, 20*, 958–975.

Deutsch, J. A., & Deutsch, D. (1963). Attention: Some theoretical considerations. *Psychological Review, 70*, 80–90.

Dirlam, D. K. (1972). Most efficient chunk sizes. *Cognitive Psychology, 3*, 355–359.

Dosajh, N. L. (1959). Intelligence and span of apprehension. *Indian Journal of Psychology, 34*, 132–134.

Dosher, B. A., & Ma, J.-J. (1998). Output loss or rehearsal loop? Output time vs. pronunciation time limits in immediate recall for forgetting-matched materials. *Journal of Experimental Psychology: Learning, Memory, and Cognition, 24*, 316–335.

Drewnowski, A., & Murdock, A. B., Jr. (1980). The role of auditory features in memory span for words. *Journal of Experimental Psychology: Human Learning and Memory, 6*, 319–332.

Driver, J., Davis, G., Russell, C., Turatto, M., & Freeman, E. (2001). Segmentation, attention and phenomenal visual objects. *Cognition, 80*, 61–95.

Duncan, J., Seitz, R. J., Kolodny, J., Bor, D., Herzog, H., Ahmed, A., et al. (2000). A neural basis for general intelligence. *Science, 289*, 457–460.

Ebbinghaus, H. (1885/1913). *Memory: A contribution to experimental psychology.* Translated by H. A. Ruger & C. E. Bussenius. New York: Teachers College, Columbia University. (Originally in German, *Ueber das gedächtnis: Untersuchen zur experimentellen psychologie.*)

Einstein, G. O., McDaniel, M. A., Manzi, M., Cochran, B., & Baker, M. (2000). Prospective memory and aging: Forgetting intentions over short delays. *Psychology and Aging, 15*, 671–683.

Einstein, G. O., McDaniel, M. A., Williford, C. L., Pagan, J. L., Dismukes, R. K. (2003). Forgetting of intentions in demanding situations is rapid. *Journal of Experimental Psychology: Applied, 9*, 147–162.

Ellis, N. C., & Hennelly, R. A. (1980). A bilingual word-length effect: Implications for intelligence testing and the relative ease of mental calculation in Welsh and English. *British Journal of Psychology, 71*, 43–51.

Elman, J. L. (1993). Learning and development in neural networks: the importance of starting small. *Cognition, 48*, 71–99.

Engel, A. K., & Singer, W. (2001). Temporal binding and the neural correlates of sensory awareness. *Trends in Cognitive Sciences, 5,* 16–25.

Engle, R. W. (1996). Working memory and retrieval: An inhibition-resource approach. In J. T. E. Richardson, R. W. Engle, L. Hasher, R. H. Logie, E. R. Stoltzfus, & R. T. Zacks (Eds.), *Working memory and human cognition* (pp. 89–119). New York: Oxford University Press.

Engle, R. W. (2002). Working memory capacity as executive attention. *Current Directions in Psychological Science, 11,* 19–23.

Engle, R. W., Cantor, J., & Carullo, J. J. (1992). Individual differences in working memory and comprehension: A test of four hypotheses. *Journal of Experimental Psychology: Learning, Memory, & Cognition, 18,* 972–992.

Engle, R. W., Tuholski, S. W., Laughlin, J. E., & Conway, A. R. A. (1999). Working memory, short-term memory, and general fluid intelligence: A latent-variable approach. *Journal of Experimental Psychology: General, 128,* 309–331.

Ericsson, K. A. (1985). Memory skill. *Canadian Journal of Psychology, 39,* 188–231.

Ericsson, K. A., Chase, W. G., & Faloon, S. (1980). Acquisition of a memory skill. *Science, 208,* 1181–1182.

Ericsson, K. A., Delaney, P. F., Weaver, G., & Mahadevan, R. (2004). Uncovering the structure of a memorist's superior "basic" memory capacity. *Cognitive Psychology, 49,* 191–237.

Ericsson, K. A., & Kintsch, W. (1995). Long-term working memory. *Psychological Review, 102,* 211–245.

Ericsson, K. A., & Kintsch, W. (2000). Shortcomings of generic retrieval structures with slots of the type that Gobet (1993) proposed and modelled. *British Journal of Psychology, 91,* 571–590

Ericsson, K. A., & Kirk, E. P. (2001). The search for fixed generalizable limits of "pure STM" capacity: Problems with theoretical proposals based on independent chunks. *Behavioral and Brain Sciences, 24,* 120–121.

Eriksen, C. W., & St. James, J. D. (1986). Visual attention within and around the field of focal attention: A zoom lens model. *Perception & Psychophysics, 40,* 225–240.

Feigenson, L., Carey, S., & Hauser, M. (2002a). The representations underlying infants' choice of more: Object files versus analog magnitudes. *Psychological Science, 13,* 150–156.

Feigenson, L., Carey, S., & Spelke, E. (2002b). Infants' discrimination of number vs. continuous extent. *Cognitive Psychology, 44,* 33–66.

Fisher, D. L. (1982). Limited-channel models of automatic detection: Capacity and scanning in visual search. *Psychological Review, 89,* 662–692.

Fisher, D. L. (1984). Central capacity limits in consistent mapping, visual search tasks: Four channels or more? *Cognitive Psychology, 16,* 449–484.

Flavell, J. H., Beach, D. H., & Chinsky, J. M. (1966). Spontaneous verbal rehearsal in a memory task as a function of age. *Child Development, 37,* 283–299.

Frey, P. W., & Adesman, P. (1976). Recall memory for visually presented chess positions. *Memory & Cognition, 4,* 541–547.

Friedman, N. P., & Miyake, A. (2004). The Relations among inhibition and interference control functions: A latent variable analysis. *Journal of Experimental Psychology: General, 133,* 101–135.

Frye, D., Zelazo, P. D., & Burack, J. A. (1998). Cognitive complexity and control: I. Theory of mind in typical and atypical development. *Current Directions in Psychological Science, 7,* 116–120.

Gallistel, C. R., & Gelman, R. (2000). Non-verbal numerical cognition: From reals to integers. *Trends in Cognitive Sciences, 4,* 59–65.

Garavan, H. (1998). Serial attention within working memory. *Memory & Cognition, 26,* 263–276.

Gardner, H. (1985). *The mind's new science: A history of the cognitive revolution.* New York: Basic Books.

Garlick, D. (2003). Integrating brain science research with intelligence research. *Current Directions in Psychological Science, 12,* 185–189.

Garner, W. R. (1951). The accuracy of counting repeated short tones. *Journal of Experimental Psychology, 41,* 310–316.

Garner, W. R. (1974). *The processing of information and structure.* Potomac, MD: Erlbaum.

Gathercole, S. E., & Baddeley, A. D. (1993). *Working memory and language.* Hove, UK: Erlbaum.

Gathercole, S. E., Willis, C. S., Baddeley, A. D., & Emslie, H. (1994). The Children's Test of Nonword Repetition: A test of phonological working memory. *Memory, 2,* 103–127.

Gavens, N., & Barrouillet, P. (2004). Delays of retention, processing efficiency, and attentional resources in working memory span development. *Journal of Memory and Language, 51,* 644–657.

Geary, D. C. (2004). *The origin of mind: Evolution of brain, cognition, and general intelligence.* Washington, DC: American Psychological Association.

Geary, D. C., & Widaman, K. F. (1992). Numerical cognition: On the convergence of componential and psychometric models. *Intelligence, 16,* 47–80.

Gernsbacher, M. A. (1993). Less skilled readers have less efficient suppression mechanisms. *Psychological Science, 4,* 294–298.

Glanzer, M., & Cunitz, A. R. (1966). Two storage mechanisms in free recall. *Journal of Verbal Learning & Verbal Behavior, 5,* 351–360.

Glanzer, M., & Razel, M. (1974). The size of the unit in short-term storage. *Journal of Verbal Learning & Verbal Behavior, 13,* 114–131.

Gobet, F. (2000). Some shortcomings of long-term working memory. *British Journal of Psychology, 91,* 551–570.

Gobet, F. (2001). Is experts' knowledge modular? *Proceedings of the 23rd meeting of the Cognitive Science Society* (pp. 336–431). Mahwah, NJ: Erlbaum.

Gobet, F., & Clarkson, G. (2004). Chunks in expert memory: Evidence for the magical number four … or is it two? *Memory, 12,* 732–747.

Gobet, F., & Jackson, S. (2002). In search of templates. *Cognitive Systems Research, 3,* 35–44.

Gobet, F., & Simon, H. A. (1996). Templates in chess memory: A mechanism for recalling several boards. *Cognitive Psychology, 31,* 1–40.

Gobet, F., & Simon, H. A. (1998). Expert chess memory: Revisiting the chunking hypothesis. *Memory, 6,* 225–255.

Gobet, F., & Simon, H. A. (2000). Five seconds or sixty? Presentation time in expert memory. *Cognitive Science, 24,* 651–682.

Goldinger, S. D., Kleider, H. M., Azuma, T., & Beike, D. R. (2003). "Blaming the victim" under memory load. *Psychological Science, 14,* 81–85.

Goldman-Rakic, P. S. (1992, September). Working memory and the mind. *Scientific American,* 111–117.

Graesser II, A., & Mandler, G. (1978). Limited processing capacity constrains the storage of unrelated sets of words and retrieval from natural categories. *Journal of Experimental Psychology: Human Learning and Memory, 4,* 86–100.

Grant, D. A. (1962). Testing the null hypothesis and the strategy and tactic of investigating theoretical models. *Psychological Review, 69,* 54–61.

Gray, C. M., König, P., Engel, A. K., and Singer, W. (1989). Oscillatory responses in cat visual cortex exhibit inter-columnar synchronization which reflects global stimulus properties. *Nature, 338,* 334–337.

Gray, J. R. (2001). Emotional modulation of cognitive control: Approach-withdrawal states double-dissociate spatial from verbal two-back task performance. *Journal of Experimental Psychology: General, 130,* 436–452.

Gray, J. R., Chabris, C. F., & Braver, T. S. (2003). Neural mechanisms of general fluid intelligence. *Nature Neuroscience, 6,* 316–322.

Guttentag, R. E. (1984). The mental effort requirement of cumulative rehearsal: A developmental study. *Journal of Experimental Child Psychology, 37,* 92–106.

Haarman, H. J., Davelaar, E. J., & Usher, M. (2003). Individual differences in semantic short-term memory capacity and reading comprehension. *Journal of Memory and Language, 48,* 320–345.

Hale, S., Bronik, M. D., & Fry, A. F. (1997). Verbal and spatial working memory in school-age children: Developmental differences in susceptibility to interference. *Developmental Psychology, 33,* 364–371.

Halford, G. S., Baker, R., McCredden, J. E., & Bain, J. D. (in press). How many variables can humans process? *Psychological Science.*

Halford, G. S., Maybery, M. T., & Bain, J. D. (1988). Set-size effects in primary memory: An age-related capacity limitation? *Memory & Cognition, 16,* 480–487.

Halford, G. S., Phillips, S., & Wilson, W. H. (2001). Processing capacity limits are not explained by storage limits. *Behavioral and Brain Sciences, 24,* 123–124.

Halford, G. S., Wilson, W. H., & Phillips, S. (1998). Processing capacity defined by relational complexity: Implications for comparative, developmental, and cognitive psychology. *Behavioral and Brain Sciences, 21,* 723–802.

Hambrick, D. Z., & Engle, R. W. (2001). Effects of domain knowledge, working memory capacity, and age on cognitive performance: An investigation of the knowledge-is-power hypothesis. *Cognitive Psychology, 44,* 339–387.

Hasher, L., Stolzfus, E. R., Zacks, R. T., & Rypma, B. (1991). Age and inhibition. *Journal of Experimental Psychology: Learning, Memory, & Cognition, 17,* 163–169.

Hasher, L., & Zacks, R. T. (1988). Working memory, comprehension, and aging: A review and a new view. In G. H. Bower (Ed.), *The psychology of learning and motivation* (Vol. 22) (pp. 193–225). San Diego, CA: Academic Press.

Healy, A. F., & McNamara, D. S. (1996). Verbal learning and memory: Does the modal model still work? *Annual Review of Psychology, 47,* 143–172.

Hebb, D. O. (1949). *Organization of behavior.* New York: Wiley.

Hedden, T., & Park, D. C. (2003). Contributions of source and inhibitory mechanisms to age-related retroactive interference in verbal working memory. *Journal of Experimental Psychology: General, 132,* 93–112.

Henry, L. A. (1991). The effects of word length and phonemic similarity in young children's short-term memory. *Quarterly Journal of Experimental Psychology, 43A,* 35–52.

Herrmann, C. S., Munk, M. H. J., & Engel, A. (2004). Cognitive functions of gamma-band activity: memory match and utilization. *Trends in Cognitive Sciences, 8,* 347–355.

Hester, R., & Garavan, H. (in press). Working memory and executive function: The influence of content and load on the control of attention. *Memory & Cognition.*

Hitch, G. J., Burgess, N., Towse, J. N., & Culpin, V. (1996). Temporal grouping effects in immediate recall: A working memory analysis. *Quarterly Journal of Experimental Psychology, 49A,* 116–139.

Hitch, G. J., Halliday, S., Schaafstal, A. M., & Schraagen, J. M. C. (1988). Visual working memory in young children. *Memory & Cognition, 16,* 120–132.

Hitch, G. J., Towse, J. N., & Hutton, U. (2001). What limits children's working memory span? Theoretical accounts and applications for scholastic development. *Journal of Experimental Psychology: General, 130,* 184–198.

Hockey, R. (1973). Rate of presentation in running memory and direct manipulation of input-processing strategies. *Quarterly Journal of Experimental Psychology (A), 25,* 104–111.

Hulme, C., Maughan, S., & Brown, G. D. A. (1991). Memory for familiar and unfamiliar words: Evidence for a long-term memory contribution to short-term memory span. *Journal of Memory & Language, 30,* 685–701.

Hulme, C., Stuart, G., Brown, G. D. A., & Morin, C. (2003). High-and low-frequency words are recalled equally well in alternating lists: Evidence for associative effects in serial recall. *Journal of Memory and Language, 49,* 500–518.

Hulme, C., Surprenant, A., Bireta, T. J., Stuart, G., & Neath, I. (2004). Abolishing the word-length effect. *Journal of Experimental Psychology: Learning, Memory, and Cognition, 30,* 98–106.

Hulme, C., Thomson, N., Muir, C., & Lawrence, A. (1984). Speech rate and the development of short-term memory span. *Journal of Experimental Child Psychology, 38,* 241–253.

Hutton, U. M. Z., & Towse, J. N. (2001). Short-term memory and working memory as indices of children's cognitive skills. *Memory, 9,* 383–394.

Jacoby, L. L., Woloshyn, V., & Kelly, C. (1989). Becoming famous without being recognized: Unconscious influences of memory produced by divided attention. *Journal of Experimental Psychology: General, 118,* 115–125.

James, W. (1890). *The principles of psychology.* New York: Henry Holt.

Jefferies, E., Lambon Ralph, M. A., & Baddeley, A. D. (2004). Automatic and controlled processing in sentence recall: The role of long-term and working memory. *Journal of Memory and Language, 51,* 623–643.

Jenkins, L., Myerson, J., Hale, S., & Fry, A. F. (1999). Individual and developmental differences in working memory across the life span. *Psychonomic Bulletin & Review, 6,* 28–40.

Jevons, W. S. (1871). The power of numerical discrimination. *Nature, 3,* 281–282.

Jiang, Y., & Song, J.-H. (2004, November). *fMRI adds constraints to models of visual STM.* Paper presented at the annual convention of the Psychonomic Society, Minneapolis.

Johnson, N. F. (1969). The role of chunking and organization in the process of recall. In G. H. Bower & J. T. Spence (Eds.), *Psychology of learning and motivation* (Vol. 4, pp. 171–247). Oxford, England: Academic Press.

Johnson, N. F. (1978). The memorial structure of organized sequences. *Memory & Cognition, 6,* 233–239.

Jones, D. M., Farrand, P., Stuart, G., & Morris, N. (1995). Functional equivalence of verbal and spatial information in serial short-term memory. *Journal of Experimental Psychology: Learning, Memory, and Cognition, 21,* 1008–1018.

Jones, D. M., & Macken, W. J. (1993). Irrelevant tones produce an 'irrelevant speech effect': Implications for phonological coding in working memory. *Journal of Experimental Psychology: Learning, Memory, & Cognition, 19,* 369–381.

Jones, D. M., & Macken, W. J. (1995). Phonological similarity in the irrelevant speech effect: Within- or between-stream similarity? *Journal of Experimental Psychology: Learning, Memory, & Cognition, 21,* 103–115.

Jou, J. (2001). The magic number four: Can it explain Sternberg's serial memory scan data? *Behavioral and Brain Sciences, 24,* 126.

Just, M. A., Carpenter, P. A., Keller, T. A., Emery, L., Zajac, H., & Thulborn, K. R. (2001). Interdependence of nonoverlapping cortical systems in dual cognitive tasks. *NeuroImage, 14,* 417–426.

Kahana, M. J., & Caplan, J. B. (2002). Associative asymmetry in probed recall of serial lists. *Memory & Cognition, 30,* 841–849.

Kahneman, D., Treisman, A., & Gibbs, B. J. (1992). The reviewing of object files: Object-specific integration of information. *Cognitive Psychology, 24,* 175–219.

Kail, R., & Hall, L. K. (2001). Distinguishing short-term memory from working memory. *Memory & Cognition, 29,* 1–9.

Kane, M. J., Bleckley, M. K., Conway, A. R. A., & Engle, R. W. (2001). A controlled-attention view of working-memory capacity. *Journal of Experimental Psychology: General, 130,* 169–183.

Kane, M. J., & Engle, R. W. (2002). The role of prefrontal cortex in working-memory capacity, executive attention, and general fluid intelligence: An individual-differences perspective. *Psychonomic Bulletin & Review, 9,* 637–671.

Kane, M. J., & Engle, R. W. (2003). Working-memory capacity and the control of attention: The contributions of goal neglect, response competition, and task set to Stroop interference. *Journal of Experimental Psychology: General, 132,* 47–70.

Kane, M. J., Hambrick, D. Z., Tuholski, S. W., Wilhelm, O., Payne, T. W., & Engle, R. E. (2004). The generality of working-memory capacity: A latent-variable approach to verbal and visuo-spatial memory span and reasoning. *Journal of Experimental Psychology: General, 133,* 189–217.

Kareev, Y. (2000). Seven (indeed, plus or minus two) and the detection of correlations. *Psychological Review, 107,* 397–402.

Kareev, Y., Lieberman, I., & Lev, M. (1997). Through a narrow window: Sample size and the perception of correlation. *Journal of Experimental Psychology: General, 126,* 278–287.

Kaufman, E., Lord, M., Reese, T., & Volkmann, J. (1949). The discrimination of visual number. *American Journal of Psychology, 62,* 498–525.

Keller, T. A., Cowan, N., & Saults, J. S. (1995). Can auditory memory for tone pitch be rehearsed? *Journal of Experimental Psychology: Learning, Memory, & Cognition, 21,* 635–645.

Keppel, G., & Underwood, B. J. (1962). Proactive inhibition in short-term retention of single items. *Journal of Verbal Learning and Verbal Behavior, 1,* 153–161.

Kersten, A. W., & Earles, J. L. (2001). Less really is more for adults learning a miniature artificial language. *Journal of Memory and Language, 44,* 250–273.

Killeen, P. R. (2001). The four causes of behavior. *Current Directions in Psychological Science, 10,* 136–140.

Kintsch, W., & van Dijk, T. A. (1978). Toward a model of text comprehension and production. *Psychological Review, 85,* 363–394.

Klapp, S. T., Marshburn, E. A., & Lester, P. T. (1983). Short-term memory does not involve the "working memory" of information processing: The demise of a common assumption. *Journal of Experimental Psychology: General, 112,* 240–264.

Klein, K., & Boals, A. (2001). Expressive writing can increase working memory capacity. *Journal of Experimental Psychology: General, 130,* 520–533.

Klein, K., & Fiss, W. H. (1999). The reliability and stability of the Turner and Engle working memory task. *Behavior Research Methods, Instruments, and Computers, 31,* 429–432.

Kleinberg, J., & Kaufman, H. (1971). Constancy in short-term memory: Bits and chunks. *Journal of Experimental Psychology, 90,* 326–333.

Köhler, W. (1917, 1924, 1927). *The mentality of apes.* Berlin: Royal Academy of Sciences; New York: Harcourt Brace.

Kosslyn, S. M., Brown, H. D., & Dror, I. E. (1999). Aging and the scope of visual attention. *Gerontology, 45,* 102–109.

Kucera, H. and Francis, W. N. (1967). Computational analysis of present-day American English. Providence, RI: Brown University Press.

Kyllonen, P. C., & Christal, R. E. (1990). Reasoning ability is (little more than) working-memory capacity?! *Intelligence, 14,* 389–433.

Kynette, D., Kemper, S., Norman, S., & Cheung, H. (1990). Adults' word recall and word repetition. *Experimental Aging Research, 16,* 117–121.

LaBerge, D., & Brown, V. (1989). Theory of attentional operations in shape identifications. *Psychological Review, 96,* 101–124.

Lakha, L., & Wright, M. J. (2004). Capacity limitations of visual memory in two-interval comparison of Gabor arrays. *Vision Research, 44,* 1707–1716.

Lamme, V. A. F. (2003). Why visual attention and awareness are different. *Trends in Cognitive Sciences, 7,* 12–18.

Landauer, T. K. (1962). Rate of implicit speech. *Perceptual & Motor Skills, 15,* 646.

Landman, R., Spekreijse, H., & Lamme, V. A. F. (2003). Large capacity storage of integrated objects before change blindness. *Vision Research, 43,* 149–164.

LaPointe, L. B., & Engle, R. W. (1990). Simple and complex word spans as measures of working memory capacity. *Journal of Experimental Psychology: Learning, Memory, & Cognition, 16,* 1118–1133.

LeCompte, D. C., & Shaibe, D. M. (1997). On the irrelevance of phonology to the irrelevant speech effect. *Quarterly Journal of Experimental Psychology, 50A,* 100–118.

Lépine, R., Barrouillet, P., & Camos, V. (in press). What makes working memory spans so predictive of high level cognition ? *Psychonomic Bulletin & Review.*

Lewandowsky, S., Duncan, M., & Brown, G. D. A. (in press). Time does not cause forgetting in short-term serial recall. *Psychonomic Bulletin & Review.*

Linnenbrink, E. A., Ryan, A. M., & Pintrich, P. R. (1999). The role of goals and affect in working memory functioning. *Learning and Individual Differences, 11,* 213–230.

Lisman, J. E., & Idiart, M. A. P. (1995). Storage of 7 + 2 short-term memories in oscillatory subcycles. *Science, 267,* 1512–1515.

Locke, J. (1690). *An essay concerning human understanding.* London: Thomas Bassett.

Logan, G. D. (1979). On the use of a concurrent memory load to measure attention and automaticity. *Journal of Experimental Psychology: Human Perception and Performance, 5,* 189–207.

Logan, G. D. (1988). Toward an instance theory of automatization. *Psychological Review, 95,* 492–527.

Logan, G. D. (2004). Working memory, task switching, and executive control in the task span procedure. *Journal of Experimental Psychology: General, 133,* 218–236.

Logan, G. D., & Klapp, S. T. (1991). Automatizing alphabet arithmetic: I. Is extended practice necessary to produce automaticity? *Journal of Experimental Psychology: Learning, Memory, and Cognition, 17,* 179–195.

Logan, G. D., & Zbrodoff, N. J. (2003). Subitizing and similarity: Toward a pattern-matching theory of enumeration. *Psychonomic Bulletin & Review, 10,* 676–682.

Logie, R. H. (1995). Visuo-spatial working memory. Hove, UK: Erlbaum.

Logie, R. H. (1996). The seven ages of working memory. In J. T. E. Richardson, R. W. Engle, L. Hasher, R. H. Logie, E. R. Stoltzfus, and R. T. Zacks (Eds.), *Working memory and human cognition* (pp. 31–65). New York: Oxford University Press.

Logie, R. H., & Baddeley, A. D. (1987). Cognitive processes in counting. *Journal of Experimental Psychology: Learning, Memory, & Cognition, 13*, 310–326.

Logie, R. H., Cocchini, G., Della Sala, S., & Baddeley, A. D. (2004). Is there a specific executive capacity for dual task co-ordination ? Evidence from Alzheimer's disease. *Neuropsychology, 18*, 504–513.

Logie, R. H., Della Sala, S., Wynn, V., & Baddeley, A. D. (2000). Visual similarity effects in immediate verbal recall. *Quarterly Journal of Experimental Psychology, 53A*, 626–646.

Lovatt, P., Avons, S. E., & Masterson, J. (2000). The word-length effect and disyllabic words. *Quarterly Journal of Experimental Psychology, 53A*, 1–22.

Lovatt, P., Avons, S. E., & Masterson, J. (2002). Output decay in immediate serial recall: Speech time revisited. *Journal of Memory and Language, 46*, 227–243.

Lovett, M. C., Reder, L. M., & Lebière, C. (1999). Modeling working memory in a unified architecture: An ACT-R perspective. In A. Miyake & P. Shah (Eds.), *Models of working memory: Mechanisms of active maintenance and executive control* (pp. 135–182). Cambridge: Cambridge University Press.

Luck, S. J. (2004, November). *Visual short-term memory for features and objects: A synthesis of recent research*. Paper presented at the annual convention of the Psychonomic Society, Minneapolis.

Luck, S. J., & Vogel, E. K. (1997). The capacity of visual working memory for features and conjunctions. *Nature, 390*, 279–281.

Luck, S. J., & Vogel, E. K. (1998). Response from Luck and Vogel. (A response to "Visual and auditory working memory capacity," by Cowan, N., in the same issue.) *Trends in Cognitive Sciences, 2*, 78–80.

Luck, S. J., & Zhang, W. (2003, November). *Fixed resolution, slot-like representations in visual working memory*. Paper presented at the annual convention of the Psychonomic Society, Vancouver, CA.

Lustig, C., May, C. P., & Hasher, L. (2001). Working memory span and the role of proactive interference. *Journal of Experimental Psychology: General, 130*, 199–207.

MacGregor, J. N. (1987). Short-term memory capacity: Limitation or optimization? *Psychological Review, 94*, 107–108.

Macken, W. J., & Jones, D. M. (1995). Functional characteristics of the inner voice and the inner ear: Single or double agency? *Journal of Experimental Psychology: Learning, Memory, and Cognition, 21*, 436–448.

Macken, W. J., Tremblay, S., Houghton, R. J., Nicholls, A. P., & Jones, D. M. (2003). Does auditory streaming require attention? Evidence from attentional selectivity in short-term memory. *Journal of Experimental Psychology: Human Perception and Performance, 29*, 43–51.

Mandler, G. (1967). Organization and memory. In K. W. Spence & J. T. Spence (Eds.), *The psychology of learning and motivation: I* (pp. 327–372). New York: Academic Press.

Mandler, G. (1985). *Cognitive psychology: An essay in cognitive science*. Hillsdale, NJ: Erlbaum.

Mandler, G., & Shebo, B. J. (1982). Subitizing: An analysis of its component processes. *Journal of Experimental Psychology: General, 111*, 1–22.

Marcel, A. J. (1983). Conscious and unconscious perception: Experiments on visual masking and word recognition. *Cognitive Psychology, 15*, 197–237.

May, C. P., Hasher, L., & Kane, M. J. (1999). The role of interference in memory span. *Memory & Cognition, 27*, 759–767.

May, C. P., Hasher, L., & Stoltzfus, E. R. (1993). Optimal time of day and the magnitude of age differences in memory. *Psychological Science, 4*, 326–330.

McElree, B. (1998). Attended and non-attended states in working memory: Accessing categorized structures. *Journal of Memory and Language, 38*, 225–252.

McElree, B. (2001). Working memory and focal attention. *Journal of Experimental Psychology: Learning, Memory, and Cognition, 27*, 817–835.

McElree, B., & Dosher, B. A. (2001). The focus of attention across space and across time. *Behavioral and Brain Sciences, 24*, 129–130.

McGeoch, J. A. (1932). Forgetting and the law of disuse. *Psychological Review, 39*, 352–370.

McKone, E. (1995). Short-term implicit memory for words and nonwords. *Journal of Experimental Psychology: Learning, Memory, & Cognition, 21,* 1108–1126.

McKone, E. (1995). Short-term implicit memory for words and nonwords. *Journal of Experimental Psychology: Learning, Memory, & Cognition, 21,* 1108–1126.

McKone, E. (2001). Capacity limits in continuous old-new recognition and in short-term implicit memory. *Behavioral and Brain Sciences, 24,* 130–131.

McNulty, J. A. (1966). The measurement of "adopted chunks" in free recall learning. *Psychonomic Science, 4,* 71–72.

Meehl, P. E. (1967). Theory testing in psychology and physics: A methodological paradox. *Philosophy of Science, 34,* 103–115.

Melton, A. W. (1963). Implications of short-term memory for a general theory of memory. *Journal of Verbal Learning and Verbal Behavior, 2,* 1–21.

Meyer, D. E., & Kieras, D. E. (1997). A computational theory of executive processes and multiple-task performance: Part 1. Basic mechanisms. *Psychological Review, 104,* 3–65.

Miller, G. A. (1956). The magical number seven, plus or minus two: Some limits on our capacity for processing information. *Psychological Review, 63,* 81–97.

Miller, G. A. (1962). *Psychology: The science of mental life.* New York: Harper.

Miller, G. A. (1989). George A. Miller. In L. Gardner (Ed.), *A history of psychology in autobiography* (Vol. VIII) (pp. 391–418). Stanford, CA: Stanford University Press.

Miller, G. A., Galanter, E., & Pribram, K. H. (1960). *Plans and the structure of behavior.* New York: Holt, Rinehart and Winston.

Milner, P. M. (1974). A model for visual shape recognition. *Psychological Review, 81,* 521–535.

Miltner, W. H. R., Braun, C., Arnold, M., Witte, H., & Taub, E. (1999). Coherence of gamma-band EEG activity as a basis for associative learning. *Nature, 397,* 434–436.

Miyake, A., Friedman, N. P., Emerson, M. J., Witzki, A. H., & Howerter, A. (2000). The unity and diversity of executive functions and their contributions to complex "frontal lobe" tasks: A latent variable analysis. *Cognitive Psychology, 41,* 49–100.

Miyake, A., Friedman, N. P., Rettinger, D. A., Shah, P., & Hegarty, M. (2001). How are visuospatial working memory, executive functioning, and spatial abilities related? A latent variable analysis. *Journal of Experimental Psychology: General, 130,* 621–640.

Moray, N. (1959). Attention in dichotic listening: Affective cues and the influence of instructions. *Quarterly Journal of Experimental Psychology, 11,* 56–60.

Morey, C. C., & Cowan, N. (2004). When visual and verbal memories compete: Evidence of cross-domain limits in working memory. *Psychonomic Bulletin & Review, 11,* 296–301.

Morey, C. C., & Cowan, N. (in press). When do visual and verbal memories conflict? The importance of working-memory load and retrieval. *Journal of Experimental Psychology: Learning, Memory, and Cognition.*

Morton, J., Crowder, R. G., & Prussin, H. A. (1971). Experiments with the stimulus suffix effect. *Journal of Experimental Psychology, 91,* 169–190.

Mueller, S. T., Seymour, T. L., Kieras, D. E., & Meyer, D. E. (2003). Theoretical implications of articulatory duration, phonological similarity, and phonological complexity in verbal working memory. *Journal of Experimental Psychology: Learning, Memory, and Cognition, 6,* 1353–1380.

Mukunda, K. V., & Hall, V. C. (1992). Does performance on memory for order correlate with performance on standardized measures of ability? A meta-analysis. *Intelligence, 16,* 81–97.

Murray, D. J. (1966). Vocalization-at-presentation and immediate recall, with varying recall methods. *Quarterly Journal of Experimental Psychology, 18,* 9–18.

Näätänen, R. (1992). *Attention and brain function.* Hillsdale, NJ: Erlbaum.

Nairne, J. S. (1991). Positional uncertainty in long-term memory. *Memory & Cognition, 19,* 332–340.

Nairne, J. S. (2002). Remembering over the short-term: The case against the standard model. *Annual Review of Psychology, 53,* 53–81.

Nairne, J. S., & Neath, I. (2001). Long-term memory span. *Behavioral and Brain Sciences, 24,* 134–135.

Naveh-Benjamin, M., & Ayres, T. J. (1986). Digit span, reading rate, and linguistic relativity. *Quarterly Journal of Experimental Psychology, 38A,* 739–751.

Naveh-Benjamin, M., Guez, J., & Marom, M. (2003). The effects of divided attention at encoding on item and associative memory. *Memory & Cognition, 31,* 1021–1035.

Naveh-Benjamin, M., Hussain, Z., Guez, J., & Bar-On, M. (2003). Adult age differences in episodic memory: Further support for an associative-deficit hypothesis. *Journal of Experimental Psychology: Learning, Memory, and Cognition, 29,* 826–837.

Naveh-Benjamin, M., & Jonides, J. (1984). Maintenance rehearsal: A two-component analysis. *Journal of Experimental Psychology: Learning, Memory, and Cognition, 10,* 369–385.

Neath, I., Bireta, T. J., & Surprenant, A. M. (2003). The time-based word length effect and stimulus set specificity. *Psychonomic Bulletin & Review, 10,* 430–434.

Neath, I., & Surprenant, A. (2003). *Human memory* (2nd ed.). Belmont, CA: Wadsworth.

Nelson, D. L., & Goodman, L. B. (2003). Disrupting attention: The need for retrieval cues in working memory theories. *Memory & Cognition, 31,* 65–76.

Neubauer, A. C., Grabner, R. H., Freudenthaler, H. H., Beckmann, J. F., & Guthke, J. (2004). Intelligence and individual differences in becoming neurally efficient. *Acta Psychologica, 116,* 55–74.

Newport, E. L. (1990). Maturational constraints on language learning. *Cognitive Science, 14,* 11–29.

Nipher, F. E. (1878). On the distribution of errors in numbers written from memory. *Transactions of the Academy of Science of St. Louis, 3,* ccx–ccxi.

Norman, D. A. (1968). Toward a theory of memory and attention. *Psychological Review, 75,* 522–536.

Oberauer, K. (2002). Access to information in working memory: exploring the focus of attention. *Journal of Experimental Psychology: Learning, Memory, and Cognition, 28,* 411–421.

Oberauer, K., Demmrich, A., Mayr, U., & Kliegl, R. (2001). Dissociating retention and access in working memory: An age-comparative study of mental arithmetic. *Memory & Cognition, 29,* 18–33.

Oberauer, K., Lange, E., & Engle, R. E. (2004). Working memory capacity and resistance to interference. *Journal of Memory and Language, 51,* 80–96.

Oberauer, K., Süβ, H. M., Wilhelm, O., & Wittmann, W. W. (2003). The multiple faces of working memory—storage, processing, supervision, and coordination. *Intelligence, 31,* 167–193.

Okada, R., & Burrows, D. (1978). The effects of subsidiary tasks on memory retrieval from long and short lists. *Quarterly Journal of Experimental Psychology, 30,* 221–233.

Ornstein, P. A., Naus, M. J., & Liberty, C. (1975). Rehearsal and organizational processes in children's memory. *Child Development, 46,* 818–830.

Pascual-Leone, J. A. (1970). Mathematical model for the transition rule in Piaget's developmental stages. *Acta Psychologica, 32,* 301–345.

Pascual-Leone, J. (2001). If the magical number is 4, how does one account for operations within working memory? *Behavioral and Brain Sciences, 24,* 136–138.

Pascual-Leone, J., & Smith, J. (1969). The encoding and decoding of symbols by children: A new experimental paradigm and a neo-Piagetian model. *Journal of Experimental Child Psychology, 8,* 328–355.

Pashler, H. (1988). Familiarity and visual change detection. *Perception & Psychophysics, 44,* 369–378.

Pashler, H. (1994). Dual-task interference in simple tasks: Data and theory. *Psychological Bulletin, 116,* 220–244.

Penney, C. G. (1989). Modality effects and the structure of short-term verbal memory, *Memory & Cognition, 17,* 398–422.

Peterson, L. R. & Peterson, M. J. (1959). Short-term retention of individual verbal items. *Journal of Experimental Psychology, 58,* 193–198.

Peterson, S. A., & Simon, T. J. (2000). Computational evidence for the subitizing phenomenon as an emergent property of the human cognitive architecture. *Cognitive Science, 24,* 93–122.

Phillips, S., & Niki, K. (2002). Separating relational from item load effects in paired recognition: Tempoparietal and middle frontal gyral activity with increased associates, but not items during encoding and retention. *Neuroimage, 17,* 1031–1055.

Phillips, S., & Niki, K. (2003). Increased bilateral occipitoparietal activity during retention of binary versus unary indexed lists in pair recognition. *NeuroImage, 20,* 1226–1235.

Pollack, I., Johnson, I. B., & Knaff, P. R. (1959). Running memory span. *Journal of Experimental Psychology, 57*, 137–146.

Posner, M. I., & Peterson, S. E. (1990). The attention system of the human brain. *Annual Review of Neuroscience, 13*, 25–42.

Posner, M. I., & Rothbart, M. K. (1991). Attentional mechanisms and conscious experience. In A. D. Milner & M. D. Rugg (Eds.), *The neuropsychology of consciousness* (pp. 91–111). London: Academic Press.

Postle, B. R., & D'Esposito, M. (1999). "What"—then—"where" in visual working memory: An event-related fMRI study. *Journal of Cognitive Neuroscience, 11*, 585–597.

Postle, B. R., Druzgal, T. J., & D'Esposito, M. (2003). Seeking the neural substrates of visual working memory storage. *Cortex, 39*, 927–946.

Postman, L., & Phillips, L. W. (1965). Short-term temporal changes in free recall. *Quarterly Journal of Experimental Psychology, 17*, 132–138.

Poulton, E. C. (1954). Eye-hand span in simple serial tasks. *Journal of Experimental Psychology, 47*, 403–410.

Prabhakaran, V., Narayanan, K., Zhao, Z. & Gabrieli, J. D. E. (2000). Integration of diverse information in working memory within the frontal lobe. *Nature Neuroscience, 3*, 85–90.

Pylyshyn, Z., Burkell, J., Fisher, B., Sears, C., Schmidt, W., & Trick, L. (1994). Multiple parallel access in visual attention. *Canadian Journal of Experimental Psychology, 48*, 260–283.

Pylyshyn, Z. W., & Storm, R. W. (1988). Tracking multiple independent targets: Evidence for a parallel tracking mechanism. *Spatial Vision, 3*, 179–197.

Raaijmakers, J. G. W., & Shiffrin, R. M. (1981). Search of associative memory. *Psychological Review, 88*, 93–134.

Raffel, G. (1937). Grouping and the span of apprehension. *American Journal of Psychology, 49*, 101–104.

Ratcliff, R. (1978). A theory of memory retrieval. *Psychological Review, 85*, 59–108.

Reid, L. S., Lloyd, K. E., Brackett, H. R., & Hawkins, W. F. (1961). Short-term retention as a function of average storage load and average load reduction. *Journal of Experimental Psychology, 62*, 518–522.

Reisberg, D., Rappaport, I., & O'Shaughnessy, M. (1984). Limits of working memory: The digit-digit span. *Journal of Experimental Psychology: Learning, Memory, & Cognition, 10*, 203–221.

Rensink, R. A. (2002). Change detection. *Annual Review of Psychology, 53*, 245–277.

Rensink, R. A., O'Regan, J. K., & Clark, J. J. (1997). To see or not to see: The need for attention to perceive changes in scenes. *Psychological Science, 8*, 368–373.

Reuter-Lorenz, P. A., Jonides, J., Smith, E. E., Hartley, A., Miller, A., Marshuetz, C., et al. (2000). Age differences in the frontal lateralization of verbal and spatial working memory revealed by PET. *Journal of Cognitive Neuroscience, 12*, 174–187.

Rhode, D. L. T. & Plaut, D. C. (1999). Language acquisition in the absence of explicit negative evidence: How important is starting small? *Cognition, 72*, 67–109.

Rickard, T. C. & Grafman, J. (1998). Losing their configural mind: Amnesic patients fail on transverse patterning. *Journal of Cognitive Neuroscience, 10*, 509–524.

Rodriguez, E., George, N., Lachaux, J.-P., Martinerie, J., Renault, B., & Varela, F. J. (1999). Perception's shadow: long-distance synchronization of human brain activity. *Nature, 397*, 430–433.

Roeber, U., & Kaernbach, C. (2004). Memory scanning beyond the limit—if there is one. In C. Kaernbach, E. Schröger, & H. Müller (Eds.), *Psychophysics beyond sensation: Laws and invariants of human cognition*. Mahwah, NJ: Erlbaum.

Romani, C., & Martin, R. (1999). A deficit in the short-term retention of lexical-semantic information: Forgetting words but remembering a story. *Journal of Experimental Psychology: General, 128*, 56–77.

Rose, S. A., Feldman, J. F., & Jankowski, J. J. (2001). Visual short-term memory in the first year of life: Capacity and recency effects. *Developmental Psychology, 37*, 539–549.

Rosen, V. M., & Engle, R. W. (1997). The role of working memory capacity in retrieval. *Journal of Experimental Psychology: General, 126*, 211–227.

Ross-Sheehy, S., Oakes, S. M., & Luck, S. J. (2003). The development of visual short-term memory capacity in infants. *Child Development, 74*, 1807–1822.

Ruchkin, D. S., Grafman, J., Cameron, K., & Berndt, R. S. (2003). Working memory retention systems: A state of activated long-term memory. *Behavioral and Brain Sciences, 26,* 709–777.

Rundus, D. (1971). Analysis of rehearsal processes in free recall. *Journal of Experimental Psychology, 89,* 63–77.

Ryan, J. (1969). Grouping and short-term memory: Different means and patterns of groups. *Quarterly Journal of Experimental Psychology, 21,* 137–147.

Saito, S., & Miyake, A. (2004). On the nature of forgetting and the processing-storage relationship in reading span performance. *Journal of Memory and Language, 50,* 425–443.

Sakai, K., & Inui, T. (2002). A feature-segmentation model of short-term visual memory. *Perception, 31,* 579–590.

Salamé, P., and Baddeley, A. (1982). Disruption of short-term memory by unattended speech: Implications for the structure of working memory. *Journal of Verbal Learning and Verbal Behavior, 21,* 150–164.

Salthouse, T. A. (1996). The processing-speed theory of adult age differences in cognition. *Psychological Review, 103,* 403–428.

Salthouse, T. A., Babcock, R. L., & Shaw, R. J. (1991). Effects of adult age on structural and operational capacities in working memory. *Psychology and Aging, 6,* 118–127.

Sanders, A. F., & Schroots, J. J. F. (1969). Cognitive categories and memory span. III. Effects of similarity on recall. *Quarterly Journal of Experimental Psychology, 21,* 21–28.

Sarnthein, J., Petsche, H., Rappelsberger, P., Shaw, G. L., & von Stein, A. (1998). Synchronization between prefrontal and posterior association cortex during human working memory. *Proceedings of the National Academy of Sciences USA, 95,* 7092–7096.

Schacter, D. L. (1989). On the relation between memory and consciousness: Dissociable interactions and conscious experience. In H. L. Roediger & F. I. M. Craik (Eds.), *Varieties of memory and consciousness: Essays in Honor of Endel Tulving.* Hillsdale, NJ: Erlbaum.

Schacter, D. L. (2001). *The seven sins of memory: how the mind forgets and remembers.* Boston: Houghton Mifflin.

Scholl, B. J. (2001). Objects and attention: The state of the art. *Cognition, 80,* 1–46.

Schweickert, R., & Boruff, B. (1986). Short-term memory capacity: Magic number or magic spell? *Journal of Experimental Psychology: Learning, Memory, and Cognition, 12,* 419–425.

Schweizer, K., & Moosbrugger, H. (2004). Attention and working memory as predictors of intelligence. *Intelligence, 32,* 329–347.

Service, E. (1998). The effect of word length on immediate serial recall depends on phonological complexity, not articulatory duration. *Quarterly Journal of Experimental Psychology, 51A,* 283–304.

Shah, P., & Miyake, A. (1996). The separability of working memory resources for spatial thinking and language processing: An individual differences approach. *Journal of Experimental Psychology: General, 125,* 4–27.

Shallice, T., & Warrington, E. K. (1970). Independent functioning of verbal memory stores: A neuropsychological study. *Quarterly Journal of Experimental Psychology, 22,* 261–273.

Shastri, L., & Ajjanagadde, V. (1993). From simple associations to systematic reasoning: A connectionist representation of rules, variables, and dynamic bindings using temporal synchrony. *Behavioral and Brain Sciences, 16,* 417–494.

Shiffrin, R. M. (1988). Attention. In R. C. Atkinson, R. J. Herrnstein, G. Lindzey, & R. D. Luce (Eds.), *Stevens' handbook of experimental psychology* (Vol. 2) (pp. 739–811). New York: Wiley.

Shiffrin, R. M., & Geisler, W. S. (1973). Visual recognition in a theory of information processing. In R. L. Solso (Ed.), *Contemporary issues in cognitive psychology: The Loyola symposium.* Washington, DC: V. H. Winston & Sons.

Shiffrin, R. M., & Schneider, W. (1977). Controlled and automatic human information processing: II. Perceptual learning, automatic attending, and a general theory. *Psychological Review, 84,* 127–190.

Simon, H. A. (1974). How big is a chunk? *Science, 183,* 482–488.

Simons, D. J. (2000). Attentional capture and inattentional blindness. *Trends in Cognitive Sciences, 4,* 147–155.

Simons, D. J., & Levin, D. T. (1998). Failure to detect changes to people during a real-world interaction. *Psychonomic Bulletin & Review, 5,* 644–649.

Sirevaag, E. J., Kramer, A. F., Coles, M. G. H., & Donchin, E. (1989). Resource reciprocity: An event-related brain potentials analysis. *Acta Psychologica, 70,* 77–97.

Slak, S. (1970). Phonemic recoding of digital information. *Journal of Experimental Psychology, 86,* 398–406.

Sokolov, E. N. (1963). *Perception and the conditioned reflex.* New York: Pergamon Press.

Sperling, G. (1960). The information available in brief visual presentations. *Psychological Monographs, 74* (11, Whole No. 498.)

Sperling, G. (1967). Successive approximations to a model for short-term memory. *Acta Psychologica, 27,* 285–292.

Sperling, G., Budiansky, J., Spivak, J. G., & Johnson, M. C. (1971). Extremely rapid visual search: The maximum rate of scanning letters for the presence of a numeral. *Science, 174,* 307–311.

Spieler, D. H., Balota, D. A., & Faust, M. E. (1996). Stroop performance in healthy younger and older adults and in individuals with dementia of the Alzheimer's type. *Journal of Experimental Psychology: Human Perception & Performance, 22,* 461–479.

Sternberg, S. (1966). High-speed scanning in human memory. *Science, 153,* 652–654.

Stevanovski, B., & Jolicoeur, P. (2003, November). *Attentional limitations in visual short-term memory.* Poster presented at the annual convention of the Psychonomic Society, Vancouver, British Columbia, Canada.

Stevens, S. S. (1975). *Psychophysics: Introduction to its perceptual, neural, and social prospects.* New York: Wiley.

Stigler, J. W., Lee, S.-Y., & Stevenson, H. W. (1986). Digit memory in Chinese and English: Evidence for a temporally limited store. *Cognition, 23,* 1–20.

Stolzfus, E. R., Hasher, L., & Zacks, R. T. (1996). Working memory and retrieval: An inhibition-resource approach. In J. T. E. Richardson, R. W. Engle, L. Hasher, R. H. Logie, E. R. Stoltzfus, and R. T. Zacks (Eds.), *Working memory and human cognition* (pp. 66–88). New York: Oxford University Press.

Strayer, D. L., & Johnston, W. A. (2001). Driven to distraction: Dual-task studies of simulated driving and conversing on a cellular telephone. *Psychological Science, 12,* 462–466.

Stroop, J. R. (1935). Studies of interference in serial verbal reactions. *Journal of Experimental Psychology, 18,* 643–662.

Stuart, G., & Hulme, C. (2000). The effects of word co-occurrence on short-term memory: Associative links in long-term memory affect short-term memory performance. *Journal of Experimental Psychology: Learning, Memory, and Cognition, 26,* 796–802.

Süß, H. M., Oberauer, K., Wittmann, W. W., Wilhelm, O., & Schulze, R. (2002). Working-memory capacity explains reasoning ability—and a little bit more. *Intelligence, 30,* 261–288.

Swanson, H. L. (1999). What develops in working memory? A life-span perspective. *Developmental Psychology, 35,* 986–1000.

Tallon-Baudry, C. Bertrand, O., Peronnet, F., & Pernier, J. (1998). Induced (-band activity during the delay of a visual short-term memory task in humans. *Journal of Neuroscience, 18,* 4244–4254.

Tallon-Baudry, C., Kreiter, A., & Bertrand, O. (1999). Sustained and transient oscillatory responses in the gamma and beta bands in a visual short-term memory task in humans. *Visual Neuroscience, 16,* 449–459.

Tan, L., & Ward, G. (2000). A recency-based account of the primacy effect in free recall. *Journal of Experimental Psychology: Learning, Memory, and Cognition, 26,* 1589–1625.

ten Hoopen, G., & Vos, J. (1979). Effect of numerosity judgment of grouping of tones by auditory channels. *Perception & Psychophysics, 26,* 374–380.

Thompson, C. P., Cowan, T. M., & Frieman, J. (1993). *Memory search by a memorist.* Hillsdale, NJ: Erlbaum.

Thorndike, E. L. (1910). The relation between memory for words and memory for numbers, and the relation between memory over short and long intervals. *American Journal of Psychology, 21,* 487–488.

Tiitinen, H., Sinkkonen, J., Reinikainen, K., Alho, K., Lavikainen, J., & Näätänen, R. (1993). Selective attention enhances the auditory 40-Hz transient response in humans. *Nature, 364,* 59–60.

Todd, J. J., & Marois, R. (2004). Capacity limit of visual short-term memory in human posterior parietal cortex. *Nature, 428,* 751–754.

Towse, J. N., Hitch, G. J., & Hutton, U. (1998). A reevaluation of working memory capacity in children. *Journal of Memory and Language, 39,* 195–217.

Towse, J. N., Hitch, G. J., & Hutton, U. (2000). On the interpretation of working memory span in adults. *Memory & Cognition, 28,* 341–348.

Towse, J. N., Hitch, G. J., & Skeates, S. (1999). Developmental sensitivity to temporal grouping effects in short-term memory. *International Journal of Behavioral Development, 23,* 391–411.

Treisman, A. (1988). Features and objects: The fourteenth Bartlett Memorial Lecture. *Quarterly Journal of Experimental Psychology, 40A,* 201–237.

Treisman, A. M., & Gelade, G. (1980). A feature integration theory of attention. *Cognitive Psychology, 12,* 97–136.

Trick, L. M., Audet, D., & Dales, L. (2003). Age differences in enumerating things that move: Implications for the development of multiple-object tracking. *Memory & Cognition, 31,* 1229–1237.

Trick, L. M., & Pylyshyn, Z. W. (1993). What enumeration studies can show us about spatial attention: Evidence for limited capacity preattentive processing. *Journal of Experimental Psychology: Human Perception and Performance, 19,* 331–351.

Tuholski, S. W., Engle, R. W., & Baylis, G. C. (2001). Individual differences in working memory capacity and enumeration. *Memory & Cognition, 29,* 484–492.

Tulving, E., & Patkau, J. E. (1962). Concurrent effects of contextual constraint and word frequency on immediate recall and learning of verbal material. *Canadian Journal of Psychology, 16,* 83–95.

Tulving, E., & Pearlstone, Z. (1966). Availability versus accessibility of information in memory for words. *Journal of Verbal Learning and Verbal Behavior, 5,* 381–391.

Turkheimer, E., Haley, A., Waldron, M., D'Onofrio, B., & Gottesman, I. I. (2003). Socioeconomic status modifies heritability of IQ in young children. *Psychological Science, 14,* 623–628.

Turner, M. L., & Engle, R. W. (1989). Is working memory capacity task dependent? *Journal of Memory and Language, 28,* 127–154.

Tzeng, O. J. L. (1973). Positive recency effect in a delayed free recall. *Journal of Verbal Learning & Verbal Behavior, 12,* 436–439.

Unsworth, N., Schrock, J. C., & Engle, R. W. (2004). Working memory capacity and the antisaccade task: Individual differences in voluntary saccade control. *Journal of Experimental Psychology: Learning, Memory, and Cognition, 30,* 1302–1321.

Usher, M., Haarmann, H., Cohen, J. D., & Horn, D. (2001). Neural mechanism for the magical number 4: competitive interactions and non-linear oscillations. *Behavioral and Brain Sciences, 24,* 151–152.

Van Zandt, T., & Townsend, J. T. (1993). Self-terminating vs exhaustive processes in rapid visual, and memory search: An evaluative review. *Perception & Psychophysics, 53,* 563–580.

Verhaeghen, P., Cerella, J., & Basak, C. (2004). A Working-memory workout: How to expand the focus of serial attention from one to four items, in ten hours or less. *Journal of Experimental Psychology: Learning, Memory, and Cognition, 30,* 1322–1337.

Verleger, R. (1988). A critique of the context updating hypothesis and an alternative interpretation of P3. *Behavioral and Brain Sciences, 11,* 343–427.

Vernon, P. E. (1965). Ability factors and environmental influences. *American Psychologist, 20,* 723–733.

Vogel, E. K., & Machizawa, M. G. (2004). Neural activity predicts individual differences in visual working memory capacity. *Nature, 428,* 749–751.

Vogel, E., McCollough, A., & Machizawa, M. (2004, November). *Visual short term memory capacity and the efficiency of attentional control.* Paper presented at the annual meeting of the Psychonomic Society, Minneapolis.

Vogel, E. K., Woodman, G. F., & Luck, S. J. (in press). The time course of consolidation in visual working memory. *Journal of Experimental Psychology: Human Perception and Performance.*

Ward, L. M. (2003). Synchronous neural oscillations and cognitive processes. *Trends in Cognitive Sciences, 7*, 553–559.

Watkins, M. J. (1974). Concept and measurement of primary memory. *Psychological Bulletin, 81*, 695–711.

Watson, D. G., & Humphreys, G. W. (1999). The magic number four and temporo-parietal damage: Neurological impairments in counting targets amongst distractors. *Cognitive Neuropsychology, 16*, 609–629.

Waugh, N. C. (1961). Free versus serial recall. *Journal of Experimental Psychology, 62*, 496–502.

Waugh, N. C., & Norman, D. A. (1965). Primary memory. *Psychological Review, 72*, 89–104.

Wegge, J., Kleinbeck, U., & Schmidt, K.-H. (2001). Goal setting and performance in working memory and short-term memory tasks. In E. Miriam, U. Kleinbeck, & H. Thierry (Eds.), *Work motivation in the context of a globalizing economy* (pp. 49–72). Mahwah, NJ: Erlbaum.

Wheeler, M. E., & Treisman, A. M. (2002). Binding in short-term visual memory. *Journal of Experimental Psychology: General, 131*, 48–64.

Wickelgren, W. A. (1964). Size of rehearsal group and short-term memory. *Journal of Experimental Psychology, 68*, 413–419.

Wickelgren, W. A. (1966). Phonemic similarity and interference in short-term memory for single letters. *Journal of Experimental Psychology, 71*, 396–404.

Wickelgren, W. A. (1975). The long and the short of memory. In D. Deutsch and A. J. Deutsch (Eds.), *Short-Term Memory* (pp. 41–63). New York: Academic Press.

Wickelgren, W. A., Corbett, A. T., & Dosher, B. A. (1980). Priming and retrieval from short-term memory: A speed-accuracy tradeoff analysis. *Journal of Verbal Learning and Verbal Behavior, 19*, 387–404.

Wickens, C. D. (1984). Processing resources in attention. In. R. Parasuraman & D. R. Davies (Eds.), *Varieties of attention* (pp. 63–102). New York: Academic Press.

Wickens, D. D., Born, D. G., & Allen, C. K. (1963). Proactive inhibition and item similarity in short-term memory. *Journal of Verbal Learning and Verbal Behavior, 2*, 440–445.

Wilken, P., & Ma, W. J. (2004). A detection theory account of change detection. *Journal of Vision, 4*, 1120–1135.

Winkler, I., Schröger, E., & Cowan, N. (2001). The role of large-scale memory organization in the mismatch negativity event-related brain potential. *Journal of Cognitive Neuroscience, 13*, 59–71.

Wilson, F. A. W., O'Scalaidhe, S. P., & Goldman-Rakic, P. S. (1993). Dissociation of object and spatial processing domains in primate prefrontal cortex. *Science, 260*, 1955–1958.

Winch, W. H. (1904). Immediate memory in school children. *British Journal of Psychology, 7*, 127–134.

Wood, N., & Cowan, N. (1995). The cocktail party phenomenon revisited: How frequent are attention shifts to one's name in an irrelevant auditory channel? *Journal of Experimental Psychology: Learning, Memory, & Cognition, 21*, 255–260.

Wood, N. L., Stadler, M. A., & Cowan, N. (1997). Is there implicit memory without attention? A re-examination of task demands in Eich's (1984) procedure. *Memory & Cognition, 25*, 772–779.

Woodman, G. F., & Vogel, E. K. (in press). Fractionating working memory: Consolidation and maintenance are independent processes. *Psychological Science*.

Woodman, G. F., Vogel, E. K., & Luck, S. J. (2001). Visual search remains efficient when visual working memory is full. *Psychological Science, 12*, 219–224.

Wundt, W. (1894/1998). *Lectures on human and animal psychology*. Translated from the second German edition by J. E. Creighton & E. B. Titchener. Bristol, UK: Thoemmes Press.

Xu, Y. (2004, November). *Representing objects in visual short-term memory: Features, parts, and possible neural mechanisms.* Paper presented at the annual meeting of the Psychonomic society, Minneapolis.

Yantis, S. (1992). Multielement visual tracking: Attention and perceptual organization. *Cognitive Psychology, 24*, 295–340.

Zelazo, P. D., & Frye, D. (1998). Cognitive complexity and control: II. The development of executive function in childhood. *Current Directions in Psychological Science, 7*, 121–126.

Zhang, G., & Simon, H. A. (1985). STM capacity for Chinese words and idioms: Chunking and acoustical loop hypotheses. *Memory and Cognition, 13*, 193–201.

Author Index

Subject Index

A

Activated memory, 40–41, 43–45, 146, 159–160, 191
Active vs. passive sets, 160
"Adopted chunks," 87, 107
Age-related memory issues
  attentional capacity, 172–173
  attention spans, 26–29, 120, 174–175
  in binding, 181–182, 186
  chunking, 101
  control of attention, 171
  inhibitory processes, 60–61
  prospective memory, 208
  rehearsal processes, 57
  subitizing, 9
American Sign Language (ASL), 132
Antisaccade tasks, 65
Apprehension, span of, 10–12, 22–23
Articulatory suppression; *see also*
  Interference
  definition, 32, 121
  and flexibility of attention, 70
  as phonological buffer evidence, 47–48
  and recall speed, 34
  as rehearsal blocker, 47–48, 69–70, 121–123
  and word-length effect, 36

ASL (American Sign Language), 132
Associative links in serial recall, 87
Asymmetrical chunk formation, 82
Asymptotic limit, 115, 154
Attention; *see also* Focus of attention
  vs. awareness, 117–120
  and binding, 177
  capacity of, 41, 70, 171–174, 203
  control of, 62–66, 72–73, 171, 174, 193–195
  frontal and parietal systems for, 187–190
  span of, 26–29, 120, 174–175
Awareness vs. attention, 117–120

B

Behavioral and Brain Sciences, 139
Binding; *see also* Chunking
  and brain activity, 189
  and individual differences, 181–182
  model of, 184–186
  overview, 176–177
  unpacking, 180, 182, 184
  and working memory capacity, 177–181
Binding-limit view, 163
Brain physiology
  and control of attention, 72–73
  and counting vs. subitizing, 124